The Modern

Consumer Movement

references and resources

Reference Publications on

American Social Movements

Irwin T. Sanders, Editor

The Modern

Consumer Movement

references and resources

STEPHEN BROBECK

G.K. Hall & Co.

70 Lincoln Street, Boston, Massachusetts

First published 1990
by G.K. Hall & Co.
70 Lincoln Street
Boston, Massachusetts 02111

10 9 8 7 6 5 4 3 2 1

Library of Congress Cataloging-in-Publication Data

Brobeck, Stephen.
    The modern consumer movement: references and resources /
Stephen Brobeck.
        p. cm. – (Reference publications on American social
movements)
    Includes bibliographical references and index.
    ISBN 0-8161-1833-7
    1. Consumer protection – United States –
Bibliography. 2. Consumer protection – United States –
Societies, etc. 3. Consumer affairs directors –
United States – Biography. 4. Consumer protection.
I. Title. II. Series.
Z7164.C92B76   1990
[HC110.C63]
016.3813'2'0973 – dc20   90-40054
                                                          CIP

The paper used in this publication meets the minimum requirements of
American National Standard for Information Sciences – Permanence of
Paper for Printed Library Materials. ANSI Z39.48-1984   ∞™
MANUFACTURED IN THE UNITED STATES OF AMERICA

To Mother and Dad

Contents

Contents

Acknowledgments

Many persons made essential contributions to this book. It is a pleasure to acknowledge my indebtedness to them.

I could not have undertaken this project without taking a leave from my day-to-day responsibilities at the Consumer Federation. Cornell University made that possible. Scott Maynes urged me to consider a sabbatic in the College of Human Ecology's Department of Consumer Economics and Housing. The department's chairman, Keith Bryant, persuaded the college to offer me a visiting appointment and four companies to contribute funds for this position. Meredith Layer and Peggy Haney of American Express, Roger Nunley of Coca Cola, Grace Richardson of Colgate-Palmolive, and Cheryl Ragland of AT&T provided this support.

The research could not have been completed without access to several of the nation's finest research libraries – the Library of Congress and university libraries at Cornell, American, Georgetown, George Washington, and Maryland. The staff of these institutions were always helpful. So were Elizabeth Hamilton of the Consumers Union library and Anthony Crawford of the Kansas State University library, who supplied information about their collections and even lent me sources.

Jieyu Li, Mary Jesukiewicz, Stewart Lee, Lee Richardson, Tom Garman, and many colleagues in the advocacy community assisted in tracking down sources. Rob Mayer reviewed the entire manuscript and passed on seven instructive pages of recommended improvements. Bob Herrmann made several constructive criticisms of the literature review. My father, Dr. John Brobeck, provided the kind of thorough editing of my writing that he has generously made available to me for more than thirty years.

I am also grateful to those associated with G. K. Hall. Executive editor Elizabeth Holthaus invited me to submit a proposal for the manuscript and advised me at each stage of its preparation. Series editor Irwin Sanders made many useful suggestions. Manuscript editor Ara Salibian skillfully oversaw copyediting of the book.

Ann Lower deserves special recognition for helping me design and create a computer data-base that allowed easy organization and editing of entries. Ann, Sarah Gardner, and Pat Baker also provided essential assistance in data inputting and manipulation.

Finally, I wish to thank my wife Susan for tolerating my weekly commutes to Cornell and my many evenings and weekends spent in D.C.-area libraries, and also for providing much-needed moral support.

Introduction

The consumer movement has been a powerful force in our society. It has been instrumental in the enactment of hundreds of consumer protection laws and regulations, and in the creation of dozens of consumer agencies, at federal, state, and local levels. More important, it has played a central role in the transformation of buyer-seller relations. By fostering the development of *consumer consciousness* – an awareness among buyers that they have interests distinct from sellers and have rights in transactions with these vendors – the consumer movement has helped equalize these relationships. Moreover, by institutionalizing itself, the movement has ensured that there will continue to be an advocate for consumer interests in our society.

There is both a scholarly and a popular literature on this movement. Much of it was utilized by Robert Mayer in the preparation of *The Consumer Movement: Guardians of the Marketplace* (see entry 57), the first comprehensive analysis of the subject, which was released last year. These sources, however, are not easily accessible to scholars, let alone to others interested in learning more about consumerism, because they have been written by researchers from many different fields. Articles on the movement, for instance, can be found in journals of marketing, economics, consumer economics, political science, social psychology, and history. Other important sources have been published privately and thus have not circulated widely. Also, informative articles in the popular press can be located only by checking hundreds of citations from newspaper and magazine indexes. In brief, there is a growing need for a guide to sources about the consumer movement.

This book attempts to meet that need. Its 943 entries identify, describe, and, in the case of scholarly works, evaluate these sources. The way these entries have been organized and cross-referenced, along with the literature review in the following chapter, suggest relationships among the sources. The literature review also recommends directions for future research. While the book is intended primarily as a guide to sources, it also reveals much about the consumer movement itself. It identifies and describes important consumer organizations and leaders. It provides information about the movement's internal and external relationships, and about its advocacy and impacts. In addition, it outlines how our society–especially business, the press, and the public–view consumerism.

A critical issue in developing an annotated bibliography on the consumer movement is the scope of such a work. Three questions must be addressed. First, what is the consumer movement? Does it, for example, include proconsumer legislators, journalists, and educators, as well as advocates? Second, what time period will receive emphasis? Scholars agree that consumerism emerged at the end of the last century but has been more influential since the 1960s. Should one give equal attention to the past ten decades or only to the past three? Third, what types of sources will be included? Academic research certainly should be treated. But how is one to select among the thousands of newspaper articles on the movement or an equally voluminous set of documents produced by the movement itself?

A distinction that is useful in answering the first question is between *consumerism* and the *consumer movement*. Consumerism, on the one hand, embraces all individuals and organizations who are consciously seeking to advance the consumer interest. Thus, it can include legislators who pass consumer protection laws, regulators who enforce these statutes, consumer agency staffers who handle complaints, consumer educators who train future consumers, researchers who define the consumer interest more precisely, product evaluators who disseminate specific information about products, and cooperative organizations that supply consumer services, as well as Ralph Nader and advocacy groups. The consumer movement, on the other hand, is made up only of nonprofit advocacy groups and individual advocates who seek to advance the consumer interest by "reforming" governmental and/or corporate policies and practices. Although the movement is only a subset of consumerism, it is a very important part. At present, it includes some dozen national organizations and several hundred state or local groups that aggressively seek change.

In selecting a time period for emphasis, there are limited choices. Scholars identify three eras of consumerism in our nation's history: the late nineteenth and early twentieth centuries, when food and drug safety legislation was enacted and the Food and Drug Administration and Federal Trade Commission were established; the late 1920s and 1930s, when these laws and agencies were strengthened, consumers were given some representation in government, and Consumers Union was founded; and the "modern period," beginning in the 1960s and continuing today, during which hundreds of consumer laws have been passed, dozens of consumer agencies have been established, and scores of advocacy groups have been organized.

Although this book includes a chapter on secondary sources treating the first two periods, it concentrates on the third. Before 1960, the movement was not well organized. In the first era the only groups were consumer leagues, and their principal purpose was to protect the rights of woman and child workers. In the second, the nation's largest consumer organization was founded, but it mainly served educational and informational functions. It was not until the third era that a well-developed set of advocacy groups was established. Not surprisingly, then, a large majority of secondary sources on consumerism focuses on the last period.

The selection of sources was a more difficult issue. Historical bibliographies typically begin with primary sources located in archives. But few documents about the past thirty years of the consumer movement can be found in these repositories; nearly all are held privately by consumer organizations or their leaders. Accordingly, this work includes no separate listing of primary materials. In almost all cases, scholars must seek access to these documents from movement participants.

The choice of secondary works was especially problematic. Scholarly books, articles, and published papers on the movement are of course included. But which of the thousands of mass-market books, newspaper and magazine articles, and writings by advocates should be brought in? I answered this question by identifying aspects of the consumer movement that are generally believed to deserve attention. Feature articles on consumer advocacy groups, their leaders, their advocacy, or the movement as a whole are included. But because it was so extensive, most of the news coverage of specific movement activities is not. Each year, each major national advocacy group generates from a half to a couple dozen stories and several times that number of articles reporting on them. Constraints of time and space did not permit inclusion of these sources.

Secondary sources on related topics are also included. Research on public opinion is treated because it helps explain the movement's strengths and weaknesses and its priorities. So are the major publications of advocates, since these reveal how the movement views government, business, consumer needs, public policy, and itself. In addition, representative sources on the role of advocates in public policy changes and the economic impacts of these policies are given attention, even though consumer advocacy has been only one "cause" of these reforms – and not always an important one. A selection of sources describing business responses to consumer advocacy and criticisms of the movement from different viewpoints is also included. Finally, to provide a sense of perspective, articles and books in English on the consumer movement throughout the world were brought in.

To identify sources that meet all of these criteria, several strategies were used. Bibliographies in major works on the movement and consumer newsletters were consulted. Mayer's *Consumer Movement* and issues of the *American Council on Consumer Interests Newsletter* were especially helpful. Card catalogues at the Library of Congress, Cornell University, and several Washington-area university libraries were also searched. So were standard reference works – *Social Sciences Index, Public Affairs Information Service Bulletin, Dissertation Abstracts International Index, Reader's Guide to Periodical Literature*, and indexes to the *New York Times, Wall Street Journal*, and *Washington Post*. The two major consumer movement archives, at Consumers Union and Kansas State University, were contacted. So were some two dozen national consumer leaders and their organizations, as well as some eighty of the most active state and local advocacy groups. The latter were asked to pass on copies of feature articles or studies about themselves and their organizations and to indicate whether personal papers or organizational records had been given to archives.

Identifying sources proved to be easier than locating them. Fortunately, the Library of Congress and libraries of several accessible universities – Cornell, Georgetown, George Washington, American, and Maryland – each hold many of these documents. Several others were tracked down by calling journals or authors. A few, however, were never found. On the assumption that other researchers probably could not find them either, they are not listed.

Having read the sources, I made decisions about how to annotate them that led to the following conventions: Annotations for scholarly works are nearly always longer than those for popular and movement sources. Moreover, the former frequently contain evaluations, as well as summaries, of the books and journal articles. The annotations range in length from one sentence to about 1,000 words. When sources are listed in more than one chapter or section, the annotation accompanies only one citation but is cross-referenced in the others. Annotations on dissertations are based only on abstracts in *Dissertation Abstracts International (DAI)*, which are referenced.

The most challenging decisions in the preparation of the bibliography involved organizing sources into meaningful categories. This was because, for a variety of reasons, many works did not fit neatly into any category. Articles in marketing and business journals that briefly address many aspects of the movement were particularly difficult to classify. When there was doubt, sources were listed more than once.

The fifteen chapters address subjects that parallel the topics selected for treatment. These subjects are organized in what I believe to be a logical progression. Chapter 1 lists or describes important information sources. These sources consist of descriptions of archival collections, newsletters, and directories. Chapter 2 describes and evaluates general works on the movement, most of which were written by academics. Chapter 3 includes material from a variety of sources – books, dissertations, and articles – that deal with consumerism before 1960. And chapter 4 treats public opinion surveys, conducted by academics and pollsters, that reveal consumer attitudes about consumerism.

Chapter 5 includes sources on national consumer organizations. Only those organizations for which I found sources meeting the criteria defined above are listed. The White House consumer office is included not only because there were many such sources but also because, for much of the period being studied, it functioned as a consumer advocate within the executive branch and worked closely with movement groups. Groups such as the National Insurance Consumer Organization are conspicuous by their absence. They were not featured in articles in major newspapers, magazines, or scholarly studies. The chapter also includes descriptions of the major advocacy groups still active.

It should be noted that there are separate sections on Nader Raiders, the Nader network, and groups in this network such as Public Citizen. The raiders were individuals recruited by Ralph Nader in 1969 and 1970 to conduct investigative research. The network consists of the many organizations established by Nader after 1970, including Public Citizen. Those researching these groups should also consult the sources listed under "Nader Network."

Chapter 6 focuses on state and local consumer organizations. Because so few have been subjects of national news articles or academic research, the creation of this chapter depended somewhat on the submission of information and materials by grass-roots organizations. Several did so conscientiously, but many could not or would not. Many of these organizations do not keep careful records, in part because of rapid turnover of leadership. Also, while the press frequently reports on specific activities, it rarely prints feature articles on these groups or their leaders.

Chapter 7 lists and describes sources that reveal the relationship of the consumer movement to other organizations – business, academic, environmentalist, and government groups. It also contains several articles on relations between movement organizations or their leaders.

Chapter 8 treats leaders of both national and grass-roots consumer organizations. In addition to listing sources, it includes brief biographies of selected national leaders. Criteria used in making this selection were leadership of an advocacy organization for at least ten years, the influence of the organization, and the availability of related sources. The only exceptions to these rules were: the three heads of the White House consumer office – Esther Peterson, Betty Furness, and Virginia Knauer; two regulators who also had worked with movement groups – Michael Pertschuk and R.

David Pittle; and Bess Myerson. Each was treated by the press as a consumer advocate and as a leader of the movement.

Chapter 9 lists major publications by consumer advocates that address public policy issues or the movement itself. It excludes the consumer advice books prepared by organizations such as Public Citizen's Health Research Group and Consumer Federation of America. Such publications, however, represent only a small fraction of all testimony, reports, op-ed essays, trade-press articles, and other writing by movement activists.

Chapter 10 includes sources on movement advocacy. These consist mainly of analyses by political scientists and articles from newspapers and magazines. It is organized chronologically by presidential administrations since most sources treated the activities of national groups that were strongly influenced by whomever was in the White House.

Chapters 11 and 12 consist of selections from the most interesting academic research on the political and economic impacts of the movement. The first treats mainly studies by political scientists on the role of consumer advocates in shaping public policy. The second samples the extensive literature, written mainly by economists, on the economic impacts of these policies. While most of this research assesses the costs and benefits of safety regulations, a good portion examines the consumer and market impacts of required information disclosures.

Chapter 13 treats sources that reveal business responses to the movement. Some of these works investigate the attitudes of members of the business community toward consumerism. Others describe related changes in business policies or practices. Still others examine the political mobilization of business against the movement.

Chapter 14 presents critiques of the consumer movement by academics, business executives, the press, conservatives, and radicals. Nonscholarly works by academics with a political bias were grouped in the latter two categories.

Chapter 15 contains sources published in English available in this country about the international consumer movement. A number, many of them focusing on the International Organization of Consumers Unions, treat consumer advocacy throughout the world. Others deal with the movement in three regions – the Americas, Asia, and Europe – and in their countries.

The book contains both author and subject indexes. The latter consists mainly of movement leaders and organizations. Both identify entries by their serial numbers, not by pages. When researching a topic, it is important to consult the subject index as well as relevant chapters and sections.

Finally, the question of my own biases should be addressed because of my participation in both the academic and advocacy communities. I was trained as a social historian and have published in that field. After earning a Ph.D. from the University of Pennsylvania, I taught for nine years in the

American studies department at Case Western Reserve University. During the same period, I cofounded and coordinated a grass-roots consumer organization, Cleveland Consumer Action. In the mid-1970s, I was elected to the board of the Consumer Federation of America. Since 1980, I have directed this organization. Last fall, I spent a sabbatical leave at Cornell University, where I held the position of visiting associate professor in the Department of Consumer Economics and Housing and began work on this bibliography.

In the preparation of this book, I have been very aware of the possibility that my past and current involvement in the movement would bias my selection of topics and sources and the way both were treated. I can say only that I have tried to be objective and impartial. Readers can judge for themselves whether I have succeeded.

This work has benefited significantly, however, by my dual role of researcher and advocate. Because of my participation in the consumer movement for twenty years, I have much greater experience with, and possibly insight into, this movement than do uninvolved researchers. As is evident in the annotations, this understanding informed my evaluations of major secondary sources.

A Review of the Literature

There are a surprisingly large number of secondary sources on the U.S. consumer movement, and they are extremely varied. These sources were published in several forms, address many subjects, and were written by movement participants, journalists, and academics, among others. Moreover, the researchers were trained in diverse fields including history, sociology, social psychology, political science, law, economics, consumer economics, marketing, and business administration.

The sources listed in this bibliography illustrate several of these points. Although focused mainly on the modern U.S. consumer movement, 1960-89, they are 786 in number (see table below). Over half of these sources (50.5 percent) are newspaper or magazine articles; 159 (20.2 percent) are journal articles; 93 (11.8 percent), books; 46 (5.9 percent), chapters in books; 34 (4.3 percent), papers read at conferences and then published; and 18 (2.3 percent), dissertations. Because of the large number of newspaper and magazine articles, it is not surprising that journalists wrote nearly half (48.9 percent) of all the sources listed. But academics have also extensively researched the consumer movement. They authored 243 (30.9 percent) of the sources. Also worthy of note is the fact that movement participants and sympathizers have published so many writings. They wrote 132 (16.8 percent) of the sources in the bibliography, and many of these works treat the movement itself, not marketplace problems.

TABLE 1: SOURCES ON THE CONSUMER MOVEMENT

	Academics	Journalists	Movement Participants	Other*	Total	
Dissertations	18	0	0	0	18	(2.3%)
Books	36	12	36	9	93	(11.8%)
Chapters	24	1	20	1	46	(5.9%)
Journal articles	136	0	22	1	159	(20.2%)
Magazine articles	3	177	24	1	205	(26.1%)
Newspaper articles	0	191	0	1	192	(24.4%)
Papers	21	0	13	0	34	(4.3%)
Other**	5	3	17	14	39	(5.0%)
TOTAL	243	384	132	27	786	
	(30.9%)	(48.9%)	(16.8%)	(3.4%)		(100.0%)

*Businesspeople, government officials, conservative critics affiliated with think tanks, among others.
**Mainly reports.

While invaluable as sources of information and interpretation, most articles and books by journalists and movement participants do not consistently build on or reference other publications; only works by academics usually do. Thus, the core of the literature on the consumer movement is made up of these scholarly sources. Yet, as will be shown later in the chapter, this academic literature fails to address adequately many important subjects related to the movement. Furthermore, a number of activists, many of whom were trained as academics, have written informatively about this movement. Accordingly, this review treats selected works by journalists and by movement participants and sympathizers as part of the literature on the consumer movement.

The chapter has three purposes. It identifies and describes major types of secondary sources on the movement. In general, authors with the same academic training have tended to address the same subjects using the same approach. The chapter also identifies and describes the most valuable single sources on the movement. A surprisingly large number were written by movement participants or sympathizers. Finally, this review identifies deficiencies in the literature and proposes research to remedy these deficiencies. Although many of these research needs can be met by specialized studies using the methods of a single discipline, some can only be addressed by interdisciplinary research.

In this review, sources are neither cited nor described in detail. Since the first time they are mentioned they are referenced by their serial number, both citations and annotations can easily be consulted.

Types of Sources

Most of the sources that make up the literature of the consumer movement can be categorized as one of a number of types. Each of these types, and several subtypes, are described below. The types are listed in the order in which related sources are found in the bibliography.

General Works by Social Scientists: Academics have written more than a dozen general works on the consumer movement, past and present. Most of these studies were published as articles – Aaker and Day in *Consumerism* (entry 19), Anderson and Hair in *Mississippi Business Review* (21), Anthony and Haynes in *University of Michigan Business Review* (23), Bloom and Greyser in *Harvard Business Review* (29), Buskirk and Rothe in *Journal of Marketing* (32), Cravens and Hills in *Business Horizons* (35), Finch in *Journal of Consumer Studies and Home Economics* (38), Forbes in *Journal of Consumer Policy* (40), Gaedeke in *University of Washington Business Review* (41), Herrmann et al. in *Frontier of Research* (47), Herrmann in *Journal of Marketing* (44), Herrmann in *Current History* (46), Kahalas in *Akron Business and Economic Review* (50), and Markin in *Business and Society* (56). Scholars have published only two books about the U.S. movement – Creighton's *Pretenders to the Throne* (36) and Mayer's *Consumer Movement* (57).

These works have several characteristics. Each of the authors was trained as a social scientist. Most of the sources (nine of sixteen) are articles published in business or marketing journals. The large majority, especially those in these journals, are primarily derivative; they are based solely or mainly on other secondary sources. Moreover, a large number are not adequately referenced. In general, however, these works have built on each other. The two most useful sources, Mayer's book and Herrmann's article in *Frontier of Research*, both published recently, skillfully utilize earlier research.

Dissertations by Historians: Eight doctoral dissertations have been written by historians about the consumer movement – Harrison (74), Samson (78), Silber (80), Athey (85), Okun (89), Gilmartin (101), Katz (102), and Orlin (64). They were prepared by graduate students at major eastern or midwestern universities that include Yale and Chicago. Two of these studies treat Consumers Union; two, the National Consumers League; and the remaining four, the rise of consumerism and the consumer movement. Only two, those by Silber and Okun, were published in revised form as books.

These dissertations share a number of traits that reflect the training of their authors as historians. First, they focus on change over decades. For most, this period of time is twenty to thirty years. Only Samson and Orlin treat longer periods. Second, the studies examine the relationship of the consumer movement, or parts of it, to the larger society, especially to broad reform movements such as Progressivism and the New Deal. Athey, for example, researched the National Consumers League as part of the Progressive movement, while Silber investigated the societal impacts of Consumers Union's product testing. Third, all the dissertations incorporate exhaustive empirical research in primary sources. Such research of course is required of doctoral candidates. Fourth, in part because of this expectation, all the studies focus most of their attention on the consumer movement before 1960, the beginning of its modern era. Primary sources usually are not given to archives, where they are easily accessible to historians, until they are at least twenty or thirty years old. Also, most historians believe that it is difficult to study the recent past with sufficient objectivity.

Historical Accounts by Movement Participants: Given the incompleteness and inaccessibility of this historical research, accounts by movement participants assume great importance. Activists Colston Warne (191 and 192), Ware (82 and 105), Peterson (256), Campbell (100), Newman (103), Keyserling (75), Wiley (92), and Matthews (98) have all written informatively about the consumer movement before its modern era. Each of these activists participated in the movement before 1960. Each wrote about his or her experiences in the movement. Thus, it is not surprising that six of the nine sources focus mainly on the 1930s, 1940s, and/or 1950s. Also, most authors wrote about the organization or organizations with which they identified—Warne on Consumers Union, Campbell on the New York Consumers Counsel, Newman on various D.C. grass-roots groups, Keyserling on the National Consumers League, Ware on federal consumer advisory boards, and Matthews on Consumers Research. Six of the articles appear in Angevine's *Consumer Activists* (22).

Survey Research by Social Scientists: In the past two decades, academics trained in the social sciences have published a number of articles on public attitudes toward consumerism and the consumer movement—Barksdale and Darden (106), Gaski and Etzel (110), Herrmann and Warland (114), Hustad and Pressemier (115), Kroll and Stampfl (119), Mason and Bearden (123), Stanley and Robinson (125), and Gazda and Gourley (112). Nearly all of these researchers were associated with business schools or schools of human ecology.

Most of the eight articles were published in journals devoted to research on consumer topics. Five appeared in the *Journal of Consumer Affairs*, one in the *Journal of Consumer Studies and Home Economics*, and another was printed in a book on consumerism. These studies address public opinion about two general subjects – marketplace practices and the consumer movement. Barksdale and Darden, Gaski and Etzel, and Hustad and Pressemier, for example, focus mainly on attitudes toward marketing and advertising. Most of the other research concentrates on views of consumer advocacy.

Analyses by Movement Participants and Sympathizers: Movement activists and sympathizers have published more than twenty analyses of the modern consumer movement. Some of these sources treat individual organizations or organizational networks – Boyte et al. on Citizen Action (138), Angevine on the Consumer Federation of America (145 and 146), Warne on Consumers Union (191), Warne (212) and Bollier (195) on the Nader network, Peterson on the White House consumer office (256), Griffin on public interest research groups (PIRGs) (300), Smaby on CAPUR (295), and Caplan on the Connecticut Citizen Action Group (287). Others examine grass-roots consumer groups – Brobeck and Nishimura (264), Nelson (482), Warne (273), and Sorenson (271). Still others focus attention on the consumer movement as a whole – Boyte (263), Morse (555), Pertschuk (611), National Consumers League (62), and *At Home with Consumers* (7). And several discuss the relation of the consumer movement to other groups – Brobeck (310) to academics, Simmons (319) to the civil rights movement, and Clinton Warne (337) to the labor movement.

Few of these sources were published in the early 1970s when the movement was most visible and influential. Fifteen of the twenty-two did not appear in print until the 1980s, when consumer groups were less powerful. In this latter period, perhaps some of the activists who were writing sought to regain lost public recognition and appreciation.

Most of these movement participants were or are national leaders – Warne, Pertschuk, Peterson, Angevine, Brobeck, National Consumers League, and Booth and Max (who collaborated with Boyte). Others were grass-roots activists who held academic positions – Clinton Warne, Nelson, and Morse. Bollier, Sorenson, and Griffin were movement sympathizers who received full cooperation from the organizations they examined.

Biographies of Nader by Journalists: Journalists have written a half-dozen biographies of Ralph Nader – Acton and Le Mond (407), Buckhorn (414), De Toledano (424), Gorey (432), McCarry (448), and Sanford (471). All were published between 1972 and 1976, so apparently they were written at or just after the peak of Nader's prestige and power. Most were based largely on extensive interviews with Nader, his colleagues, his opponents, and observers. Four are highly sympathetic while two are sharply critical – De Toledano and Sanford.

Political Analyses by Social Scientists: Since the consumer movement has achieved its greatest visibility trying to influence national public policy, it is to be expected that social scientists have examined the participation of consumer advocates in the public policy-making process. Vogel (617, 619, and 763), Nadel (609 and 619), and Mayer (316, 327, and 735) have written seven of the ten sources of this type. Berry (24), Snow and Weisbrod (614), and Handler (753) have contributed the others.

Most of these academics were trained in political science or public policy. They published all but one of their studies after 1975. Most of those works focus on legislative processes – Berry, Nadel (609), Vogel (617), Vogel and Nadel (619), and Mayer (316 and 735). This research treats public interest lobbyists (Berry), the relation of these lobbyists to business lobbyists (Mayer, 316), specific legislative issues (Mayer, 735, and Vogel/Nadel), consumer policy-making in general (Nadel, 609), and its impact on business (Vogel, 763). Two other works examine public interest litigation (Snow/Weisbrod and Handler). One looks at consumer participation in the regulatory process (Mayer, 327).

Cost-Benefit Studies by Economists: The chapter on economic impacts (12) describes a representative sample of cost-benefit studies, most by economists, of consumer laws and regulations. Because public policies are influenced by many factors beyond the consumer movement, this research represents that which is least central to the study of the movement. The large majority of sources were published as journal articles.

This research can be divided into two subtypes. Several articles that are highly critical of consumer regulations were published in major economics journals – *Journal of Political Economy* (796 and 797), *American Economic Review* (803), *Journal of Law and Economics* (802), and *Review of Economics and Statistics* (805). Most were written by Viscusi or Pelzman. Only two studies published in mainstream economic journals (795 and 800) present data supportive of regulations. Most studies that are neutral or favorable to these regulations were published in journals of consumer economics, agricultural economics, marketing, or public policy – *Journal of Marketing* (770 and 780), *Journal of Consumer Policy* (783, 785 and 806), *Journal of Public Policy and Marketing* (772), *Journal of Consumer Research* (771 and 775), *Journal of Marketing Research* (778), *Journal of Retailing* (777), *American Journal of Agricultural Economics* (790), and *Journal of Consumer Affairs* (786, 787, 791, and 801). Only one article very critical of regulation (794) appeared in these publications.

The correlation between conclusions about regulations and type of journal raises questions about political bias. Research by Viscusi and Pelzman has been supported and published by the conservative American

Enterprise Institute, which was established to promote free markets. A number of studies neutral or favorable to consumer regulations were written by researchers affiliated with the American Council on Consumer Interests, an organization that seeks to promote these interests. Yet all the research in academic journals was independently reviewed. In any event, each study must be judged on its own merits.

Conservative Critiques: Books or lengthy studies by Bennett and DiLorenzo (847), Burt (196), Grayson and Shephard (851), Isaac and Isaac (852), Peterson (853), and Winter (856) criticize the consumer movement from a conservative perspective. Most of these works are one-sided, as their titles suggest–*Destroying Democracy, Abuse of Trust, The Disaster Lobby, Coercive Utopians, The Regulated Consumer,* and *The Consumer Advocate Versus the Consumer.* Several were funded by conservative foundations. Their most frequent criticism is that the regulations advanced by the movement have imposed huge costs on business and limited consumer choices. They also argue that the government has funded consumer advocacy (Bennett and DiLorenzo) and that the movement has acted improperly (Burt).

Left-Liberal Critiques: Books or articles by Holsworth (834), Creighton (36), Edwards (863), Burlingame (415), Gartner and Riessman (864), Hornsby-Smith (865), and Lazarus (54) have criticized the movement from a leftist or liberal perspective. While most of these writers are academics, they explicitly fault consumer advocates for being weak and/or misguided. Creighton's critique is mainly Galbraithian and environmentalist; Holsworth, environmentalist; Gartner and Riessman, Burlingame, and Lazarus, populist/New Left; and Edwards and Hornsby-Smith, Marxist. The most common theme is that the consumer movement is too "reformist," failing to challenge fundamental flaws in the political and economic system.

Although there are other types of sources besides these ten, none are as cohesive or as important. For example, academics and movement participants have frequently written about the future of the consumer movement, but these works are usually highly speculative. Also, there are many collections of articles or conference papers, but such anthologies frequently address a variety of topics and contain reprinted articles.

Essential Sources

Among the 786 sources listed in this bibliography, a few are essential to understanding the consumer movement. All these works treat the movement in general, its organizations, its leaders, or its activities. Most were published in the 1980s. Mainly because the academic research on the movement is incomplete, a number of works by movement participants or sympathizers are included. Although often biased in favor of their subject, these sources are rich in detailed descriptions and explanatory hypotheses about the movement.

The Movement as a Whole: All but one of the most valuable general works are by academics. Herrmann's 1970 *Journal of Marketing* article (44) represents the first well-researched study of the history of the consumer movement. It proposes the division of this history into three periods distinguished by widespread reform efforts. Although Mayer's treatment of the movement's history (57) is more fully developed than this article, it is based largely on this source.

Creighton's *Pretenders to the Throne* was the first book by an academic on the modern consumer movement. While its principal purpose is to criticize the movement for failing to understand the modern economy and for failing to address broad issues such as income distribution, quality of life, and the environment, it contains useful analysis of the history and then-current character of consumer advocacy.

Angevine's *Consumer Activists* (1982) is a unique collection of recollections and analysis by movement participants. The most useful chapters draw heavily from the personal experiences of the authors – Colston Warne on Consumers Union, Ware on federal consumer advisory boards, Angevine on the Consumer Federation of America, Keyserling on the National Consumers League, and Newman on grass-roots groups in D.C. in the 1930s and 1940s.

Herrmann, Walsh, and Warland's article on the "organization of the consumer movement" (1988) is a well-researched treatment of four major consumer groups – the Nader network, Consumers Union, the American Council on Consumer Interests, and local boycott groups. Its analysis of the groups' emergence, tactics, resources, and relations to other groups draws on the best academic research and movement sources.

The most useful source of information on the consumer movement is also one of the most recent – Mayer's *Consumer Movement* (1989). Incorporating nearly all of the earlier research, it addresses a broad range of topics including the movement's history, organization, worldview, political success, and economic impacts. It is the first source that those interested in learning about the consumer movement should consult.

Organizations: Most works on movement organizations have been written by consumer leaders or sympathizers. There are two key sources on Consumers Union. Warne's lengthy article in Angevine (1982) on the history of this organization up to the 1970s is extremely valuable because it draws on his experiences as president of Consumers Union for forty years and reflects his academic training. It provides information and insights available from no other source. An essential complement to this article is Silber's *Test and Protest* (1983), which is based on the author's doctoral dissertation in history. While it primarily explains how Consumers Union has used product testing as a form of social protest, it also contains well-documented analysis of the emergence of consumerism, the origins of Consumers Union, and the societal impact of its advocacy. Supplementing and updating both of these sources is the article by Herrmann et al. described above.

This article also represents the best academic analysis of the Nader network, but it addresses a limited number of topics in only a few pages. The most useful sources of information on this network are both highly biased, one pro and the other con, yet together they present a fairly complete description of this cluster of organizations. Bollier's *Citizen Action* (1989) is an authorized history of the network by a sympathetic journalist. It identifies participating groups, their leaders, a chronology of events, and claimed accomplishments. Burt's *Abuse of Trust* (1982), an unsatisfactory exposé of Nader-related organizations, nevertheless contains useful information about dozens of these groups, including their finances and their interrelationships.

Boyte, Booth, and Max's *Citizen Action and the New American Populism* (1986) is the only book on the most powerful consumer/citizen grass-roots network in the country. Written by three supporters of this network, the work discusses origins, leaders, member organizations, resources, and advocacy campaigns.

Griffin's *More Action for Change* (1987) is the only book about another active and influential grass-roots network, the public interest research groups (PIRGs). Written by a PIRG sympathizer, it contains useful information on the network's history, advocacy, and impacts. It also profiles two PIRGs and several PIRG leaders.

Few sources contain good analysis of individual state and local consumer organizations. One of these, Wilson and Brydoff's article (308) in *No Access to Law*, examines one of the most successful groups outside the PIRG and Citizen Action networks, San Francisco Consumer Action. This study focuses most of its attention on the complaint-handling methods of the organization, but it also discusses the group's origins, staffing, activities, and funding.

Leaders: Except for newspaper articles, there are few secondary sources on movement leaders, and most of these treat Nader. The best of the biographies is probably McCarry's (1973), but this work treats only the first quarter of Nader's life as a consumer advocate. Since then, numerous articles have been published about the man. Those by Whiteside (1973, entry 221), Rowe (1984, entry 469), and Fisher (1989, entry 429) are especially useful. Two academic articles, however, use survey data to analyze the views and characteristics of a group of consumer leaders. Friedman's *Journal of Consumer Affairs* article (1971, entry 268), on leaders of the 1964 consumer boycotts, and Lichter and Rothman's *Public Opinion* article (1983, entry 349), on national public interest advocates, are excellent sources of information and analysis.

Activities: There are several good sources on congressional lobbying by consumer activists. Two were written by academics. Nadel's *Politics of Consumer Protection* (1971) is a valuable study of the making of federal consumer policy in the late 1960s. It examines Nader's role in this policy-making and also that of the National Consumers League, Consumer Federation of America, Consumers Union, and the AFL-CIO, all of which worked closely together. Berry's *Lobbying for the People* (1977) uses mainly survey responses from public interest lobbyists, many of them consumer advocates, to understand how they lobby, their influence, and the organizations that support them.

Two other sources on congressional lobbying were written by an advocate and former regulator, Michael Pertschuk. His *Revolt against Regulation* (1982) represents the most useful account of the role of consumer advocates in shaping legislation in the late 1960s and the 1970s. His more recent *Giant Killers* (1986, entry 740) contains perceptive case studies of the role of activists in congressional consideration of cigarette labeling legislation and a bill that would have granted the medical profession an antitrust exemption.

The most useful analysis of consumer litigation is included in Handler's *Social Movements and the American Legal System* (1978). Fourteen of the thirty-eight cases filed by public interest organizations that this study examines concern consumer issues.

The best research on consumer boycotts has been completed by Friedman. His 1971 *Journal of Consumer Affairs* article has already been mentioned. His 1985 article in the same journal (605) analyzes ninety consumer boycotts in the 1970s. The large majority of these campaigns, however, were not initiated by consumer organizations.

Research Needs

Although the literature on the modern consumer movement raises all the important questions and contains much insight, it is incomplete. Most importantly, it is not grounded in sufficient empirical research on consumer organizations, their interrelations, their relations with other groups, movement leaders, the advocacy of these organizations and leaders, and their changes over the past thirty years. As evaluations in the annotations suggest, some academic studies are not informed by important published research. Other scholarly works, which adequately reference the literature, rely too heavily on biased assessments of the movement by its participants. In addition to making "global" attempts to understand and interpret the consumer movement, academics must produce the detailed empirical research that represents the only firm foundation for these understandings and interpretations. This research must utilize not only the sources in this bibliography but also the records of organizations and individuals.

Organizations: There are some two dozen national organizations and several hundred grass-roots groups. The large majority were established after 1960. We need to learn much more about these organizations – especially those at the state and local levels – how and why they were established, and how and why they have changed since then in terms of their organization, structure, staffing, leadership, resources, priorities, advocacy, impact, and relation to other consumer groups and to government, business, the press, and other nongovernmental institutions.

The sources in this bibliography represent a starting point for such an examination. For national groups in the 1970s, *National Journal* articles are a particularly valuable source of information. Yet researchers must not limit themselves to research in secondary materials. It is essential that they gain access to organizational records, almost all of which are still held by the groups themselves. Important sources here are annual reports, minutes of board meetings, newsletters and other regular publications, special studies, legislative testimony, regulatory petitions and comments, other official statements, financial statements, press clips, and any unique sources. For example, the executive directors of both Public Voice for Food and Health Policy and the Consumer Federation of America prepare monthly reports for their boards that represent an invaluable record of the activities of these two organizations.

Consumers Union and the Nader network need additional academic study, especially for the period comprising the last fifteen years. But researchers must reserve the highest priority for other organizations about which little has been written. For national groups, they should probably start with the organizations that have been active the longest – National Consumers League, Consumer Federation of America, Center for Auto Safety, Center for Science in the Public Interest, and Action for Children's Television. At the grass roots, they should also look at the older groups, particularly those with good and accessible records, such as the Consumer Education and Protective Association and Cleveland Consumer Action.

Leaders: The only consumer leader who has been adequately researched is Nader. But our current understanding of Nader could still benefit from an academic synthesis and interpretation of existing secondary sources. The leaders who probably should be researched first are Colston Warne, Esther Peterson, Virginia Knauer, Michael Pertschuk, and Rhoda Karpatkin. Warne's and Peterson's papers can be found in archives. Other leaders who deserve attention are Max Weiner, Louise Trubek, Helen Nelson, Harry Snyder, Betty Furness, Joan Claybrook, Sid Wolfe, Alan Morrison, Clarence Ditlow, John Banzhaf, Michael Jacobson, Ellen Haas,

Bob Brandon, Stephen Brobeck, Peggy Charren, David Pittle, and Mark Silbergeld. As longtime activists, each has made his or her mark.

Research on these leaders should begin with the sources treated by this bibliography. It should extend to relevant organizational records and to personal papers, including daily calendars when available. It should also include interviews with the subject and with colleagues, allies, opponents, and neutral observers.

Activities: As well as monographs on organizations and leaders, studies of movement activities are needed. Several subjects should be pursued. Resource development: How do organizations raise funds to support their advocacy? What constraints do funding sources impose? Management: How are staffs of these groups organized? How do the offices function? Advocacy: To what extent do these groups use research, news coverage, grass-roots networking, coalition building, and lobbying to advance their issues? How have these groups worked together on single issues? There is a great need for case studies of legislation and regulations proposed by advocates. Congressional consumer banking protections, state lemon laws, and state initiative campaigns could each be usefully researched.

External Relations: As advocates, consumer groups and leaders depend greatly on their relationships with government, the press, business, labor, consumer researchers and educators, and other activists. Although they are not easy to research, all of these relationships need more careful study. Case studies of movement advocacy should prove especially illuminating here.

Impacts: There is surprisingly little research on the role of the consumer movement in influencing legislative and regulatory bodies, business, the press, and public opinion. To what extent have advocates influenced the public agenda? What has been their specific role in approval of consumer laws and regulations? How has the threat of these interventions, or simply public pressure, changed business programs, policies, and practices? Again, case studies of specific campaigns can reveal these effects.

The Consumer Movement in General: Global questions about the role, influence, and prestige of the consumer movement in general can be answered satisfactorily only if the types of empirical research outlined above are undertaken. Still, specialized studies using indexes of wealth, status, and power can reveal important changes in the movement, including the extent of its institutionalization. For example, in many research libraries there are records of registered lobbyists, congressional testimony, regulatory interventions, litigation, and news coverage. These sources can reveal important characteristics of groups and how these organizations have changed. It is also important to seek to explain those changes by examining their underlying factors.

Finally, just as an earlier generation has done, current consumer leaders must take the time to write about their own experiences. Nader's memoirs could be particularly instructive. So would insightful accounts by anyone who has participated in the consumer movement. It is possible that the first account will stimulate many others.

1. Information Sources

ARCHIVAL

1 GELSTON, STEVEN W., and PASCOE, PEGGY A. *A Guide to Documents of the Consumer Movement: A National Catalog of Source Material.* Mount Vernon, N.Y.: Consumers Union Foundation, 1980. 105 pp.

A catalogue of materials about individuals and organizations associated with consumerism from the late nineteenth century to 1980. Collections are listed by individuals, organizations, and government offices. Each entry includes the dates, size, location, and description of records and a description of the subject. Most materials about consumer organizations are held by these groups; only a few have been placed in archives. Also most materials date to before 1960.

2 MORSE, RICHARD L. D. "The Consumer Movement Archives." In *Proceedings, 34th Annual Conference of the American Council on Consumer Interests*, edited by Vickie L. Hampton, 1. Columbia, Mo.: American Council on Consumer Interests, 1988.

A short paper describing the new Consumer Movement Archives at Kansas State University. Notes that Marjorie Shields, Louis Meyer, Lee Richardson, Nancy Nolf, Florence Mason, and Richard Morse have donated specific collections and that the American Council on Consumer Interests has selected the archives as the official repository of ACCI records. (The archives also contain limited holdings of papers or records of the Arizona Consumers Council, Thomas M. Brooks, Consumer Federation of America, and Alma Williams.)

Archival

3 SHAINWALD, SYBIL. "The Center for the Study of the Consumer Movement." *Journal of Consumer Affairs* 12 (Winter 1978): 393-95.

A short article on Consumers Union's Center for the Study of the Consumer Movement, which was established in 1972. The center seeks to preserve primary materials and to encourage scholarly research on the movement. Located at Consumers Union's Mount Vernon headquarters, it is open to researchers and consumerists. Contains records of Consumers Union, Consumer Federation of America (1968-71), and Helen Nelson, among other movement organizations and leaders.

NEWSLETTERS

4 AMERICAN COUNCIL ON CONSUMER INTERESTS. *American Council on Consumer Interests Newsletter*. Columbia, Mo.

The four-page newsletter of the American Council on Consumer Interests, which was edited by Stewart Lee from the late 1950s to 1989. Contains invaluable information about the activities of consumer groups and agencies, consumer laws and regulations, and consumer sources.

5 COMMISSION FOR THE ADVANCEMENT OF PUBLIC INTEREST ORGANIZATIONS. *Periodicals of Public Interest Organizations: A Citizen's Guide*. Jeannette, Pa.: Committee for the Advancement of Public Interest Organizations, 1979. 57 pp.

A listing and description of more than 100 public interest periodicals. Grouped in sections on health, housing, taxes, agriculture and food, energy, natural resources, foreign and military policy, civil liberties, citizen voices, community change, consumer access, telecommunications, appropriate technology, corporate accountability, and resources. Listings include address and subscription information and 50- to 150-word descriptions.

6 CONSUMER FEDERATION OF AMERICA. *CFA News*. Washington, D.C.

The newsletter of the Consumer Federation of America (CFA) that was published first in the early 1970s and now appears nine times annually. Most articles report CFA analysis of and advocacy on specific federal issues, as well as congressional and regulatory actions on these issues. Other articles treat grass-roots advocacy of issues on the state or local levels. Occasional "perspective" columns by CFA staff or guest writers are included.

7 DIRECT SELLING EDUCATION FOUNDATION. *At Home with Consumers*. Washington, D.C.

A periodical published two to four times annually in the 1980s by the educational foundation of the Direct Selling Association. Typically features pro and con articles on a major consumer issue. Consumer advocates are frequent contributors.

8 FEDERAL-STATE REPORTS, INC. *Of Consuming Interest*. Arlington, Va.

A newsletter published from the late 1960s to the early 1980s on consumer news in Washington, D.C. The Library of Congress holds issues from 1967 to 1968 and 1976 to 1982.

9 IDELSON, GEORGE. *The Consumer Affairs Letter*. Washington, D.C.

A monthly newsletter, published in the 1980s, with news on consumer groups and interviews with their leaders. A valuable source of information on the activities of such organizations, mainly those based in Washington, D.C., and the perspectives of their leaders.

10 NATIONAL CONSUMERS LEAGUE. *National Consumers League Bulletin*. Washington, D.C.

The newsletter of the National Consumers League, which has been published from 1934 to the present. Although its content has varied considerably over the years, it often reports news about and issues of concern to the organization.

11 PUBLIC CITIZEN. *Public Citizen*. Washington, D.C.

A magazine published first four, then six times a year by Public Citizen since 1980. Includes analysis of issues, reports on congressional and regulatory actions, commentary by Public Citizen staffers, and consumer advice. An excellent source of information on perspectives and activities of a major public interest organization. Also useful for its analyses of congressional and regulatory policy-making.

12 SOCIETY OF CONSUMER AFFAIRS PROFESSIONALS IN BUSINESS. *Mobius*. Alexandria, Va.

A quarterly journal published since 1982 for members of the Society of Consumer Affairs Professionals in Business. Includes a number of articles by advocates. For example, the fall 1989 issue, which treats the consumer agenda for the 1990s, contains essays by Ralph Nader, Joan Claybrook, Linda Golodner, Pablo Eisenberg, James Thompson, and Stephen Brobeck.

Directories

DIRECTORIES

13 BERGNER, DOUGLAS J. *Public Interest Profiles*. 5th ed. Washington, D.C.: Foundation for Public Affairs, 1986.

A lengthy, loose-leaf publication, prepared by the Foundation for Public Affairs, with profiles of more than 300 public interest organizations, nearly all national. Eighteen of these groups are classified as "consumer/health," including Center for Auto Safety, Center for Science in the Public Interest, Center for the Study of Responsive Law, Consumer Federation of America, Consumers Union, Health Research Group, International Organization of Consumers Unions, National Consumers League, National Insurance Consumer Organization, and Public Voice. Public Citizen and Congress Watch are listed in the "political/governmental process" section. Center for Community Change, Citizen Action, USPIRG, New York PIRG, Illinois Public Action Council, and Ohio Public Interest Campaign are found in the "community/grass-roots" category. Each profile includes information about budget, staff, membership, purpose, activities, current concerns, newsletters and other recent publications, board of directors, funding, and effectiveness. An invaluable source of information on many national and several state consumer groups.

14 CONSUMER FEDERATION OF AMERICA. *1983 Directory of State and Local Consumer Organizations*. Washington, D.C.: Food Marketing Institute, 1983. 41 pp.

A directory of nearly 400 nonprofit state and local groups engaged in consumer advocacy in 1983. Organizations are listed alphabetically within states. Entries include the name of a contact person, year the organization was established, 1983 membership, top three priority issues, and the name, address, and phone number of the organization.

15 CONSUMER FEDERATION OF AMERICA. *1987 Directory of State and Local Consumer Organizations*. Washington, D.C.: Food Marketing Institute, 1987. 32 pp.

A directory of more than 400 state and local nonprofit consumer groups that updates the CFA's 1983 directory.

16 CONSUMER FEDERATION OF AMERICA. *Working for Consumers – A Directory of State and Local Organizations*. Washington, D.C.: Consumer Federation of America, 1977.

A directory of some 300 state and local groups working on consumer issues in the mid-1970s. Organized by state, listings include the name, address, phone number, contact person, and priority issues of each group.

17 HARVEY, ANN P., ed. *Contacts in Consumerism*. Washington, D.C.: Fraser/Associates, 1980. 624 pp.

The third edition of a directory of organizations and agencies that deal with consumer issues. Separate sections treat the federal government, state and local government protection offices, public interest organizations, corporate consumer affairs representatives, industry and trade association consumer affairs representatives, Better Business Bureaus, consumer affairs reporters, and consumer publications. The section on public interest groups includes a description of each national organization.

18 INTERNATIONAL ORGANIZATION OF CONSUMERS UNIONS. *Consumer Directory–1987*. The Hague: International Organization of Consumers Unions, 1986. 247 pp.

A directory of more than 200 nonprofit and government consumer groups throughout the world. The selection is somewhat arbitrary as indicated by the fifteen U.S. groups listed, which include the Consumer Product Safety Commission, Consumer Federation of America, and Board of Education Employees, Local 372. Each listing includes information about officers, membership, funding sources, publications, goals, and "specific areas of work."

2. General Works

19 AAKER, DAVID A., and DAY, GEORGE S. "A Guide to Consumerism." In *Consumerism: Search for the Consumer Interest*, 4th ed., edited by David A. Aaker and George S. Day, 2-20. New York: Free Press, 1982.

The introductory chapter in Aaker and Day's *Consumerism* anthology (entry 20). Suggests that consumerism expanded from the mid-sixties to late seventies, then contracted. Discusses the four consumer rights defined by President Kennedy and adds a fifth, the right to recourse and redress. Identifies and explains nine factors that influence the evolution of consumerism. Predicts that in the next decade and beyond, consumerism will be in a mature, active stage. Specifically foresees increasing criticism of government regulation, declining influence of government agencies, expanding consumer groups and corporate consumer affairs departments, and growing sophistication in approaches to consumer problems. These predictions have proven essentially correct.

20 AAKER, DAVID A., and DAY, GEORGE S., eds. *Consumerism: Search for the Consumer Interest*. 4th ed. New York: Free Press, 1982. 500 pp.

The fourth edition of the most widely used anthology on consumerism. Consists of the following sections: 1) introduction, 2) perspectives on consumerism, 3) the prepurchase phase: consumer information, 4) the prepurchase phase: advertising, 5) the purchase phase, 6) the postpurchase phase, and 7) responding to consumerism. Each covers all aspects of a subject including different perspectives on specific issues. Many contributions by academics. Other articles by advocates, business leaders, government officials, and journalists. An excellent undergraduate text for a course on consumerism.

21 ANDERSON, ROLPH E., and HAIR, JOSEPH F., Jr. "Consumerism: A Force to Be Reconciled." *Mississippi Business Review* 33 (April 1972): 3-9.

   An examination of consumerism intended for business readers. Traces the history of the consumer movement from the end of the nineteenth century to the present. Identifies three major periods of "consumer unrest" that were characterized by consumer protests that responded to declining income or rising prices, to journalistic exposés of product hazards or inadequacies, and to the emergence of new organizations advocating government protections. Differentiates proconsumer groups as adaptationist, protectionist, or reformer. Discusses such underlying reasons for consumerism as inadequate information, rising expectations, loss of confidence in business and government, and impersonalization. Reports that business reaction to consumerism has been largely "critical and defensive." Argues that companies should try to exploit the competitive opportunities it offers. Although this article represented an informative analysis of consumerism at the time it was written, it is of less interest today because recent sources incorporate more thorough research and analysis.

22 ANGEVINE, ERMA, ed. *Consumer Activists: They Made a Difference.* Mount Vernon, N.Y.: Consumers Union Foundation, 1982. 365 pp.

   A unique collection of articles on the history of the consumer movement by movement leaders. Separate sections focus on cooperatives, product testing, product standards, federal consumer protection, participation in government, participation in business, consumer education, and organizing and lobbying. Contributors include Colston Warne and a number of persons, including the editor, who were associated with the National Consumers League. For information on selected chapters, see citations for Warne (entries 191, 212), Ware (82, 105), Peterson (256), Campbell (100), Nelson (482), Newman (103), Angevine (146), and Keyserling (75).

23 ANTHONY, WILLIAM P., and HAYNES, JOEL B. "Consumerism: A Three Generation Paradigm." *University of Michigan Business Review* 27 (November 1975): 21-26.

   A broad and largely derivative article on the "new consumerism." Distinguishes three eras in its history. Contrasts the last era with the first two to help explain why the new consumerism emerged. Discusses consumerism in terms of theory developed by Neil Smelser on social movements, but reveals lack of understanding of the consumer movement: for example, identifies Consumers Union and the Center for the Study of Responsive Law with "structural conduciveness," and Ralph Nader and third-party organizations with "precipitating factors." Considers implications of the new consumerism for business. Identifies several forces that are likely to restrain it in the future.

24 BERRY, JEFFREY M. *Lobbying for the People*. Princeton: Princeton University Press, 1977. 331 pp.

A valuable study of eighty-three national public interest groups, including thirteen consumer organizations, based largely on a survey of their lobbyists in 1972-73. Examines the development, maintenance, resources, decision making, and legislative strategies and tactics of the organizations as well as the background and recruitment of the lobbyists. Attempts to integrate these findings into the literature on interest groups and to understand better how public interest groups make decisions on issue priorities and lobbying tactics. Chapter 2 discusses the origins and maintenance of these organizations. Chapter 3 examines organizational resources such as finances and staffing. Chapter 4 investigates the background, recruitment, and career orientation of the lobbyists. Chapters 5 and 6 are case studies of nonconsumer groups. Chapter 7 treats the dynamics of organizational decision making. Chapter 8 discusses how the groups lobby and their perception of their influence. Findings include the following: Those who support these groups represent a minority who believe in their goals. Entrepreneurial theory provides a better explanation for the origins of the groups than does disturbance theory. The groups are fairly well funded. Lobbyists choose to work for the public interest for a variety of ideological and personal reasons. They tend to be less experienced but more committed than other lobbyists. Real power tends to be concentrated in the staffs rather than the members or boards of these organizations. The groups have had a "real and significant" impact in many policy areas. Concentrates on the most valuable source of information on public interest lobbying groups, the lobbyists themselves, but neglects to examine other important sources such as organizational records and perceptions of other lobbyists and congressional staffers. Consequently, some of the findings, such as the conclusion about activist influence, are not adequately supported.

25 BISHOP, JAMES R., and HUBBARD, HENRY W. *Let the Seller Beware*. Washington, D.C.: National Press, 1969. 195 pp.

A sympathetic book by two *Newsweek* reporters on the development and current status of consumerism and the problems it has addressed. Discusses its historical development in chapters on the late 1800s and early 1900s, the late 1920s and 1930s, the 1950s and early 1960s, and the late 1960s. In that last section, profiles Ralph Nader and his plans to create a Washington-based organization. In subsequent chapters, focuses on problem areas–advertising, health and safety, deception and fraud, and other problems such as poor quality, poor service, and the costs of credit and insurance. In a concluding chapter, urges business to respond affirmatively to consumer challenges and discusses favorably the proposal to establish a federal consumer protection agency. Lists no sources.

26 BLOOM, PAUL N. *Consumerism and Beyond: Research Perspectives on the Future Social Environment*. Cambridge, Mass.: Marketing Science Institute, 1982. 148 pp.

Proceedings of a conference organized by the Marketing Science Institute and Center of Business and Public Policy, University of Maryland, on the consumer movement. Contains thirty papers on the movement's organizations, current and future issues, future social environment, and corporate responses, which were prepared by academics, consultants, regulators, business executives, and advocates. The most interesting of these papers were later published by Bloom and Smith as *The Future of Consumerism* (entry 30).

27 BLOOM, PAUL N. "The Shifting Make-Up of Consumerism." In *Proceedings, 30th Annual Conference of the American Council on Consumer Interests*, edited by Karen P. Goebel, 134-38. Columbia, Mo.: American Council on Consumer Interests, 1984.

A provocative paper building on the thesis developed earlier by the author and Greyser (entry 29) that the consumer movement has experienced a productlike life cycle and is now in the "mature, fragmented" stage. Anticipates that consumer demand for consumerism will remain strong. But predicts seven demand or supply-side shifts in the "consumerism industry." 1) The emergence of rich/poor consumers still concerned about the traditional rights to be safe, to be informed, to be heard, and to choose, but also interested in getting a better deal on necessities. 2) More politicized blacks and women, who will provide greater support for government consumer protection and assistance, including day-care and child-care subsidies. 3) Shorter attention and interest time spans of consumers, which will require consumerists frequently to develop new "products." 4) A glut of lawyers that will result in their marketing of consumer services and more litigation. 5)

The much more rapid growth of grass-roots consumer activism as compared with Washington-based advocacy. 6) The restructuring of big business, which could lead to more efficient, consumer-oriented companies and/or to highly publicized wheeling and dealing that disgusts consumers. 7) Increased corporate sophistication in responding to consumer concerns through communications.

28 BLOOM, PAUL N., and GREYSER, STEPHEN A. *Exploring the Future of Consumerism*. Cambridge, Mass.: Marketing Science Institute, 1981. 49 pp.

A working paper on the current status and future of consumerism. A revised and more succinct version of this report was published in the *Harvard Business Review* (entry 29).

29 BLOOM, PAUL N., and GREYSER, STEPHEN A. "The Maturing of Consumerism." *Harvard Business Review* 59 (November-December 1981): 130-39.

An influential article on the current status and future of consumerism. Suggests that it has entered the mature stage of its product life cycle and thus has experienced considerable market fragmentation. Many organizations and individuals are offering different "brands" of consumerism that compete for resources, media attention, and public support. Identifies eight different types of organizations in the consumerism industry – nationals, feds, deregulators, locals, co-ops, corporates, antiindustrialists, and reindustrialists. Predicts a "quieter but still active consumer movement" in the 1980s, in part because the public still supports many of its goals. Suggests that the future looks brighter for locals and co-ops and bleaker for nationals. Discusses the implications of this analysis for business. It is unclear why groups like the reindustrialists are identified with the consumerism industry. It also appears that the authors may not understand all the groups they are examining: For example, the umbrella organization Public Citizen is identified as a "national" and its lobbying arm, Congress Watch, as an "antiindustrialist." Moreover, even though its budget and staff are smaller, the Consumer Federation of America is classified as a "large broad-based group" and Public Citizen as a "smaller multiissue organization." In retrospect, the prediction about a quieter but active consumer movement has proven correct. But nationals have fared much better than many co-ops and locals: the two largest consumer co-ops – Berkeley and Greenbelt – have gone bankrupt, and many local protection agencies have lost substantial funding. By comparison, by the late 1980s national consumer groups had never been better funded and were advocating many new policy initiatives.

30 BLOOM, PAUL N., and SMITH, RUTH BELK. *The Future of Consumerism*. Lexington, Mass.: Lexington Books, 1986. 220 pp.

An anthology of sixteen papers on the consumer movement, most of which were written by academics. In sections on "perspectives on the movement" and "relevant empirical findings," the papers generally agree that the movement will survive because of continuing public support and more skillful management, but it will receive less support from the middle-aged middle class and more from the elderly and disadvantaged. In the section on "emerging issues," papers suggest that future issues will concern necessities, new technologies, big institutions, and Third World consumer problems. In a final section on "the response of business," the two papers stress that business will need to adapt to a changing consumer movement. For a summary of selected articles, see Mitchell (entry 321), Peterson (591), Post (886), Richardson (65), Smith (69), and Warland (70).

31 BLOOM, PAUL N., and STERN, LOUIS W. "Consumerism in the Year 2000: The Emergence of Anti-Industrialism." In *Consumerism: New Challenges for Marketing*, edited by Norman Kangun and Lee Richardson, 183-97. Chicago: American Marketing Association, 1978.

Drawing from literature on the postindustrial society, argues that consumerism as it exists today will probably disappear by the end of the century, to be replaced by a much broader antiindustrial movement. By 1990, rather than having disappeared, consumer organizations have institutionalized themselves, and they continue to concentrate on traditional priorities.

32 BUSKIRK, RICHARD H., and ROTHE, JAMES T. "Consumerism – An Interpretation." *Journal of Marketing* 34 (October 1970): 55-65.

An effort by two marketing professors to explain consumerism and its implications for corporations. Treats the causes, catalysts, and impacts of consumerism. Recommends that to prevent government intervention, businesses should establish effective programs to improve communications with consumers. Subsequent research and interpretation have gone beyond that of this article.

33 CARLSON, LES, and KANGUN, NORMAN. "Demographic Discontinuity: Another Explanation for Consumerism?" *Journal of Consumer Affairs* 22 (Summer 1988): 55-73.

An imaginative but tenuous attempt to explain the success or failure of contemporary consumerism partly in terms of demographic factors. Specifically, argues that the civil unrest of the 1960s and 1970s, including consumerism, may be partially accounted for by growing numbers of baby boomers socialized more by peers than by adults and thus "more resistant to the authority of government." Predicts that since the youth of the 1980s were socialized to a greater extent by adults, any consumerism of the 1990s will be less militant than that of the 1960s and early 1970s. A more adequate test would compare the socialization experiences of consumerist leaders and strong supporters with those of nonsupporters in the same generation. Also, more precise indices of socialization than birth rates and family size must be developed. For example, would not the rising participation of mothers in the labor force tend to increase peer socialization?

34 CONSUMERS UNION. *America at Risk: A History of Consumer Protest*. Film. Mount Vernon, N.Y.: Consumers Union, 1984.
 A one-hour documentary funded in part by Consumers Union and hosted by Edwin Newman on the history of the consumer movement. Uses archival footage, still photos, and contemporary interviews to examine the major events, personalities, and institutions that have had a significant impact on American consumers. Chronicles the passage of consumer protection laws in the areas of food, drugs, and auto safety, as well as the fight for truth in packaging and pricing. Includes interviews with Esther Peterson, Caroline Ware, Michael Pertschuk, Ralph Nader, Senator Robert Packwood, James C. Miller III, and Stuart Chase.

35 CRAVENS, DAVID W., and HILLS, GERALD E. "Consumerism: A Perspective for Business." *Business Horizons* 13 (August 1970): 21-28.
 An article on consumerism for businesspeople written by two business administration professors. Treats its origins, nature and scope, goals, and interrelationships. Argues that consumerism was inevitable and must be seriously dealt with by corporations, in part by developing relationships with consumerists and involving top management. Contains little specific information on consumerism, mainly generalizations. Includes only three references.

36 CREIGHTON, LUCY BLACK. *Pretenders to the Throne: The Consumer Movement in the U.S.* Lexington, Mass.: D. C. Heath, 1976. 142 pp.
 A controversial critique of the consumer movement that contains excellent analysis of the development and character of this movement. Chapter 1 outlines the critique: Advocates have largely failed to organize consumers and establish consumer sovereignty because of their acceptance of the classical microeconomic theory of the rational consumer operating in competitive markets. Chapter 2 outlines this

economic theory and the social and economic forces that gave the movement impetus. Chapter 3 examines the consumer movement in the period from the late 1920s to the 1950s. Chapter 4 summarizes recent congressional, presidential, and state support for consumer protection. Chapter 5 examines the work of Ralph Nader. Chapter 6 discusses the efforts of the Consumer Federation of America, Consumers Research, Consumers Union, the labor movement, and consumer educators on behalf of the consumer interest. Chapter 7 argues that, by operating under an outmoded economic theory, consumer advocates have failed to come to grips with "the new industrial state." Also, they have failed to deal with broader quality of life issues. Chapter 8 recommends that these advocates address broader issues of income distribution, environmental quality, and identity and community. The critique can be faulted for neglecting well-documented impacts of consumerism and for inaccurately characterizing the views and activities of advocates. It ignores the rise of consumer consciousness, the expansion of grass-roots activism, the institutionalization of remedies for individual consumers with problems, and the positive effects of government interventions that have been demonstrated by research. Moreover, most modern consumerists, including virtually all Naderites, assume a Galbraithian view of the economy and the state, which is why they seek to toughen antitrust enforcement, break up monopolies, and empower citizens through the organization of citizen action (e.g., citizen utility boards) and cooperative (e.g., Buyers Up) organizations. Furthermore, the advocates view as important and in various ways are seeking to address the broader issues, albeit not always with success. In fact, there is some evidence that consumer organizations lose public support when they seek to broaden the consumer agenda to structural, class, and environmental issues. Nevertheless, this book is a serious one that supplies valuable information and raises important questions about the theory and priorities of the consumer movement.

37 FELDMAN, LAURENCE P. *Consumer Protection: Problems and Prospects*. 2d ed. St. Paul, Minn: West Publishing, 1980. 299 pp.
    An analysis of consumer protections and the seller-consumer conflict that underlies it. Examines the evolution of this protection, sources of conflict in the seller-buyer relationship, federal regulation related to products, advertising, and special groups, and the future of consumer protection. Contains interesting comments in the introductory and concluding chapters on the status of the consumer movement.

38 FINCH, JAMES E. "A History of the Consumer Movement in the United States: Its Literature and Legislation." *Journal of Consumer Studies and Home Economics* 9 (March 1985): 23-33.

An analysis of the history of U.S. consumerism to determine when "a sustained and lasting consumer movement first thrived." Identifies the necessary characteristics of such a movement as popular support for it, recognition of its influence, and the continuing and sustained impact of its activities. After examining the history of consumerism in this century, concludes that a movement did not appear until the 1960s. Predicts that it is likely to endure because of widespread popular support, the existence of TV, and the establishment of federal consumer agencies and offices. While the conclusion of the study is probably correct, it is based on an incomplete analysis that includes only one page on the consumer movement of the 1960s and 1970s. Important research on the modern consumer movement is not cited, and no referenced sources date after 1976.

39 FORBES, J[AMES] D. *The Consumer Interest: Dimensions and Policy Implications*. London: Croom Helm, 1987. 341 pp.

An ambitious and useful attempt to clarify the meaning, scope, and dimensions of the consumer interest. Analyzes this interest from the perspectives of activist groups and academic disciplines. Chapter 1 outlines the history of consumerism and explains the complex nature of the consumer interest. Chapter 2 discusses consumerist and researcher views on the consumer interest, which emphasize health and safety, information, environmental quality, and representation. Chapter 3 examines business views of consumer advocates, which claim that these activists do not really reflect the attitudes and beliefs of consumers. Chapter 4 analyzes the consumer viewpoint from the perspective of microeconomics, consumer behavior, and information processing. It highlights the problems of consumers' obtaining and processing useful information. Chapter 5 treats this interest from the perspective of industrial organization theory, which stresses the competitiveness and efficiency of businesses. Chapter 6 examines the functions of consumer laws and the character of consumer redress mechanisms in OECD countries. Chapter 7 discusses the consumer movement in OECD countries – its organizations, origins, membership, structure, internal problems, and interaction with other organizations. Chapter 8 outlines an analytical and conceptual consumer policy framework to assist policy evaluation, prioritization of issues, and development of legislative agendas. Chapter 9 discusses the future of consumerism. The author draws on a broad range of research, but because of its incompleteness he is sometimes forced to base judgments mainly on his own experience.

40 FORBES, JAMES D. "Organizational and Political Dimensions of Consumer Pressure Groups." *Journal of Consumer Policy* 8 (June 1985): 105-31.

A review and synthesis of research and theories about the participation of consumer advocacy groups in the political process. Discusses the genesis of these groups, motivation for joining them, organizational structure, organizational maintenance and operations, and interactions with other organizations. Finds that most of these topics are neither well studied nor well understood. Yet, reports several interesting findings – for example, that research has overestimated economic motivations for membership and understated social, altruistic, and status benefits of participation. Uses dozens of studies on organizations from the United States, Canada, and Western Europe, though neglects relevant work by Mayer, Herrmann, and others on U.S. advocates. Thus, neglects all leading Washington-based consumer advocacy organizations and erroneously treats Consumers Union, primarily a product-testing organization, as the leading consumer pressure group. Nevertheless, has value for U.S. researchers because of the questions it raises and because of the research on consumer groups in other countries that it discusses.

41 GAEDEKE, RALPH M[ORTIMER]. "The Movement of Consumer Protection: A Century of Mixed Accomplishments." *University of Washington Business Review*, Spring 1970, 31-40.

A history of consumer protection activities since the late nineteenth century. Reveals that consumerism has existed for nearly a century but that its level of activity and influence are greater today than in earlier periods. Predicts that it will "increasingly become a dynamic force in the marketplace." At the time of its publication, one of the most informative articles on consumerism. Today, less useful because more recent publications incorporate new research.

42 GAEDEKE, RALPH M[ORTIMER], and ETCHESON, WARREN W., eds. *Consumerism – Viewpoints from Business, Government, and the Public Interest*. San Francisco: Canfield Press, 1972. 401 pp.

An anthology of forty articles on consumerism organized into sections introducing the consumer movement, discussing its background and some of its major issues, examining the role of government regulation, and advising business on its response to consumerism. For a fuller discussion of individual articles, see Gaedeke (entry 88), Magnuson (554), McLaughlin (253), and Warne (190, 891).

43 HENDON, DONALD W. "Towards a Theory of Consumerism." *Business Horizons*, August 1975, 16-24.

An interdisciplinary analysis that tries to develop a "theory of consumerism." Identifies factors in modern society that have shifted legal responsibility from lawyers to sellers. Suggests that Maslow's theory of a needs hierarchy and the unique aspects of the U.S. experience help explain consumerism. Proposes a general theory of consumerism, based on Thacker's theory of social adaptation to innovation, and advances eight specific hypotheses that are described but not tested. Contends inaccurately that the United States is not a leader in the international consumer movement: Consumers Union has been the major force behind and funder of the International Organization of Consumers Unions, the leader of international consumerism. Suggests that Marxist theory does not help explain the development of consumerism.

44 HERRMANN, ROBERT O. "Consumerism: Its Goals, Organizations, and Future." *Journal of Marketing* 34 (October 1970): 55-60.

An article based on the first useful study of the history and development of the U.S. consumer movement (entry 45). Suggests that there have been three periods of consumerism – the early 1900s, the 1930s, and the 1960s. Argues that "serious economic and social dislocation" helps explain the rise of consumerism in each. (Yet it appears the reverse is true; consumerism emerged during periods of economic growth and rising affluence.) In a lengthy discussion of the goals of consumerism, emphasizes that there is no overall philosophy and program of action, that consumerists differ about solutions and strategies, that the choice of issues largely reflects historical accidents, and that there is a lack of overall leadership. Stresses the importance of presidential support. Describes key organizations – Consumers Union, Consumer Federation of America, and state and local groups. Discusses the implications for marketing, some of which are positive. Since the study was written before the proliferation of consumer groups in the 1970s, its conclusions are dated.

45 HERRMANN, ROBERT O. "The Consumer Movement in Historical Perspective." Paper no. 88, Department of Agricultural Economics and Rural Sociology. Pennsylvania State University, University Park, Pa., February 1970. 32 pp.

The first research to distinguish three periods of consumerism – the early 1900s, the 1930s, and the 1960s – that shared important features: emergence in a period of "rapid social change and economic dislocation"; journalistic exposés that aroused the public; and legislation pushed by consumer groups and the president. Sections examine chronologically the development of the consumer movement in each period. Movement activities are described within a national political and economic context. The concluding section identifies three "persisting problem areas" that give rise to consumerism – "ill-considered applications of new technology," rising expectations regarding the social responsibilities of business, and deceptive and unconscionable business practices. Since these conditions are likely to recur together in the future, so too is an expansive consumer movement. Mayer (entry 57) and others have developed this analysis more fully.

46 HERRMANN, ROBERT O. "Consumer Protection: Yesterday, Today, and Tomorrow." *Current History* 78 (May 1980): 193-96, 226-27.

A general and largely theoretical review of consumer protection – the emergence of problems in an industrialized, mass-consumption society; the rationale for government regulation to prevent or remedy abuses; the tools of regulation including standard setting, information and education, antitrust enforcement, and complaint resolution; the potential costs and benefits of interventions that must be considered; and the performance of regulatory agencies. Briefly discusses the growth of consumerism and the response of business. Suggests that support for consumer protection appears to be declining but should survive.

47 HERRMANN, ROBERT O.; WALSH, EDWARD J.; and WARLAND, REX H. "The Organization of the Consumer Movement: A Comparative Perspective." In *The Frontier of Research in the Consumer Interest*, edited by E. Scott Maynes, 469-94. Columbia, Mo.: American Council on Consumer Interests, 1988.

Examines organizations in the consumer movement to explain how the unique characteristics of each help explain its present situation and future prospects. Focuses on local boycott groups, the Nader network, Consumers Union, and the American Council on Consumer Interests. For each, looks at the conditions underlying its historical development, tactics, source and level of resources, linkages to other organizations, and prospects for success. Concludes that the consumer movement is a "decentralized movement with no binding ideology." By including nonadvocacy groups and omitting most advocacy organizations from examination, greatly understates the ideological agreement, cooperation, and personal ties that unite some two dozen national and more than 100 grass-roots organizations. Yet, represents one of the best analyses of the consumer movement in the 1980s.

48 JENSEN, HANS RASK. "The Relevance of Alternative Paradigms as Guidelines for Consumer Policy and Organized Consumer Action." *Journal of Consumer Policy* 9 (December 1986): 389-405.

Proposes a social systems approach to the study of consumer policy and consumer activism. Defines a typology of consumer problems based on causal distinctions. Suggests three different interpretations of the interrelationship between production and consumption systems – consumer-controlled production, producer-controlled production, and interdependence between production and consumption. Concludes that the latter two are the most useful in developing consumer policy and advocacy. Also finds that the Danish consumer movement focuses on functional problems and is guided by the interdependence interpretation.

49 JONES, MARY GARDINER, and GARDNER, DAVID M. *Consumerism: A New Force in Society.* Lexington, Mass.: Lexington Books, 1976. 187 pp.

A collection of nineteen speeches delivered by academics, activists, government officials, and business leaders at a 1974 conference on consumerism. For information about selected presentations, see Green (entry 552) and Schrag (836).

50 KAHALAS, HARVEY. "The Problems and Challenges of Consumerism." *Akron Business and Economic Review* 5 (Summer 1974): 20-25.

An article on consumerism based largely on other secondary sources. Discusses its definition, economic aspects, causes, goals, and future. Suggests that consumer activists like Nader share a Galbraithian view of the world. Predicts that they will broaden their focus by moving from "clear-cut" abuses, adequate information, and protection of consumers against themselves and others to structural reforms and environmental protection.

51 KANGUN, NORMAN, and RICHARDSON, LEE, eds. *Consumerism: New Challenges for Marketing.* Proceedings of Conference on Consumerism conducted by American Marketing Association. Chicago: American Marketing Association, 1978. 214 pp.

Twelve papers, eleven by academics, given at a 1976 marketing conference on consumerism. Organized into sections on consumer regulation, product safety, gasoline marketing, government involvement in consumer programs, and the future of consumerism. Papers by Richardson (entry 66), and Bloom and Stern (31) address consumer movement topics.

52 KATZ, ROBERT N. *Protecting the Consumer Interest: Private Initiative and Public Response*. Cambridge: Ballinger Publishing Co., 1976. 277 pp.

A collection of seventeen edited versions of papers read at a 1974 conference on the role of consumer groups, the press, regulatory agencies, the courts, and industry in protecting consumers. The articles by Vogel and Nadel (entry 619) and Kass (553) are especially relevant.

53 KELLEY, WILLIAM T., ed. *The New Consumerism: Selected Readings*. Columbus, Ohio: Grid, 1973. 590 pp.

A book of forty-eight readings on consumerism intended as a supplementary textbook. These include articles from academic journals, magazines, and newspapers; papers presented at conferences; and contributions written for the anthology. Sections cover the history of consumerism, the new consumerism, consumers in the marketplace, questionable business practices, the impact of consumerism, the reaction of business, new kinds of regulation, consumerism's abuse of business, the social responsibilities of business, and the future. For a description of selected chapters, see Beem (entry 93), Kelley (776), Zanger (782), and Hansen (792).

54 LAZARUS, SIMON. *The Genteel Populists*. New York: Holt, Rinehart, and Winston, 1974. 303 pp.

A thoughtful, historically based evaluation of the new populists of the 1960s and 1970s such as Ralph Nader. Focuses not on their personalities and programs but on their ideology. Argues that this ideology, with its emphasis on reform of government to redistribute power, is similar to that of Progressives and New Dealers. Criticizes this goal as unrealistic because of its "vulnerability to subversion." Recommends instead a commitment to more modest measures. Expresses cautious optimism about the "radicalization" of Consumers Union and development of public interest law firms. In retrospect, the author greatly exaggerated this radicalization and underestimated the potential of public interest groups to institutionalize themselves.

55 McLAUGHLIN, FRANK E., ed. *The Future of Consumerism*. Proceedings of a conference held 5-6 October 1981. College Park, Md.: Center for Business and Public Policy, 1982. 176 pp.

Presentations and summaries of discussions at a conference addressed by academics, federal officials, corporate representatives, journalists, and one consumer group representative, Rhoda Karpatkin of Consumers Union. The views of most of the academics are presented in more detail in articles published elsewhere. Most speakers made presentations expressing a business or conservative point of view.

56 MARKIN, RON J. "Consumerism: Militant Consumer Behavior." *Business and Society* 12 (Fall 1971): 5-17.

A broad analysis of the sources and significance of consumerism by a professor of business administration. Devotes considerable attention to the problems and frustrations of consumers in the marketplace. Emphasizes income pressures, exposés, and changing attitudes as factors stimulating consumerism. Urges marketers and businesspeople to "become more aware and sensitive to the needs of society as vocalized by social man." Of limited usefulness to researchers today.

57 MAYER, ROBERT. *The Consumer Movement: Guardians of the Marketplace*. Boston: Twayne Publishers, 1989. 193 pp.

The best analysis of the U.S. consumer movement. Based mainly on several hundred secondary sources, this work perceptively treats the history, structure, world views, political success, economic impact, relation to international consumerism, and future of this movement. As well as many original insights, it contains the most useful summaries of the evolution of the movement, character of the current movement, and research on the economic effects of consumer policies in the literature. Its principal limitation reflects the deficiencies of this literature, the most important of which is the paucity of good empirical research on movement organizations, leaders, and advocacy, especially at the grass roots. Nevertheless, short of conducting this research himself, the author could not have written a more useful, and provocative, book on the consumer movement. Chapter 1 discusses definitions of consumerism and the question of whether it qualifies as a social movement. This discussion usefully summarizes research on both issues and raises important questions that are addressed throughout the book. Yet, by equating *consumerism* with the *consumer movement*, it misses an opportunity to distinguish consumer advocacy from other consumerist activities – such as research, education, complaint handling, and regulation – that are intended to promote consumer interests. Chapter 2 examines the three eras of consumer activism recognized by the literature. But it goes beyond other sources in its identification of characteristics shared by the periods. Its principal limitation is a failure to show how the movement progressed from era to era. For example, in the first period, there were no well-established consumer groups (the National Consumers League was primarily a labor support organization); in the second, a product-testing organization (Consumers

Union) was established; and in the third, dozens of advocacy groups with full-time staffs were organized. Chapter 3 analyzes the movement's structure. It begins by discussing definitions of the consumer movement and correctly distinguishes between *primary activists*, mainly advocates with nonprofit groups, and *secondary activists*, who include government officials and members of related social movements. This treatment would have been more useful, however, if it had been structured not around Bloom and Greyser's poorly conceived identification of eight "firms" in the movement (entry 29) but around a differentiation of consumerist functions, closely paralleling consumerist institutions, that considered the movement (mainly nonprofit advocates and advocacy organizations) to be a subset of consumerism. After briefly discussing secondary activists, the chapter describes and differentiates among primary activists in terms of an imaginative, though limited, anatomical model that, for example, identifies Ralph Nader as the head of the movement, Consumers Union as its heart, and the Consumer Federation of America as its backbone. The dozens of organizations that Nader has established and nourished may view him more as heart than head. Similarly, the public and public policymakers who view Consumers Union as the consumer group with the highest intellectual and organizational standards may think of it more as head than heart. Nevertheless, the chapter accurately describes these three and nearly a dozen single-issue national groups. Probably because the literature on the subject is deficient, the chapter then briefly and inadequately discusses state and local organizations. Finally, it perceptively assesses the movement's overall structure – its size, degree of specialization, sources of cohesion and tension, and patterns of authority and decision making. It errs, and only slightly, in suggesting that the movement "leans toward" centralization; it is highly decentralized and growing more so. Nader, for instance, now has a formal affiliation with and provides substantial financial support to only one organization, the Center for the Study of Responsive Law. Chapter 4 intelligently analyzes the worldviews of consumerists in terms of problem perception and identification, problem explanation, and solutions and tactics. Its fundamental distinction is between movement *reformers* and *radicals*. Although this distinction is useful to a point, a more accurate differentiation would be based on a multidimensional continuum with somewhat arbitrary shifts from conservative reformism to liberal reformism to radicalism. For example, in many respects the "reformist" staff of the Consumer Federation of America hold views more similar to those of "radical" Naderites than to those of "reformist" Virginia Knauer. Chapter 5 examines the political dynamics of consumer issues with special attention to the factors that influence the success of movement advocacy. The latter include environmental determinants, such as public opinion and leadership by government activists, and tactical determinants such as choice of goals, building public support, and responding to opposition. The chapter concludes with a survey of federal consumer laws. Chapter 6 draws from the literature of cost-benefit analysis to assess the economic impacts of public policies supported by the consumer movement. It begins with an excellent discussion of the limitations of this literature. It then reviews studies on product safety, information disclosure, automobile fuel efficiency, and deregulation of trucking, banking, airlines, and generic drugs. It organizes this discussion in terms of policies that were successful, those that were not, and those with mixed results. Chapter 7 analyzes international consumerism. It compares consumerism in the United States and Europe in terms of shared characteristics and differences. Here a discussion of social and economic differences would have illuminated some of the differences in consumerism, such as the more developed mechanisms for redress in the United States that probably reflect what the Europeans have called our "cowboy capitalism." The chapter also examines Third World consumerism in terms of internal and external influences. While probably beyond the scope of this book, more detailed comparisons of organizations and leaders in the United States and Europe would have effectively illustrated general themes and revealed additional similarities and differences. Chapter 8 discusses the future prospects of the consumer movement in and outside the United States. It identifies those economic and demographic forces that will define the future context of consumerism. It then speculates on whether reformist or radical consumerism will predominate; and it concludes that reformists, with their emphasis on efficiency, will prevail over radicals, who emphasize equality. This discussion is unsatisfactory in two respects. First, it equates equality and fairness, even though many consumerists strive not for equality but for equality of opportunity (or fairness). Second, those whom the author identifies as radicals emphasize redistribution of power rather than resources. In fact, it is the liberal reformists who have made helping low-income consumers a high priority. The concluding speculation on the future of the movement is provocative. The book contains an excellent bibliography.

58 MAYNES, E. SCOTT, ed. *The Frontier of Research in the Consumer Interest*. Columbia, Mo.: American Council on Consumer Interests, 1988. 889 pp.

Proceedings of the International Conference on Research in the Consumer Interest, which featured research papers by academics and comments by academics and consumerists from government, business, and consumer organizations. The seventy-three papers and comments are organized into thirty-six chapters and six sections – the right to safety, the right to be informed, the right to choose, the right to be heard, the right to redress, and the right to consumer education. Many of the papers review past and proposed research on topics such as product safety, cost-benefit analyses, price-quality relationships, the economics of information, economic deregulation, the consumer movement, consumer problems in developed and less developed countries, corporate consumer affairs departments, and consumer complaints. A unique and invaluable source of current research and consumerist perspectives on a wide range of consumer topics. For summaries of selected papers, see Lampman (entry 630), Herrmann (47), and Allain (867).

59 METZEN, EDWARD. "Consumerism in the Evolving Future." In *Future of Consumerism*, edited by Paul N. Bloom and Ruth Belk Smith, 3-15. Lexington, Mass.: Lexington Books, 1986.

A thoughtful discussion of the future of consumerism. Speculates on future conditions for consumers including inflation/recession, a declining material level of living, and greater economic uncertainty. Predicts that consumers will respond to these conditions through greater demand for consumer education, information, and satisfaction in individual purchases. Suggests that they will provide more support for local consumer organizations (less for national groups), become less dependent on commercial markets, and place a higher priority on income, tax, and environmental policies. Concludes that corporations will increasingly be held accountable by consumers, workers, and the public, and urges them to respond reasonably to the demands of these stakeholders.

60 MITCHELL, JEREMY. "The Consumer Movement and Technological Change." *International Social Science Journal* 25, no. 3 (1973): 358-69.

An article by a British social scientist/consumerist that tries to explain the rise of the consumer movement in Europe and the United States in terms of technologically induced changes in the marketplace. Outlines several of these changes. Discusses the emergence of consumer organizations focused on comparative testing, informative labeling, and quality certification. Suggests, however, that these groups may not meet low-income consumer needs. Notes that while the consumer movement is still weak politically, it is gaining strength, especially in the United States. Proposes that the role of consumerists in relation to technological change should be to assess its impacts on consumers and to help identify consumers' "unsatisfied technological needs."

61 MURRAY, BARBARA B., ed. *Consumerism: The Eternal Triangle*. Pacific Palisades, Calif.: Goodyear Publishing Co., 1973. 469 pp.

An anthology of forty-eight articles, nearly all reprints, on consumer issues and protections. Emphasizes the social, economic, and marketing aspects of consumerism as related to laws, regulation, business and marketing, and low-income consumers. Articles grouped into sections on economics and consumerism, consumerism, government and consumerism, the Federal Trade Commission and consumerism, credit lending, truth in packaging, business and consumerism, marketing and consumerism, advertising and consumerism, warranties and product liability, and low-income groups and consumerism. Many sections include a *Wall Street Journal* article as an introduction to the subject, then research by academics. Useful as a text if updated.

62 NATIONAL CONSUMERS LEAGUE. *A Look at the Current Consumer Activist Movement: 1981*. Prepared for Office of Consumers Education, Department of Education, Washington, D.C., 1981. 77 pp.

An informative insider's description and analysis of the consumer movement. Briefly discusses the changing social and political context and how advocacy groups generally have responded to these changes. Using information supplied by 226 organizations, identifies priority issues and target populations of national and grass-roots groups, and briefly describes nine of the former organizations and seven of the latter. Examines consumer group experiences in federal proceedings. Lists major national and grass-roots organizations with addresses and areas of interest.

63 OLANDER, F., and LINDHOFF, H. "Consumer Action Research: A Review of the Consumerism Literature and Suggestions for New Directions in Theoretical and Empirical Research." *Social Science Information* 4 (1976): 47-84.

Reviews studies, most of them from and about the United States, that analyze or evaluate the effects of consumer action. Notes the tremendous expansion of this literature in the past three to four years and the pragmatic, atheoretical nature of most of this research. Reports that it is being conducted by researchers from many fields and with many perspectives–marketing, economics, consumer economics, political science, sociology, and Marxism, among others. Divides this research into six categories: studies of the historical, organizational, and ideological aspects of consumer action; studies resulting from proposed or enacted laws or regulations; studies of the effects of consumer education or information campaigns; studies of disadvantaged groups;

the development of instruments for measuring consumer satisfaction; and proconsumer studies of business. Suggests a theoretical model, based on work by Schermerhorn, to help analyze consumer problems and actions. Includes a useful bibliography.

64 ORLIN, MALINDA BERRY. "The Consumer Movement: The Buyer Needs a Thousand Eyes, the Seller Only One." Ph.D. dissertation, University of Pittsburgh, 1973. 331 pp.

Examines the relationship between structural conditions and consumer activism in the United States during the Progressive period, the New Deal, and the 1960s. Argues that in this last period, a unique convergence of ideological and structural elements produced a climate favorable to the development and expansion of the consumer movement. In particular, widespread affluence is necessary for the development of consumer consciousness. Yet, predicts that because of several conditions present in the 1960s, but not earlier, in the future the consumer movement will not have a significant long-term impact on the marketplace. Perhaps they did not constitute a "significant impact," but at the time the dissertation was approved, federal and state governments were approving hundreds of new consumer protections. For a more detailed summary, see *DAI* 34 (1973): 7334A.

65 RICHARDSON, STEWART LEE, Jr. "The Evolving Consumer Movement: Predictions for the 1990s." In *The Future of Consumerism*, edited by Paul N. Bloom and Ruth Belk Smith, 17-22. Lexington, Mass.: Lexington Books, 1986.

A brief but perceptive analysis of the consumer movement and its future issues. Emphasizes that the movement is dependent on its environment and thus has had a cyclical history. Discusses those resources available to consumer organizations; chiefly, they are media access, salable ideas, and credibility. Predicts that food safety and health, product safety, sinful products, deceptive practices, insurance, and cable television will receive greater consumerist attention. From the perspective of 1990, these predictions were prescient.

66 RICHARDSON, [STEWART] LEE, [Jr.]. "A Ten-Year Agenda for Consumer Advocates." In *Consumerism: New Challenges for Marketing*, edited by Norman Kangun and Lee Richardson, 167-82. Chicago: American Marketing Association, 1978.

Reviews the history of consumerism to predict its agenda during the next decade. Identifies key issues, federal agencies, advocates, and organizations. Outlines a ten-point agenda that includes establishment of a federal consumer agency, a central national organization, and new or improved public participation mechanisms. In retrospect, the agenda fails to anticipate an antiregulatory backlash that put advocates on the defensive and allowed a far less ambitious set of priorities.

67 ROSE, LAWRENCE L. "The Role of Interest Groups in Collective Interest Policy-Making: Consumer Protection in Norway and the United States." *European Journal of Political Research* 9 (March 1981): 17-45.

A comparison of the role of interest groups in consumer policy making in Norway and the United States. Explores the characteristics of consumer protection as a collective interest. Outlines six models of consumer interest representation. Examines this representation in Norway and the United States. Finds that Norway exhibits characteristics of the corporatist, quasipublic consumer agency, and political-bureaucratic models, whereas the United States, by contrast, exhibits characteristics mainly of the independent consumer association model and elements of all the others except the corporatist one. Investigates alternative patterns of agenda setting. Suggests that Norway conforms most closely to the guardian state model and the United States to the populist state model. Concludes that the different interest groups play an important role in establishing consumer protection policies. Neglects to explore important factors such as population size, social homogeneity, and culture that help explain differences between the two countries. Inaccurately describes the U.S. consumer movement. Most useful for its discussion of consumerism in Norway.

68 RUFFAT, MICHELE. *Le Contre-Pouvoir Consommateur aux États Unis*. Paris: Presses Universitaires de France, 1987. 283 pp.

An analysis of the modern U.S. consumer movement by a French political scientist based not only on documentary research but also on interviews with many consumerists. Chapter 1 traces the history of the movement from its origins in the late nineteenth century to the 1950s. Chapter 2 examines the factors that gave rise to the consumerism of the 1960s and 1970s, with emphasis on "the revolt of the individual against private and public organizations that control his life." Chapter 3 discusses major consumer organizations, the rise of Ralph Nader, and the goals of the movement. Chapter 4 reviews legislative and regulatory reforms related to the rights to safety, information, choice, representation, and education. Chapter 5 explores the movement's future. Chapter 6 discusses the role and legitimacy of consumerism in a democratic society.

69 SMITH, DARLENE BRANNIGAN, and BLOOM, PAUL N. "Is Consumerism Dead or Alive? Some Empirical Evidence." In *The Future*

of Consumerism, edited by Paul N. Bloom and Ruth Belk Smith, 61-74. Lexington, Mass.: Lexington Books, 1986.

A useful study that examines data from surveys of consumers, federal government representatives, and national consumer organizations to assess the current and future status of consumerism. Concludes that public support for consumerism remains strong, that the most pressing consumer problems are experienced by the poor and disadvantaged, that Washington policymakers are not adequately meeting consumer protection needs, and that some consumer groups (e.g., locals) are competing more effectively in the consumerism industry than others (e.g., national organizations). The analysis of consumer activist organizations is flawed by the inclusion of Consumers Union, primarily a product-testing organization with a relatively large budget and staff, in the sample of eight national consumer groups. The result is that trend data mainly reflect changes at Consumers Union. Thus, the 49 percent increase in the budgets and 31 percent decline in staff size of the nationals can be accounted for by rising subscriptions to *Consumer Reports* and by the contracting out of services formerly supplied by a Consumers Union division with some 150 employees. Furthermore, one of the "community grass-roots consumer groups" is primarily a national support organization funded almost entirely by national foundations.

70 WARLAND, REX H.; HERRMANN, ROBERT O.; and MOORE, DAN E. "Consumer Activism, Community Activism, and the Consumer Movement." In *The Future of Consumerism*, edited by Paul Bloom and Ruth Belk Smith, 85-95. Lexington, Mass.: Lexington Books, 1986.

Uses survey data from nearly 10,000 adult Pennsylvanians to examine the relation between community activism and the potential for consumer activism. Identifies a group of people representing 17 percent of the sample who have participated in both community and consumer-redress actions. These "complete activists" tend to be from the middle to upper middle class, middle-aged, and longtime residents of their communities. Suggests that they represent a pool of persons who could be recruited into the grass-roots consumer movement.

71 WARLAND, REX H.; HERRMANN, ROBERT O.; and MOORE, DAN E. "Consumer Complaining and Community Involvement: An Exploration of Their Theoretical and Empirical Linkages." *Journal of Consumer Affairs* 19 (Summer 1984): 64-78.

Examines the relationship between complaining behavior and citizen participation using data from a survey of 9,367 Pennsylvanians. Tests hypotheses derived from a model suggesting that discretionary-time activities are highly correlated. Finds that those who complain are also active in political and community affairs. Interestingly, helps explain why groups using self-help complaint-handling procedures, such as those developed by the Consumer Education and Protective Association, succeed to the extent they do.

72 WORSNOP, RICHARD L. "Directions of the Consumer Movement." *Editorial Research Reports* (12 January 1972): 23-40.

An informative report on the growth, influence, and priorities of the consumer movement. Discusses new federal legislation and regulation, Ralph Nader and his organizations, the history of the movement, its dissatisfaction with the performance of federal regulatory agencies, and its plans to advocate the establishment of new consumer product safety and consumer protection agencies.

3. Early History

73 DAMERON, KENNETH. "The Consumer Movement." *Harvard Business Review* 18 (January 1939): 271-89.

An analysis of the early history and economic implications of the consumer movement up to the late 1930s. Describes consumer education, consumer guides and product rating services, and consumer protection at the federal and state levels. Discusses the need for informative labels and advertising. Treats the efforts of retailers, service industries, and professions to advance the consumer interest. Predicts that the consumer movement will consolidate, work more closely with business, improve consumer education and representation programs, and place greater emphasis on price and cost information.

74 HARRISON, DENNIS IRVEN. "The Consumers' League of Ohio: Women and Reform, 1909-1937." Ph.D. dissertation, Case Western Reserve University, 1975. 367 pp.

Uses detailed records of the Consumers' League of Ohio to examine this organization during the period 1909-37. Shows how the work of the league linked reform efforts in the Progressive period to those in the New Deal. In both, the league took leadership in Ohio in advocating the interests of child and female workers. Suggests that by allowing the league to become a quasipublic agency, the Committee on Women and Children in Industry, the war encouraged its reform activities. Credits the organization with stimulating a national movement for unemployment insurance in the 1930s. For a more detailed summary, see *DAI* 36 (1975): 3964.

General

75 KEYSERLING, MARY DUBLIN. "The First National Consumers Organization: The National Consumers League." In *Consumer Activists: They Made a Difference*, edited by Erma Angevine, 343-60. Mount Vernon, N.Y.: Consumers Union Foundation, 1982.

A brief history of the National Consumers League from its founding in 1899 to 1940. Reveals NCL's emphasis on worker issues during this period.

76 MAYER, ROBERT. *The Consumer Movement: Guardians of the Marketplace*. Boston: Twayne Publishers, 1989. Ch. 2.

See entry 57 for annotation.

77 ROBERTS, EIRLYS. *Consumers*. New York: International Publications Service, 1966. 220 pp.

An early but valuable analysis of the rise, current character, and significance of modern consumerism in industrialized countries. Chapters treat the early history of Consumers Research and Consumers Union, consumer protections, British consumerism, consumerism in Europe (Scandinavia, the Netherlands, Belgium, and France), the role of consumer research, the language of consumer research, the role of consumer groups in society, and the implications of future social changes for consumerism. The discussion is informed by and refers to the work of theorists such as Marx, Tawney, Veblen, and Galbraith.

78 SAMSON, PETER EDWARD. "The Emergence of a Consumer Interest in America, 1870-1930." Ph.D. dissertation, University of Chicago, 1980.

Shows how the consumer interest emerged as a major social and economic force between 1870 and 1930. After pointing out that in this period consumption was managed almost exclusively by women, traces social concern for the consumer interest first to cookbooks, then to women's magazines, and finally to the home economics profession. Demonstrates how the issue of food safety in the first decade of the twentieth century and the issue of inflation in the second decade brought to national attention important consumer concerns. The result was the passage of consumer legislation and establishment of consumer watchdog government agencies. Identifies Stuart Chase and F. J. Schlink's *Your Money's Worth* as the first comprehensive antibusiness critique from a consumer perspective. Explains how this led to the formation of Consumers Research, the "first modern consumer organization." For a more detailed summary, see *DAI* 41 (1981): 3235A.

79 SIEKMAN, P. "U.S. Business's Most Skeptical Customer: Should Manufacturers Take Consumers Union Seriously?" *Fortune* 62 (September 1960): 157-59+.

A description and evaluation of Consumers Union. Concludes that it can influence sales, usually tests products adequately, and is not biased against large manufacturers. Discusses the history of the organization, including prewar and postwar charges of its being a communist front and repudiation of these charges by a congressional committee.

80 SILBER, NORMAN ISAAC. "Consumer Protest and the Social Control of Technology: The Public Interest at Consumers Union, 1936-1964." Ph.D. dissertation, Yale University, 1978. 226 pp.

Uses newly available archival records and other sources to analyze how Consumers Union utilized scientific product testing as a form of social criticism during the first twenty-eight years of its existence. This goal was attained by relating the deficiencies of consumer products to larger economic and social problems. Contains detailed case studies of the reform of automotive design, the discouragement of smoking, and the prevention of contamination of food by radioactive fallout. Concludes that Consumers Union was an important center of consumer activism and played a key role in informing Americans about problems of environmental health and public safety. For a more detailed summary, see *DAI* 40 (1979): 422. A revised version of this study was published as *Test and Protest* (entry 81).

81 SILBER, NORMAN I[SAAC]. *Test and Protest*. New York: Holmes & Meier, 1983. 172 pp.

An examination of product testing at Consumers Union and its impacts on reform of automotive design, discouragement of smoking, and prevention of food contamination from radioactive fallout. Chapter 1 outlines the emergence of a mass consumption society and the types of criticisms made of it. Chapter 2 discusses the origins of Consumers Union and its development of product testing as a means of technological and social criticism. Chapters 3, 4, and 5 represent case studies of the role of Consumers Union's product testing in expanding public awareness about smoking, unsafe cars, and radioactive contamination of food. Chapter 6 assesses the impact and limitations of Consumers Union's product testing, including the role of this testing in building support for the consumer movement. Despite the claims of its title, this book neglects to examine the period after 1970, CU's role in promoting other consumer organizations, and its role in influencing public policy and public opinion on issues other than the three

General

examined. Nevertheless, for these three issues the study represents a valuable analysis of Consumers Union's product testing, its limitations, and its impacts on public awareness and policy making. Based on doctoral dissertation (entry 80).

82 WARE, CAROLINE. "Consumer Participation at the Federal Level." In *Consumer Activists: They Made a Difference*, edited by Erma Angevine, 171-97. Mount Vernon, N.Y.: Consumers Union Foundation, 1982.

Discusses consumer advisory boards in the federal government from the New Deal to the Kennedy administration. Notes that the first boards were established not in response to consumer pressure but because of a commitment by New Dealers to public participation. Treats advisory boards to the National Recovery Administration, Agricultural Adjustment Administration, the Bituminous Coal Consumer Counsel, the National Defense Advisory Commission, and consumer advisory committees to Office of Price Administration, Council of Economic Advisors, and President Kennedy. Reviews the strengths and weaknesses of this consumer participation.

83 WARNE, COLSTON E. "Consumers Union's Contribution to the Consumer Movement." In *Consumer Activists: They Made a Difference*, edited by Erma Angevine, 85-110. Mount Vernon, N.Y.: Consumers Union Foundation, 1982.

See entry 22 for annotation.

BEFORE 1920

84 ANDERSON, OSCAR E., Jr. *The Health of a Nation: Harvey W. Wiley and the Fight for Pure Food*. Chicago: University of Chicago Press, 1958. 333 pp.

A well-researched biography of the leading advocate for safe food and drugs in the late nineteenth and early twentieth centuries. Written by a historian, the study relies mainly on Wiley's personal and professional papers to examine his life chronologically. Provides extensive information and analysis about Wiley's life and the institutions with which he interacted. Contains little evaluation of the larger significance of his work, or analysis of the profound changes in food production and the political role of the food industry during this period.

85 ATHEY, LOUIS LEE. "The Consumers' Leagues and Social Reform, 1890-1923." Ph.D. dissertation, University of Delaware, 1965. 355 pp.

Examines consumers' leagues during the Progressive period. Despite their name, these organizations focused on improving working conditions, particularly those of women and children. In the first three chapters, traces the origin, development, and expansion of the ideas and organization of the leagues. In the next four, treats league activity on specific issues. In closing chapters, discusses the decline of the leagues and their relation to the Progressive era. Reaches the following conclusions: Members were mainly middle-class women motivated by humanitarianism. The leagues were similar to reform organizations in many European countries, in part because they participated in international conferences. Their main legacy was promoting the idea that society is responsible for the welfare of individuals harmed by industrialization. For a more detailed summary, see *DAI* 26 (1966): 7275.

86 BAILEY, THOMAS A. "Congressional Opposition to Pure Food Legislation, 1879-1906," *American Journal of Sociology*, 36 (July 1930): 52-64.

Examines the twenty-seven-year congressional debate that culminated in the passage of the Pure Food Law in 1906. Characterizes progress of pure-food legislation as a "long evolutionary process" in which the focus of attention shifted gradually from bills dealing with specific foods to a general law. Identifies three types of congressional opposition to the legislation: those who objected on Constitutional grounds (mainly states' rights advocates), those who were not aware of the seriousness of the problem, and those who had a personal interest in "perpetuating the frauds" that the legislation was designed to eliminate. Suggests that the most important factor moving the legislation forward was the publication of critical reports on food safety that aroused public opinion and persuaded the second congressional group to support protections.

87 BLUMBERG, DOROTHY ROSE. *Florence Kelley: The Making of a Social Pioneer*. New York: Augustus M. Kelley, 1966. 194 pp.

A well-researched biography of a leading advocate against child labor in the late nineteenth and early twentieth centuries. The last chapter discusses her work for the National Consumers League as general secretary. Contains little information on the last thirty years of her life.

88 GAEDEKE, RALPH M[ORTIMER]. "The Muckraking Era." In *Consumerism – Viewpoints from Business, Government, and the Public*

Before 1920

Interest, edited by Ralph M. Gaedeke and Warren W. Etcheson, 57-59. San Francisco: Canfield Press, 1972.

A brief overview of consumerism and consumer protection between the 1870s and 1930s.

89 OKUN, MITCHELL. "Fair Play in the Marketplace: Adulteration and the Origins of Consumerism." Ph.D. dissertation, City University of New York, 1983. 476 pp.

Examines the food and drug adulteration and related reform efforts in the mid- to late 1800s. Discusses the passage of adulteration laws and the establishment of professional boards of health around the time of the Civil War. Shows how new threats to the safety of food and drugs resulted from the implementation of new technologies such as the mechanization of canning, use of refrigeration cars, and introduction of new processed foods. Explains how food manufacturers and chemists defeated reform legislation at both the federal and state levels. For a more detailed summary, see *DAI* 44 (1983): 1551-A.

90 OKUN, MITCHELL. *Fair Play in the Marketplace: The First Battle for Pure Food and Drugs*. DeKalb: Northern Illinois University Press, 1986. 345 pp.

A well-documented history of the battle over adulteration of food and drugs fought between 1865 and 1886. Focuses on the methods and motives of those leaders in business, chemistry, and medicine who shaped the antiadulteration laws passed by several states. Explores related events in Washington, D.C., New Jersey, and Massachusetts, but concentrates on New York, where these laws were first proposed and where the associated controversy paralleled that of the Pure Food and Drug Act of 1906. Based on doctoral dissertation (entry 89).

91 THELEN, DAVID P. "Patterns of Consumer Consciousness in the Progressive Movement: Robert M. La Follette, the Antitrust Persuasion, and Labor Legislation." In *The Quest for Social Justice*, edited by Ralph M. Aderman, 19-47. Madison: University of Wisconsin Press, 1983.

An important article on the development of consumer consciousness in the late nineteenth and early twentieth centuries. Argues that, under the leadership of Robert M. La Follette, this consciousness developed a strong prolabor orientation. Explains how early consumer activists, especially those of the National Consumers League, advocated reforms such as improved product quality and safety that were consistent with those advocated by labor. Attributes labor support by consumer advocates to the latter's "radical resistance to and critique of industrial capitalism." This article reveals how different the worldview of consumer activists was in this early period from that in the current one.

92 WILEY, HARVEY. *An Autobiography*. Indianapolis: Bobbs-Merrill Co., 1930. 339 pp.

The fascinating autobiography of the leading advocate for pure food and drug protections in the late nineteenth and early twentieth centuries. Covers all periods of his life. Discusses his personal life and his professional work as a chemist as well as his advocacy activities. Reveals what an enormous impact a well-trained, socially concerned scientist can have.

1920s AND 1930s

93 BEEM, EUGENE R. "The Beginnings of the Consumer Movement" and "The Consumer Movement, 1930 to World War II." In *New Consumerism: Selected Readings*, edited by William T. Kelley, 13-45. Columbus, Ohio: Grid, 1973.

These two articles provide a useful overview of the early history of the consumer movement. The first discusses cooperatives, the American Home Economics Association, the Chicago Housewives League, the National Consumers League, consumer educators, the muckrakers, Harvey Wiley, business self-regulation, consumer laws, and the "guinea pig" books. The second describes organizations with secondary consumer interests and those with primary consumer interests – cooperatives, the American Home Economics Association, consumer committees and councils, and national consumer organizations. It pays insufficient attention to the most important group, Consumers Union.

94 CAMPBELL, PERSIA. *Consumer Representation in the New Deal*. New York: Columbia University Press, 1940. 298 pp.

An examination of consumer representation in selected federal government agencies during the New Deal. Focuses specific attention on the Consumer Advisory Board and the Consumers Division in the National Recovery Administration, the Consumers Counsel of the National Bituminous Coal Commission, and the Consumers Counsel in the Agricultural Adjustment Administration. Concludes that the advice of these consumer advisory groups was constructive but was not heeded because of their lack of influence and autonomy. Recommends that the consumer interest in government be "separately represented" by an independent consumer agency.

95 CHASE, STUART, and SCHLINK, FREDERICK J. *Your Money's Worth*. New York: Macmillan, 1927. 285 pp.

A major exposé of consumer exploitation that helped initiate a wave of consumerism in the late 1920s and 1930s. Criticizes modern marketing methods (advertising and sales techniques) as often deceptive and unconscionable, and finds the products they promote to be frequently overpriced, shoddy, adulterated, or useless. Advocates product standardization, government standard setting, and the establishment of a private organization to test and disseminate information about products. Responses to this book led to the founding of Consumers Research.

96 "Fifty Years Ago: What Happened When Consumerism and Unionism, Two Great Social Movements of the 1930s, Collided?" *Consumer Reports* 51 (January 1986): 8-10; (February 1986): 76-79.

Discusses the forces and people that led to the establishment of Consumers Union. Identifies mass production, electrification, national advertising, and rising prosperity as important preconditions. Points out that the values of a mass consumption society were criticized by Thorstein Veblen and the accompanying abuses exposed by Stuart Chase and Frederick Schlink. With others, the latter two authors organized the first consumer product-testing organization, Consumers Research, in 1927. Eight years later, in a dispute over wages, some employees of this organization left to form Consumers Union, the new product-testing organization that publishes *Consumer Reports*. Describes the first issue of this magazine and the problems the new group faced in its early years. Indicates that subscriptions did not rise substantially until the 1950s.

97 KALLETT, ARTHUR, and SCHLINK, F[REDERICK] J. *100,000,000 Guinea Pigs: Dangers in Everyday Foods, Drugs, and Cosmetics*. New York: Vanguard Press, 1932. 312 pp.

An exposé of health and safety threats posed by foods, drugs, and cosmetics. A best-seller, it was instrumental in building public support for the Food, Drug, and Cosmetic Act of 1938. Treats issues such as the dangers of specific foods, arsenic and lead contamination, unsafe and ineffective drugs and cosmetics, fake antiseptics, and dangerous patent medicines. Criticizes the weakness of federal law and its enforcement. Proposes a new system of regulating these products.

98 MATTHEWS, J. B. *Odyssey of a Fellow Traveler*. New York: Mount Vernon Publishers, 1938. 285 pp.

The autobiography of a radical who served on the board of directors of Consumers Research. In the chapter entitled "Dissenter Again," he recounts his efforts to oppose what he felt was a Communist party attempt to seize control of Consumers Research. He characterizes Arthur Kallet, who helped organize Consumers Union, as a functional Communist party member. See Warne (entry 191) for a different perspective on these events.

1940s AND 1950s

99 CAMPBELL, PERSIA. *The Consumer Interest*. New York: Harper and Brothers, 1949. 649 pp.

An early consumer economics textbook written by a leading consumer educator and advocate. Chapter 10 analyzes a consumer movement that was far less well organized than it is today. Discusses consumer education, consumer organization (cooperatives, testing agencies, consumer councils, attempts to establish a national organization, citizen groups with a consumer interest), and consumer representation.

100 CAMPBELL, PERSIA. "Consumer Representation at the State Level: The Pioneers, New York." In *Consumer Activists: They Made a Difference*, edited by Erma Angevine, 213-27. Mount Vernon, N.Y.: Consumers Union Foundation, 1982.

A paper on the functions and legislative program of the New York State consumer counsel in the late 1950s. Written by a leading consumer advocate of the period who held this position. Discusses the relation of this office to the state Consumer Advisory Committee. Identifies as legislative priorities reform of installment credit terms, elimination of deceptive sales practices, and regulation of chemicals in food.

101 GILMARTIN, Sister JEANINE. "A Historical Analysis of the Growth of the National Consumer Movement in the United States from 1947 to 1967." Ph.D. dissertation, Georgetown University, 1970. 188 pp.

Analyzes the history of the consumer movement between 1947 and 1967. Suggests that the movement grew as consumers tried to gain a meaningful role in politics. Emphasizes the following developments: In 1947, establishment of the National Association of Consumers. In 1950, introduction of the first congressional legislation "to establish some type of legislative machinery" to protect the consumer interest. In 1962,

1940s and 1950s

President Kennedy's consumer message to Congress. Shortly thereafter, institutionalization of consumer input in the executive branch through a special assistant to the president for consumer affairs, a President's Committee on Consumer Interests, and a Consumer Advisory Council. Passage of congressional consumer legislation. In 1967, formation of the Consumer Federation of America. For a more detailed summary, see *DAI* 31 (1970): 2306A.

102 KATZ, NORMAN DAVID. "Consumers Union: The Movement and the Magazine, 1938-1957." Ph.D. dissertation, Rutgers University, 1977. 431 pp.

Examines the history of Consumers Union from its founding in the 1930s through the 1950s. Discusses the ideology that "spawned" the product-testing organization and the influence of the writings of Thorstein Veblen on this worldview. Shows how the ideology changed over the years in response to national and world political, economic, and intellectual developments. Also traces the institutional development of the organization. For a more detailed summary, see *DAI* 38 (1979): 1973A.

103 NEWMAN, SARAH H. "Early Consumer Activities in Washington, D.C." In *Consumer Activists: They Made a Difference*, edited by Erma Angevine, 297-309. Mount Vernon, N.Y.: Consumers Union Foundation, 1982.

A review of the activities and accomplishments of local consumer groups in Washington, D.C., in the late 1930s and 1940s written by a participant. These organizations are the D.C. Milk Committee, which sought to reduce milk prices in the late 1930s; the Washington Committee for Consumer Protection, which tried to reduce consumer prices in the late 1940s; the League of Women Shoppers, which worked for price controls and rationing in the late 1930s and early 1940s; and consumer cooperatives, which began in the mid-1930s. Most of these organizations were supported by trade unions.

104 PETERSON, ESTHER. "Representing the Consumer Interest in the Federal Government." *Michigan Law Review* 64 (May 1966): 1323-28.

An article by Esther Peterson, President Johnson's newly appointed consumer adviser, on the way the executive branch represents the consumer interest. Reviews consumer representation in federal agencies during the New Deal and World War II. Discusses the need for the government to play an active role in ensuring adequate product information. Describes her position as special assistant to the president for consumer affairs and the way her office sought to define more precisely the federal role in consumer affairs.

105 WARE, CAROLINE. "The Consumer Voice: Lobbying in the Consumer Interest." In *Consumer Activists: They Made a Difference*, edited by Erma Angevine, 319-26. Mount Vernon, N.Y.: Consumers Union Foundation, 1982.

A discussion of consumer advocacy on the issues of food and drugs, resale price maintenance, and wartime price controls in the late 1930s and 1940s. Identifies advocacy groups active in this period.

4. Public Opinion

106 BARKSDALE, HIRAM C., and DARDEN, WILLIAM R. "Consumer Attitudes toward Marketing and Consumerism." *Journal of Marketing* 36 (October 1972): 28-35.

Analyzes responses to a 1971 national survey of consumer attitudes toward marketing and consumer advocacy. Concludes that consumers value many aspects of a free-market system, are dissatisfied with many business policies and marketing practices, and strongly support additional government regulation. Finds that there are few significant differences between categories of demographic variables, though younger, liberal respondents tend to be more critical of business and more supportive of consumerism. Suggests that if business does not improve customer relations, it will face increased government regulation. Survey incorporated in 1976 *Journal of Consumer Affairs* article (entry 107).

107 BARKSDALE, HIRAM C.; DARDEN, WILLIAM R.; and PERREAULT, WILLIAM D. "Changes in Consumer Attitudes toward Marketing, Consumerism, and Government Regulation: 1971-75." *Journal of Consumer Affairs* 10 (Winter 1976): 117-39.

Using responses to national surveys in 1971, 1973, and 1975, analyzes consumer attitudes toward marketing, regulation, and consumer advocacy. Sample sizes ranged from 354 to 697, slightly under half of the questionnaires mailed each year. Found no substantial swings but several discrete trends in consumer attitudes during the four-year period. Most important, discovered relatively high levels of consumer dissatisfaction and support for more active government intervention. Suggests that inflation and the "supercharged times" may help account for both.

108 CARPENTER, EDWIN HUGH. "An Exploration of the Factors Determining Support of the Consumer Movement." Ph.D. dissertation, Pennsylvania State University, 1972. 185 pp.

Uses the attitudes of 908 Pennsylvanians to try to explain why some persons support the consumer movement, others oppose it, and still others know little or nothing about it. Generates hypotheses from the theory of Neil Smelser on collective behavior, whose important concepts include beliefs in the injustice of social arrangements, in the fact of blocked or marginally effective channels for redress of grievances, and in the necessity of social reform. Examines the relationship between these three factors and support for Ralph Nader. Finds a strong association between beliefs in being treated unfairly, in being unable to obtain redress, and in giving support for social reform, on the one hand, and support for Nader, on the other. But also discovers that some nonsupporters also share the same beliefs. Thus, concludes that great frustration does not always result in support for the consumer movement. Offers suggestions to consumer advocates about holding and building support, and gives suggestions to business and government about how to respond to consumer dissatisfaction. For a more detailed summary, see *DAI* 34 (1973-74): 1369A.

109 EVERS, MYRLIE. "Consumerism in the Eighties." *Public Relations Journal*, August 1983, 24-26.

Summarizes the key findings of the 1983 *Consumerism in the Eighties* public opinion survey commissioned by ARCO and conducted by Louis Harris and Associates, Inc. Briefly explains why ARCO initiated the survey and how it was developed.

110 GASKI, JOHN F., and ETZEL, MICHAEL J. "Evolution of Consumer Attitudes toward Business, 1971-84: A Replication." In *The Future of Consumerism*, edited by Paul N. Bloom and Ruth Belk Smith, 75-83. Lexington, Mass.: Lexington Books, 1986.

A study of consumer attitudes toward business in 1984 that updates earlier research by Barksdale, Darden, and Perreault. Data analyzed were supplied by 1,428 randomly selected households throughout the United States. Concludes that consumer attitudes toward business are slightly negative but have improved since the 1970s. Notes that this finding conflicts with that of Harris (entry 120).

111 GAZDA, GREGORY MACE. "A Study of the Attitudes of Businessmen, Consumers, and Consumerists toward Consumerism." Ph.D. dissertation, Arizona State University, 1974. 195 pp.

Uses several hundred mailed questionnaires completed by consumers, consumerists, and businesspeople in Tempe, Arizona, to assess the attitudes of these three groups toward consumerism. Examines the attitudes of these respondents to product information, product safety, advertising, government protection, and the environment. Concludes that consumers, consumerists, and businesspeople hold different attitudes toward consumerism. Yet on most issues the views of consumers and consumerists are closest. Also finds that consumers do not support government protection as strongly as has been indicated in the consumerism literature, desire more and better information, do not regard advertising highly, and are less concerned about product safety than are consumerists; in addition, finds that the elderly are not very concerned about consumerism. For a more detailed summary, see *DAI* 34 (1974): 4490A. For an even more extensive summary and evaluation, see Gazda's *Journal of Consumer Affairs* article (entry 112).

112 GAZDA, GREGORY M[ACE], and GOURLEY, DAVID R. "Attitudes of Businessmen, Consumers, and Consumerists Toward Consumerism." *Journal of Consumer Affairs* 9 (Winter 1975): 176-86.

Reports the results of an early study of the attitudes of businesspeople, consumers, and consumerists. Uses data from questionnaires completed by about 400 representatives of the three groups in Arizona. Finds considerable differences in the attitudes of each but more agreement of consumerists with consumers than of businesspeople with consumers. Specifically, consumers agree with consumerists on the need for more product information, proof of product safety in advance, more truthful ads, and environmentally benign products, but they disagree with them on the desirability of government-imposed safety standards, the difficulty of obtaining product information, government regulation of business, and business responsibility for water pollution. Somewhat at odds with national surveys sponsored by Sentry Insurance and by ARCO, this research may reflect in part the conservatism of Arizona citizens. Based on a doctoral dissertation (entry 111).

113 HARRIS, LOUIS. "Nader Gets a Positive Job Rating." *Washington Post*, 23 June 1975, sec. C, p. 4.

A prominent pollster reports the results of a recent opinion survey on Ralph Nader and compares it with earlier surveys. Reveals that a majority of consumers believe he has done an "excellent" or "pretty good" job protecting their interests and that support for him is even greater than four years earlier.

114 HERRMANN, ROBERT O., and WARLAND, REX H. "Nader's Support: Its Sources and Concerns." *Journal of Consumer Affairs* 10 (Summer 1976): 1-18.

Uses data from telephone interviews with a nationwide sample of 1,215 adults to examine the extent of support for Ralph Nader and its sources. Finds that Nader has considerable support, particularly among middle-income liberals who are active complainers and supporters of other political and social causes. Concludes that support for Nader is part of a "broader pattern of social and political activism." Notes that the desire for brand-related product information is not highly correlated with support for Nader.

115 HUSTAD, THOMAS P., and PRESSEMIER, EDGAR A. "Will the Real Consumer Activist Please Stand Up: An Examination of Consumers' Opinions about Marketing Practices." *Journal of Marketing Research* 10 (August 1973): 319-24.

Analyzes the results of a survey of consumer opinion of marketing practices. The sample includes 912 husband-wife pairs from an Indiana city. Uses a cluster analysis of 115 variables to identify probusiness, antibusiness, and uncommitted groups. Correlates these three groups with values, latent occupation abilities, activities, media consumption, product usage, product ownership, and socioeconomic variables. Reports that the antibusiness group makes up 18 percent of the sample population and is associated with the "activist avant-garde segment of society with both the motivation and the capacity to institute change."

116 JACKSON, GARY BRIAN. "An Investigation of the Relationship between Perceived Risk and Consumerism." Ph.D. dissertation, University of Arkansas, 1977. 105 pp.

Uses responses from 193 mailed questionnaires to investigate the relationship between perceived risk and consumerism. In addition, examines how perceived risk in the purchase of a new car and consumerism attitudes toward the automobile industry are associated with perceived changes in real income and political preference. Questions were related to three clusters of variables: 1) the perceived risk of money, time, ego, and hazard losses; 2) consumerism attitudes toward the auto industry and its regulation; and 3) past consumerism activities such as complaining to a government agency or participating in a consumer boycott. Finds that perceptions of risk are highly correlated with consumerism attitudes and activities. Also learns that proconsumerism opinions are associated with political liberalism. Concludes that before consumerism behavior can be changed, consumerism attitudes probably must change. Suggests that auto manufacturers should seek to improve consumer opinion of their "fairness." For a more detailed summary, see *DAI* 38 (1977): 3008.

117 KROLL, ROBERT J[OSEPH]. "The Consumerism Gender Gap." In *Proceedings: 30th Annual Conference of the American Council on Consumer Interests*, edited by Karen P. Goebel, 272-78. Columbia, Mo.: American Council on Consumer Interests, 1984.

A paper investigating the nature of the political and consumerism gender gaps using 621 questionnaires completed by Madison, Wisconsin, and Rockford, Illinois, residents. Confirms the political gender gap found by pollsters. Finds a consumerism gender gap, where women are more supportive of consumer and environmental regulation than are men, that was partially a subset of the political gender gap. Discovers that the importance assigned to freedom and equality, marital status, family income, and involvement in an income-producing role help account for the two gaps.

118 KROLL, ROBERT JOSEPH. "Orientations toward Consumerism." Ph.D. dissertation, University of Wisconsin, Madison, 1982. 294 pp.

Uses responses from 621 questionnaires to classify individuals in terms of their orientations toward consumerism. Finds that across issues, respondents are consistent in their support or nonsupport for consumerism and in their preference for choice-limiting or choice-allowing solutions. Also learns that these views are related to broader political orientations and to approval ratings of Ralph Nader, Ronald Reagan, other political leaders, and political parties. Discusses implications of findings for consumer advocates and educators, business, government, and political parties. For a more detailed summary, see *DAI* 43 (1982): 1663.

119 KROLL, ROBERT J[OSEPH], and STAMPFL, RONALD W. "Orientations toward Consumerism: A Test of a Two-Dimensional Theory." *Journal of Consumer Affairs* 20 (Winter 1986): 214-30.

Using survey data from 621 respondents, attempts to resolve inconsistencies in research on orientations toward consumerism by testing a theory based on Rokeach's two-dimensional theory of political orientations. Finds that preference for choice-limiting or choice-allowing solutions helps distinguish different types of supporters of consumerism. Suggests as one "tentative" implication that consumerists should not assume that consumers concerned about a problem will support any solution that is proposed. Based on Kroll's doctoral dissertation (entry 118).

120 LOUIS HARRIS AND ASSOCIATES, INC. *Consumerism in the Eighties.* Los Angeles: Atlantic Richfield Co., 1983. 92 pp.

A major national opinion survey on consumerism that builds on the 1977 survey conducted by Harris for Sentry Insurance (entry 122). Reports and comments on consumer attitudes about the marketplace, government agencies, consumer groups, government regulation, credit, personal involvement in the consumer movement, and special groups of consumers. Finds that the public is more critical of the consumer protection activities of the federal government and of consumer organizations than in 1977. Learns that consumers are more critical of government regulation in general, yet they are very supportive of many specific regulations.

121 LOUIS HARRIS AND ASSOCIATES, INC. *A Survey of the Public, Community Leaders, and Consumer Activists on: Consumerism.* New York: Louis Harris and Associates, 1978. 73 pp.

A summary of the views of the public and of consumer advocates on definitions of consumerism, consumer problems, business, product safety, consumers, regulators, the consumer movement, corporate consumer affairs representatives, and selected issues. Fails to describe sample populations. Less useful than the Sentry and Arco surveys, also by Harris.

122 LOUIS HARRIS AND ASSOCIATES, INC., and MARKETING SCIENCE INSTITUTE. *Consumerism at the Crossroads: A National Opinion Research Survey of Public, Activist, Business, and Regulator Attitudes toward the Consumer Movement.* Boston: Sentry Insurance, 1977. 90 pp.

The first major national opinion survey on consumerism. Examines attitudes about business and the marketplace, government regulation, consumer groups, sources of consumer information, and the future. Reports that the public strongly supports the consumer movement but does not always agree with its priorities, backs a range of new consumer initiatives, and mistrusts advertising. Also includes the results of a survey of consumer activists, government consumer affairs officials, business consumer representatives, and senior business executives.

123 MASON, J. BARRY, and BEARDEN, WILLIAM O. "A Comparative Analysis of Elderly Perceptions of the Consumer Movement." *Journal of Consumer Studies and Home Economics* 5 (September 1981): 187-98.

A study of perceptions by the elderly of the consumer movement and of government and business efforts to protect consumers.

Compares views of 100 elderly couples with those of the entire adult population, as reported in the Sentry Insurance survey (entry 122). Concludes that the elderly have more negative attitudes toward the movement and toward business and government protection than do other groups. It is not clear that the small sample, drawn from a southeastern city, is representative of all elderly. Moreover, the most striking finding is that the elderly know so little about the consumer movement: 58 percent "knew nothing about" Ralph Nader. Specific agencies that are familiar such as the Food and Drug Administration and the Better Business Bureau receive high ratings.

124 MILLONES, PETER. "Consumer Indignation." *New York Times*, 30 June 1969, 29.

An article on rising consumer dissatisfaction and support for the consumer movement, especially among the young who bring a "moralistic approach" to the movement.

125 STANLEY, THOMAS J., and ROBINSON, LARRY M. "Opinions on Consumer Issues: A Review of Recent Studies of Executives and Consumers." *Journal of Consumer Affairs* 14 (Summer 1980): 207-20.

An analysis of five major attitudinal studies conducted between 1971 and 1977 to try to explain differences in the opinions of consumers and business executives. Reports a growing gap between the attitudes of the two groups on consumerism issues. Specifically, finds that consumers favor, and executives oppose, additional government regulation. Discovers that consumers believe there is a need for improved product safety and information disclosures that is not recognized by businesspeople.

5. National Organizations

ACTION FOR CHILDREN'S TELEVISION

Organized in 1968, a coalition of more than 100 organizations that supports diversity in children's television and the elimination of abuses in children's advertising. Seeks to achieve these goals through public education, publications, and national conferences and workshops. Founded and led by Peggy Charren. Based in Newtonville, Massachusetts.

126 "A Harsh Critic of Kids' TV." *Business Week*, 29 May 1978, 52.

An article on Peggy Charren, founder and president of Action for Children's Television (ACT), which is seeking to improve the quality of children's TV programs. Describes the establishment of this organization by outraged mothers and its current focus on federal regulatory agencies.

AMERICAN COUNCIL ON SCIENCE AND HEALTH

Founded in 1978 by Elizabeth Whelan to try to provide an alternative to public interest groups that emphasize dangerous products and to advocate greater health and safety regulation. Concentrates on public education. Funded largely by corporations and conservative foundations. Directed by Whelan. Based in New York City.

127 BRONSON, GAIL. "New Groups to Study Health Issues, Give Nader Competition." *Wall Street Journal*, 18 July 1978, 17.

Reports on the formation of a new nonprofit group, the American Council on Science and Health, to provide a different perspective than

American Council on Science and Health

organizations such as the Health Research Group and Center for Science in the Public Interest on health and safety issues. Identifies the leader of the New York-based organization as Elizabeth Whelan. Indicates that the organization will often defend corporations and will accept corporate funds.

CENTER FOR AUTO SAFETY

An organization established by Ralph Nader in 1970 to work for reduced deaths and injuries from motor vehicle accidents. Collects and analyzes information on auto-related consumer complaints as the basis for monitoring the performance of the National Highway Traffic Safety Administration. When CAS finds this wanting, pressures NHTSA through public education, litigation, and intervention at the agency. Directed by Clarence Ditlow. Based in Washington, D.C.

128 JENSEN, CHRISTOPHER. "This Man Gives the Auto Industry Nightmares." *Plain Dealer*, 24 July 1988, sec. D, p. 1+.
    A lengthy profile of Clarence Ditlow and the Center for Auto Safety, the organization he heads. Describes Ditlow's education, views of the auto industry, and leadership of the center. Discusses the center's goals, activities, membership, staff, and criticism from industry and the National Highway Traffic Safety Administration.

129 LOGAN, GARY J. "Steering toward Safety." *Everyday Law*, February 1989, 43-48.
    An article on the Center for Auto Safety, a Washington-based consumer advocacy organization founded by Ralph Nader. Its principal role is monitoring the performance of the National Highway Traffic Safety Administration using the thousands of auto complaints it receives annually. Describes the organization's budget, membership, publications, petitioning of NHTSA, and impacts.

130 SCHORR, BURT, and CONTE, CHRISTOPHER. "Coming of Age: Public-Interest Groups Achieve Higher Status and Some Permanence." *Wall Street Journal*, 27 August 1984, 1+.
    Examines the role of national public interest groups in the 1980s. Identifies key functions as pressuring federal regulatory agencies to enforce laws, calling attention to new problems, and supplying data to legislators and regulators. Gives special attention to Clarence Ditlow, director of the Center for Auto Safety, Dr. Sidney Wolfe, head of Health Research Group (HRG), and their organizations. The work of the center is based largely on some 30,000 complaints it receives

annually and is directed largely at the National Highway Traffic Safety Administration. The HRG focuses much of its attention on the performance of the Food and Drug Administration.

CENTER FOR COMMUNITY CHANGE

A support group for community-based citizen organizations that was established in 1967. Provides technical assistance about management, fund-raising, and advocacy. Has played an important role in initiating and advising grass-roots challenges to banks and insurance companies that discriminate against low- and moderate-income households. Directed by Pablo Eisenberg. Based in Washington, D.C.

131 JOHNSTON, DAVID. "The Poor's Voice among Philanthropists." *Los Angeles Times*, 18 December 1986, 1+.

A lengthy profile of Pablo Eisenberg, head of the Center for Community Change, which provides technical assistance to community organizations. Describes his background, his organization, and its assistance to Los Angeles groups.

132 WILLIAMS, ROGER. "Centering on the Underdog." *Foundation News*, September-October 1987, 18-24.

A lengthy article on the Center for Community Change, which provides technical assistance to community organizations and has supported consumer banking reforms. Discusses the types of assistance it renders, the types of organizations it helps, and its special projects. Includes a sidebar on Pablo Eisenberg, its president.

CENTER FOR SCIENCE IN THE PUBLIC INTEREST

Organized in 1971, an advocacy and education group for promoting a safe, healthful food supply and diet. To achieve this goal, seeks to educate the public, influence public policy, and reform corporate practices. Recently has worked on issues such as more accurate nutritional claims by food producers, reduction of fat content in "fast foods," and alcohol labeling. Directed by Michael Jacobson. Based in Washington, D.C.

133 JACQUENEY, THEODORE. "Public Interest Groups Challenge Government, Industry." *National Journal Reports* 6 (23 February 1974): 267-77.

Center for Science in the Public Interest

Profiles four public interest organizations including the Center for Science in the Public Interest, which was founded and is led by Michael Jacobson. Discusses the organization's staff, budget, goals, and priority issues.

134 MARTER, MARILYN. "A Hungry Watchdog." *Philadelphia Inquirer*, 11 May 1988, sec. F, p. 1+.

A lengthy article on Michael Jacobson and the organization he heads, Center for Science in the Public Interest. Describes the organization's origins, budget, membership, and priorities; also details Jacobson's background and eating habits. Includes comments from food industry representatives and from an academic.

135 MILLER, ANNETTA. "A Sizzling Food Fight." *Newsweek*, 20 April 1987, 56.

A report on the new marketing campaigns of beef and pork producers and criticism of them by the Center for Science in the Public Interest.

136 SEABERRY, JANE. "Consumer Crusaders Doggedly Stay on Job." *Washington Post*, 18 July 1974, 1+.

An article on the new Center for Science in the Public Interest. Reports food industry reaction to the criticisms of the center. Discusses its budget, activities, staff, and leaders such as Michael Jacobson.

137 VAN VYNCKT, VIRGINIA. "Consumer Advocate's Rage Turns to Resolve." *Chicago Sun-Times*, 1 March 1989.

A lengthy article on Michael Jacobson and the organization he directs, the Center for Science in the Public Interest. Discusses the group's accomplishments, improvements in the healthfulness of foods, Jacobson's background, his tactics, and needed improvements in industry nutritional claims.

CITIZEN ACTION

A powerful coalition, established in 1979, of more than twenty statewide organizations that seek to advance the interests of low- and moderate-income Americans. Groups include Ohio Public Interest Campaign, Illinois Public Action Council, and Florida Consumer Federation. Have worked on issues such as insurance reform, toxic wastes, and plant closings. Generate millions of dollars in revenues from door-to-door canvassing. Directed by Robert Brandon. Based in Washington, D.C.

138 BOYTE, HARRY C.; BOOTH, HEATHER; and MAX, STEVE. *Citizen Action and the New American Populism*. Philadelphia: Temple University Press, 1986. 215 pp.

The most informative source about the most powerful grass-roots consumer/citizen network in the country, Citizen Action. Discusses the ideology, origins, leaders, member organizations, support groups, fund-raising, issue campaigns, and electoral involvement of this network. Gives special attention to campaigns to oppose natural gas price deregulation and toxic waste dumping. Reveals the participation of trade unions in these efforts. Written by a progressive strongly sympathetic to Citizen Action.

139 CLOWARD, RICHARD A., and PIVEN, FRANCES FOX. "Who Should Be Organized? 'Citizen Action' vs. 'Jobs and Justice.'" *Working Papers for a New Society*, May-June 1979, 35-43.

An informative examination of recent developments in grass-roots citizen action. Describes the emergence and current work of organizations within the Citizen Action and ACORN networks. Notes that they have tended to organize around consumer issues of concern to blue-collar families, such as rising utility or auto insurance rates. Discusses the recent shift of ACORN priorities to low-income issues and the emergence of a new "jobs and justice" coalition that seeks to organize the unemployed.

CITIZEN/LABOR ENERGY COALITION

A coalition of grass-roots organizations that was established in 1978 to organize grass-roots pressure against oil companies and utilities. Seeks to restrain energy prices and promote safe, clean, and renewable energy sources. Was most active in the early 1980s when natural gas prices were escalating rapidly. Now part of Citizen Action.

140 KELSEY, JANET, and WIENER, DON. "The Citizen/Labor Energy Coalition." *Social Policy*, Spring 1983, 15-18.

An informative article by two participants about the growing citizens' movement. Central to this movement has been the Citizen/Labor Energy Coalition (CLEC), a nationwide coalition of some 300 community and labor groups, which has worked against natural gas decontrol and for new state taxes on oil companies. An overlapping network that focuses on a broader range of issues is Citizen Action, a federation of twenty statewide citizens' groups. These organizations use door-to-door canvassing to raise about $12 million annually to advance a "progressive program of change." Some take the

Citizen/Labor Energy Coalition

form of statewide organizations while others are federations of chapter-based neighborhood groups. Many staffers of these groups are trained by the Midwest Academy. Increasingly, they use not only "direct action" or "pressure politics" but also electoral organizing. Their general goal is to empower and enhance the welfare of low- and moderate-income Americans.

CONSUMER ADVISORY COUNCIL

141 CANOYER, HELEN. "The Consumer Advisory Council." *Journal of Home Economics* 55 (March 1963): 160-62.

A short article on the newly established Consumer Advisory Council written by the organization's chairman. Briefly discusses the council's origins, uniqueness, role, issue priorities, and limitations.

142 CONSUMER ADVISORY COUNCIL. *First Report*. Washington, D.C.: Executive Office of the President, 1963.

The first report of the Consumer Advisory Council to President Kennedy. The ten-person council included Persia Campbell, Colston Warne, Helen Nelson, and Richard Morse. The report includes a survey of the council's activities and recommendations concerning safety, information, competition, representation, and general economic policy. Summarizes the results of various council studies. An appendix summarizes the activities of four council committees.

143 "An Official Consumer Voice in Washington." *Consumer Reports* 27 (September 1962): 463-65.

An article on the new Consumer Advisory Council created by President Kennedy. Reports on business opposition to the concept. Notes that there are New Deal precedents for such an advisory committee. Indicates that states such as Massachusetts and several European countries have taken leadership in establishing consumer organizations. Lists the members of the committee, who include Colston Warne, Persia Campbell, Helen Nelson, Richard Morse, and Caroline Ware.

144 "Panel Asks More Federal Guidance for Consumers." *Wall Street Journal*, 9 October 1963, 3.

Discusses the Kennedy administration's Consumer Advisory Council report on the role of the federal government in serving consumer needs. The report recommends conducting special studies on consumer issues, supplying more information to consumers, and providing the CAC with a permanent staff and better access to the president.

CONSUMER FEDERATION OF AMERICA

A coalition of more than 200 consumer, cooperative, labor, and other proconsumer groups. Established in 1968, attempts to advance the consumer interest in Washington before Congress and federal regulatory agencies. Also seeks to educate consumers and to provide technical and financial assistance to its state and local members. Focuses most attention on telephone, banking, insurance, energy, product safety, and product liability issues. Directed by Stephen Brobeck. Based in Washington, D.C. Some early records of CFA are held by Consumers Union's library.

145 ANGEVINE, ERMA. "The Consumer Federation of America." *Journal of Consumer Affairs* 3 (Winter 1969): 152-55.
    A short article on the Consumer Federation of America by its executive director. Credits Esther Peterson with proposing the creation of such a coalition. Reports that it includes 140 organizations in thirty-seven states and the District of Columbia. Describes the federation's recent legislative and regulatory activity. Identifies current high-priority issues.

146 ANGEVINE, ERMA. "Lobbying and Consumer Federation of America." In *Consumer Activists: They Made a Difference*, edited by Erma Angevine, 331-42. Mount Vernon, N.Y.: Consumers Union Foundation, 1982.
    An account of the formation and early work of the Consumer Federation of America by its first executive director. Discusses CFA's activities related to the Uniform Consumer Credit Code and to several federal issues.

147 CERRA, FRANCES. "A Lobbyist for Consumers." *New York Times*, 31 November 1976, sec. III, p. 7.
    An article on the Consumer Federation of America (CFA) and its executive director, Carol Tucker Foreman. Describes her family background, education, and personal life. Suggests that the consumer movement has matured and is focusing on structural reforms, which are hard to achieve. Describes CFA and Congress Watch's criticism of President Ford and their advocacy of a consumer protection agency. Discusses the problem CFA has with the diverse interests of its member organizations and inability to mobilize large numbers of individuals.

Consumer Federation of America

148 "Connubial Consumerism." *Wall Street Journal*, 31 August 1976, 10.

An editorial arguing that the Consumer Federation of America has a conflict of interest on universal product code and item-pricing issues. Points out the participation of the retail clerks union in the federation and the marriage of its executive director to an official of the union.

149 "Consumer Action." *New York Times*, 28 January 1976, 22.

A short article on the discussion at the Consumer Federation of America's Consumer Assembly on how to organize and maintain grass-roots consumer groups. Leaders agreed that it is easiest to base these groups on the self-help complaint-handling methods used by the Consumer Education and Protective Association and by Consumer Action (California).

150 CONSUMER FEDERATION OF AMERICA. *CFA News*. Washington, D.C.

See entry 6 for annotation.

151 "Consumers Try to Organize." *Business Week*, 11 November 1967, 56.

A short article on a meeting, addressed by President Johnson, of 500 representatives from sixty organizations who are establishing the Consumer Federation of America. Identifies the Reverend Robert McEwen as a leader of this effort. Discusses fund-raising efforts. Outlines the proposed activities and goals of the new organization.

152 "Fifty Six Groups Set Up a Consumers Union." *New York Times*, 29 April 1968, 43.

A short article reporting the creation of the Consumer Federation of America. Lists the officers and their affiliations.

153 GOLD, GERALD. "Things to Fight about besides Food Prices." *New York Times*, 25 August 1973, 30.

An article on the Consumer Federation of America's annual convention, held in Milwaukee. Identifies rising food prices, antitrust enforcement, and consumer education as priority issues.

154 KRAMER, LARRY. "Chamber Suit Hits Consumer Funding." *Washington Post*, 16 August 1978, sec. E, p. 5.

An article on a lawsuit filed by the U.S. Chamber of Commerce against the Department of Energy and Department of Agriculture for compensating Consumer Federation of America participation in regulatory proceedings. Reports agency and CFA reactions.

Consumer Federation of America

155 LEONARD, MARY. "US 'Food Lady'–More Spice Than Sugar." *Detroit News*, 5 December 1977, sec. A, p. 1+.

A lengthy front-page article on Carol Tucker Foreman, an assistant secretary of agriculture and former executive director of the Consumer Federation of America. Discusses her accomplishments at the Department of Agriculture, industry reaction, her accomplishments at CFA, her disagreement with Ralph Nader on the issue of deboned meat, her goal of forging a consumer-farmer alliance, her management style, and her personal life.

156 LEVINE, RICHARD J. "Cigar-Puffing Priest May Steal Spotlight at Consumer Parley." *Wall Street Journal*, 27 October 1967, 13.

A short article describing plans for the formation of a Consumer Federation of America (CFA) with the Reverend Robert McEwen from Massachusetts as the "driving force" behind the new organization. Reports that CFA is intended to function mainly as a supporter of state and local consumer groups.

157 LOGAN, GARY J. "Profile: The Consumer Federation of America." *Everyday Law*, May 1988, 48-52.

A description of the Consumer Federation of America based on interviews with several CFA staffers and analysis of its publications. Includes sidebars on CFA's legislative achievements and the organization's officers.

158 MIROW, DEENA. "Brobeck's Battle for Consumers Moves to Higher Level." *Plain Dealer*, 8 September 1982, sec. C, p. 4.

An article based on an interview with Stephen Brobeck, former Cleveland consumer activist who now heads the Consumer Federation of America. He discusses his work in Cleveland, the condition of the consumer movement, and his priorities for CFA.

159 MYLER, KATHLEEN. "Activist Trades Signs for Briefcase." *Houston Chronicle*, 21 February 1988.

A profile of Stephen Brobeck, executive director of the Consumer Federation of America and a former grass-roots consumer organizer. Discusses his views of big business, changes in the consumer movement, his work with Cleveland Consumer Action, and the work of CFA.

160 "A New 'Consumer Federation' Sets Up Shop." *Changing Times*, April 1968, 19-20.

A report on the organization of a new national consumer organization, Consumer Federation of America. Identifies its principal

Consumer Federation of America

activity not as lobbying but as encouraging consumers to communicate with their representatives. Lists the first twenty-one organizations to join the federation.

161 SCHORR, BURT. "Winning Friends: When Carol Foreman Talks Consumerism, Congressmen Listen." *Wall Street Journal,* 9 April 1975, 1+.

A feature article on Carol Foreman, executive director of the Consumer Federation of America (CFA). Suggests that consumer lobbyists are increasingly sophisticated and that members of Congress have become more sympathetic to consumerism. Discusses proconsumer legislators and their legislative agenda. Reports on Foreman's family background and the challenges she faces within CFA.

162 SOLOMON, GOODY C. "Carol Foreman: Status for the Consumer Movement." *Washington Star,* 12 March 1977, sec. C, p. 1+.

An article on Carol Foreman, executive director of Consumer Federation of America, who was just appointed as an assistant secretary of agriculture. Describes her background, work at CFA, reputation in Congress, and responsibilities in the Department of Agriculture.

163 SWANSTON, WALTERENE. "Consumer Federation Waging Spirited Battle for Survival." *National Journal* 4 (8 July 1972): 1126-36.

A lengthy article on the Consumer Federation of America with sidebars on executive director Erma Angevine, major dues contributors, federation officers, and CFA's congressional scorecard. Describes the organization's staffing, goals, structure, and influence. Emphasizes the internal conflict between state and local groups and large national organizations. Reports that although Angevine is an effective lobbyist, the organization moves too slowly on issues, often taking a compromise position. Concludes that the future of the group depends on expanding resources and resolving internal conflicts.

164 "The Unmobilized Consumer." *Wall Street Journal,* 30 November 1967, 18.

An editorial suggesting that the members of the new Consumer Federation of America (CFA) have conflicting views about the structure and goals of the organization. Also wonders, given the small number of letters consumers write to Congress, whether the public supports new federal legislation CFA plans to promote.

CONSUMERS UNION

Established in 1936, primarily as an organization to test products and disseminate the results of these tests to consumers through Consumer Reports. *Today, with a budget approaching $100 million, represents the largest consumer organization in the world. As well as consumer information programs, supports advocacy offices in Washington, D.C.; Austin, Texas; and San Francisco. The Washington office, which was created in 1972, is directed by Mark Silbergeld. The larger organization is led by Rhoda Karpatkin. Its library houses past records of the organization.*

165 "Advocate's Advance." *Time* 103 (28 January 1974): 66.
    A short article on the selection of Rhoda Karpatkin as head of Consumers Union. Discusses her background and the challenge she faces in resolving the dispute over emphasizing testing or advocacy.

166 BAILEY, JEFF. "Altering the Product at *Consumer Reports*." *Wall Street Journal*, 5 June 1987, 29.
    A report on Consumers Union's new policy of including articles on social issues in *Consumer Reports*. Describes the background and organizational plans of executive director Rhoda Karpatkin. Discusses the organization's past and present labor problems.

167 CERRA, FRANCES. "Consumer Organizations over Nation Hurt by Loss of Grants." *New York Times*, 8 July 1975, 16.
    An article on the sharp reduction in grants to consumer advocacy groups by Consumers Union, which is having financial problems. Discusses the effect of these cutbacks on Consumer Federation of America, Center for Auto Safety, and National Consumers Congress.

168 CIMONS, MARLENE. "A Slow Move to Activism." *Washington Post*, 2 January 1980, sec. D, p. 14.
    An article on the history and current activities of Consumers Union that focuses attention on Colston Warne, a founder and president of the organization for forty years. Acknowledges Warne's courage and skill in keeping Consumers Union alive in the early years, when it was attacked by the right wing. Quotes Ralph Nader as suggesting Warne was reluctant to expand the organization's advocacy. But suggests that in recent years it has become more activist.

169 "Consumers Union Puts on Muscle." *Business Week*, 23 December 1967, 84-86.

Consumers Union

Discusses the growing size and activism of Consumers Union. Notes plans to sue government agencies for information, to set up a Washington office, and to pass consumer legislation. Provides information on subscriptions and budgets. Examines the organization's product testing.

170 "Fifty Years Ago: What Happened When Consumerism and Unionism, Two Great Social Movements of the 1930s, Collided?" *Consumer Reports* 51 (January 1986): 8-10; (February): 76-79.
See entry 96 for annotation.

171 GOLD, GERALD. "Consumers Union Picks Lawyer to Be Its First Woman Director." *New York Times*, 13 January 1974, 41.
An article on Rhoda Karpatkin, the new executive director of Consumers Union. Notes the disagreement within the organization over whether to emphasize advocacy or consumer information. Reports Karpatkin as intending to stress both and, more specifically, auto testing, evaluation of services, and the intrinsic value of products. Indicates she wants Consumers Union to do more to "reach" low-income consumers.

172 GREER, WILLIAM. "The Third World Looks at Consumerism." *New York Times*, 31 May 1986, 52.
An article on two related events–the fiftieth anniversary of Consumers Union and a meeting of Third World consumer activists, both held in New York City. Reports that the consumer movement is growing in developing countries. Briefly discusses efforts in China, India, Taiwan, and Brazil.

173 HOROWITZ, SARI. "Consumers Union Bounces Back." *Washington Post*, 10 February 1985, sec. G, p. 3+.
An article on the financial recovery of Consumers Union and its future plans. Indicates that contributions allowed it to keep open its advocacy offices. Discusses a 1984 strike of employees and how the organization coped. Notes the influence of its product ratings.

174 KARPATKIN, RHODA. "Memo to Members." *Consumer Reports* 40 (September 1975): 524.
A memo from Consumers Union's executive director to members on the resignation of Ralph Nader from the organization's board. Nader resigned because of the group's insufficient commitment to consumer action. Karpatkin responds that Consumers Union has a long history of supporting and undertaking advocacy, but she maintains that this

activism must be "ancillary to ... an impartial product-testing and reporting program."

175 KATZ, NORMAN DAVID. "Consumers Union: The Movement and the Magazine, 1938-1957." Ph.D. dissertation, Rutgers University, 1977. 431 pp.
   See entry 102 for annotation.

176 KERR, PETER. "*Consumer Reports* Is Recovering." *New York Times*, 8 January 1983, 48.
   Discusses the status of Consumers Union a year after declining subscriptions forced it to begin cutting expenses. Lists these cost-cutting measures. Quotes executive director Rhoda Karpatkin as saying finances have improved and no more cutbacks are necessary. Mentions other highlights of the year at Consumers Union.

177 KINKEAD, GWEN. "Soulful Trouble at Consumers Union." *Fortune* 105 (22 February 1982): 119-20+.
   A report on financial problems of Consumers Union. Suggests that they have been caused by poor management and spending on advocacy and a children's magazine. Discusses the strained relations between labor and management.

178 LEVY, ROBERT. "The Other Ralph Nader." *Dun's Review*, December 1971, 42-43.
   Discusses Consumers Union and its executive director, Walker Sandbach. Includes comments from Sandbach on sources of consumer dissatisfaction, the recent increase in subscriptions to *Consumer Reports*, the market impacts of the magazine, criticism of the organization's testing, and the performance of the consumer movement.

179 MAYER, CAROLINE E. "Consumers Union Closes Three Offices." *Washington Post*, 24 December 1981, sec. D, p. 5+.
   An article on the financial crisis at Consumers Union that is forcing it to lay off employees and close all three advocacy offices. In fact, funds were raised that allowed all offices to remain open.

180 MAYER, CAROLINE E. "Consumers Union Confronts Own Crisis of Pocketbook." *Washington Post*, 17 January 1982, sec. G, p. 1+.
   A lengthy article on the financial difficulties of Consumers Union. Notes that employees are trying to get rid of executive director Rhoda Karpatkin but that the board supports her. Briefly discusses the first lawsuit the organization has lost. Explains the financial problems in

Consumers Union

terms of the recession and a postal increase. Describes cost-cutting measures such as a freeze on salaries, a reduction in the size of *Consumer Reports*, and the closing of the three advocacy offices [which did not occur].

181 MINTZ, MORTON. "Consumers Union: Institution in Trouble." *Washington Post*, 22 April 1973, sec. A, p. 1; 23 April, sec. A, p. 1; 24 April, sec. A, p. 2; 25 April, sec. A, p. 3.

An informative, four-part series on the difficulties faced by Consumers Union. Part 1 discusses problems such as low renewal rates, poor subscriber service, acrimonious labor relations, disagreement on the board as to whether the organization should emphasize product testing or advocacy, and the poor performance of executive director Walker Sandbach, who had just resigned. Part 2 evaluates the effectiveness and impact of the organization's product testing. Part 3 reports on the debate within the organization on whether to emphasize product testing or advocacy. It describes the activities of Consumers Union's Washington advocacy office and the organization's funding of other advocacy groups. Part 4 examines the future of the organization. It discusses what activist board members such as Ralph Nader and Herb Denenberg would like Consumers Union and its magazine to become.

182 "Nader Quits CU." *New York Times*, 23 August 1975, 10.

A short article on Ralph Nader's resignation from Consumers Union and his reasons for it. Includes a response from Consumers Union's executive director Rhoda Karpatkin.

183 O'BRIEN, TIM. "A New Director at Consumers Union." *Washington Post*, 14 January 1974, sec. B, p. 3.

An article on the appointment of Rhoda Karpatkin as the new executive director of Consumers Union. Reports the disagreement over the organization's support for advocacy and Karpatkin's intention to expand both advocacy and product testing.

184 QUEENAN, JOE. "Bitter Taste-Tester Strike Sours This Consumer." *Wall Street Journal*, 8 September 1988, 30.

A semiserious op-ed article about the labor-management disagreement at Consumers Union and its decision to contract out taste testing of products. Reveals details about the dispute.

185 RICKLEFS, ROGER. "Consumers Union Is in Consumer Trouble." *Wall Street Journal*, 9 May 1975, 1+.

Consumers Union

Discusses financial problems experienced by Consumers Union that forced layoffs. Attributes the crisis to rising paper costs and a new computerized subscription and processing system that works poorly. Reports on the internal controversy over whether the organization should support consumer advocacy.

186 SIEKMAN, P. "U.S. Business' Most Skeptical Customer: Should Manufacturers Take Consumers Union Seriously?" *Fortune* 62 (September 1960): 157-59+.
See entry 79 for annotation.

187 SILBER, NORMAN ISAAC. "Consumer Protest and the Social Control of Technology: The Public Interest at Consumers Union, 1936-1964." Ph.D. dissertation, Yale University, 1978. 226 pp.
See entry 80 for annotation.

188 SILBER, NORMAN I[SAAC]. *Test and Protest.* New York: Holmes & Meier, 1983. 172 pp.
See entry 81 for annotation.

189 SOLOMON, BURT. "A Consumer Advocate Who Isn't a Shouter." *National Journal* 19 (18 April 1987): 956.
See entry 508 for annotation.

190 WARNE, COLSTON E. "Consumer Action Programs of the Consumers Union of United States." In *Consumerism – Viewpoints from Business, Government, and the Public Interest*, edited by Ralph M. Gaedeke and Warren W. Etcheson, 99-109. San Francisco: Canfield Press, 1972.
A description and assessment of Consumers Union by its most important leader. Discusses its founding, operation, limitations, and achievements, which include encouraging product testing in other countries, U.S. consumer protection measures, and the U.S. consumer movement, as well as dissemination of product-specific information to consumers. Urges government agencies to release the results of their product tests. Recommends developing new technologies to extend the benefits of consumer testing to the poor.

191 WARNE, COLSTON E. "Consumers Union's Contribution to the Consumer Movement." In *Consumer Activists: They Made a Difference*, edited by Erma Angevine, 85-110. Mount Vernon, N.Y.: Consumers Union Foundation, 1982.

Consumers Union

An invaluable article on Consumers Union's early history and contributions, written by its president during the organization's first forty years. Credits mass production and marketing, Herbert Hoover's emphasis on product simplification and standardization, Thorstein Veblen's theory of "conspicuous consumption," Edward Bellamy's *Looking Backward*, and the muckrakers for laying the groundwork for modern consumerism. Discusses the contributions of Stuart Chase and Frederick Schlink, who wrote popular critiques of the marketplace and organized Consumers Research. Treats the "utopian trend in consumer testing." Recounts the growing friction between Schlink and Consumers Research employees that led the latter to establish Consumers Union in 1936. Notes that J. B. Matthews (entry 98), who influenced Schlink, saw communist plots that did not exist. Discusses the severe problems of the new organization in its first ten years. Describes the attempt of the Dies Committee, featuring Matthews as a key witness, to smear Consumers Union in the 1930s and the renewal of this attack by McCarthy in the early 1950s. Mentions that during the latter time, the Consumers Union board became more academic and national in character. Outlines grants from Consumers Union to support consumerist activities. Discusses the group's efforts to promote consumer education in the schools, research, and consumer associations. Examines the relationships of Consumers Union to settlement workers, to home economists, and to journalists. Summarizes the organization's litigation activities. Discusses at length the international consumer movement and Consumers Union's promotion of it. This article represents a unique source of information on Consumers Union from its founding up to the 1970s.

192 WARNE, COLSTON E. "The Impact of Consumerism on the Market." *San Diego Law Review* 8 (February 1971): 30-46.
    An article by Consumers Union's president on the impact and limits of his organization. Reports that its magazine has affected consumer purchases and corporate behavior. Acknowledges that this publication serves principally the affluent and is of little benefit to the poor. Discusses a proposal for the government to support consumer product testing.

193 WHITNEY, CRAIG R. "Consumers Union, 33-Year-Old Watchdog, Still Has Sharp Teeth." *New York Times*, 5 November 1969, 49.
    An article on the status of Consumers Union that reports it has grown substantially in the past few years. Briefly discusses its lawsuit against the Veterans Administration on hearing aids.

NADER NETWORK

194 BENDER, MARILYN. "Capitalism Lives–Even in Naderland." *New York Times*, 7 January 1973, 49+.

A lengthy article on the new public interest organizations that Ralph Nader has created or inspired. Suggests that Nader is moving "from study to litigation and legislation" and from "flashy" issues to structural reform.

195 BOLLIER, DAVID. *Citizen Action and Other Big Ideas: A History of Ralph Nader and the Modern Consumer Movement*. Washington, D.C.: Center for Study of Responsive Law, 1989. 111 pp.

An authorized history of Ralph Nader and the consumer organizations he established, published by the group Nader heads. The appendix lists organizations founded and books and reports published by Nader and his Raiders.

196 BURT, DAN M. *Abuse of Trust: A Report on Ralph Nader's Network*. Chicago: Regnery Gateway, 1982. 269 pp.

A critical report by a conservative on those organizations that have some relation to Ralph Nader. Argues that ten primary groups and nine subgroups form a network characterized by interoganizational income transfers, shared personnel and facilities, shared ideology, interlocking directorates, and links to Nader. Maintains that an additional fifty groups have or had substantial ties to Nader and his network. Reports that the Nader network had gross income and assets of several million dollars and that it made questionable stock investments. Suggests that Public Citizen apparently violates the charitable solicitation laws in many states and refused to provide information to the author, who represents a conservative legal foundation. In appendices, describes the network groups and others with ties to the network. The contention that there is a Nader network is correct. Yet, the threat of a network with net income far less than that of any large industry trade association, and only a minuscule fraction of the resources of all business lobbyists, is not immediately evident. The "questionable" stock investments did not involve the use of any proprietary information. Public Citizen did not comply with state solicitation laws but claimed federal jurisdiction, and the issue, at the time of publication, was being considered by the Supreme Court. The book contains a number of errors. For example, it places the Consumer Federation of America in the Nader network because of distant board links while ignoring the intention of CFA founders to organize a group independent of Nader and the disagreement between CFA and Nader

Nader Network

on issues such as no-fault insurance. Also, it erroneously identifies Marc Caplan as a former executive director of the federation.

197 CHARLTON, LINDA. "Ralph Nader's Conglomerate Is Big Business." *New York Times*, 29 January 1978, sec. IV, p. 2.

An assessment of the current influence of Ralph Nader. Briefly describes (and charts) the network of organizations he established and some of their contributions. Reports recent failures and criticisms. Concludes he is "still important enough to stir argument."

198 CLAIRBORNE, WILLIAM L. "Tedious Study Is Key Tool of Nader's Raiders." *Washington Post*, 16 August 1971, sec. A, p. 3.

A lengthy article on how Nader-related organizations such as the Center for Auto Safety conduct research. Suggests that these groups do not have the resources to test products but conduct extensive library research and interviews with government and industry "insiders." Also notes that the auto safety group relies heavily on industry complaint letters. A related article describes the experience of interns who carry out most of the research.

199 DICKSON, PAUL. "What Makes Ralph Run? The Nader Story." *Progressive* 34 (January 1970): 28-32.

Discusses the "phenomenal success" of Ralph Nader. Describes four facets of the emerging Nader organization – auto safety, Nader's Raiders, Center for the Study of Responsive Law, and secret information network. Reviews Nader's background, personality, life-style, and goals.

200 GROSS, SUSAN. "The Nader Network." *Business and Society Review* 13 (Spring 1975): 5-15.

An informative article on the network of public interest groups that Ralph Nader helped establish. Traces the development of these some dozen Nader-controlled groups in Washington and others that have been spun off or are satellites. Explains that Public Citizen, the largest group run by Nader, is funded by small donations solicited through the mail, and that three others – the Corporate Accountability Research Group, the National Public Interest Research Group, and the Public Interest Research Group – are financed by Nader personally. Nader functions as chief executive officer for all these groups, but he manages the network informally, delegating some authority to Joan Claybrook, Mark Green, and Ted Jacobs. Most staffers are young and work a relatively short time, in part because salaries are low. Includes profiles of the size, budget, leadership, goals, and activities of fifteen of these organizations.

201 IGNATIUS, DAVID. "Stages of Nader." *New York Times Magazine*, 19 January 1976, 8-9+.

A "stylized history" of Ralph Nader and his organizations over the past decade written by a former Nader staffer. Identifies four stages: Nader alone (1965-67); institutionalization through exposés and the Center for the Study of Responsive Law (1968-70); promotion of a federal consumer protection agency (1970-72); and traditional advocacy—litigation, lobbying, grass-roots organizing (1972-present). Suggests that Nader's views have grown more radical and that he now believes in a "decentralized socialism" where workers control manufacturing and consumers control retailing (cooperatives).

202 JACQUENEY, THEODORE. "Nader Network Switches Focus to Legal Action, Congressional Lobbying." *National Journal* 5 (9 June 1973): 840-49.

A detailed description of the network of groups established or inspired by Ralph Nader. Focuses special attention on Congress Watch, the Public Citizen Litigation Group, the Freedom of Information Clearinghouse, and public interest research groups. Discusses other organizations such as the Health Research Group in a section titled "Nader reports." Concludes that virtually everyone agrees that Nader and his groups are effective in shaping public policy. Contains a confusing chart on Nader network funding that inaccurately suggests Nader helps fund Consumers Union. Includes sidebars on the funding of Nader organizations and the salaries they pay employees.

203 LELYVELD, JOSEPH. "Nader Undaunted by Setbacks to Consumer Drive." *New York Times*, 24 November 1975, 1+.

A lengthy front-page article on the status of Ralph Nader and his organizations. Emphasizes that they have experienced recent setbacks and failure to grow. Discusses steps Nader has taken to strengthen consumer advocacy, including founding Public Citizen and proposing checkoff-funded utility advocacy groups. Describes the network of Nader organizations.

204 LICHTENSTEIN, GRACE. "New Groups Are Serving as Watchdogs for Consumers." *New York Times*, 3 January 1972, 41+.

An article on new consumer advocates it calls "mini-Naders." Briefly describes Lowell Dodge, head of the Center for Auto Safety, and

Nader Network

Robert Choate, founder of the Council on Children, Media, and Merchandising.

205 MARSHALL, ELIOT. "St. Nader and His Evangelists." *New Republic*, 23 October 1971, 13-14.

Discusses the impact of Ralph Nader through the publication of critical reports, researched largely by students, and through congressional lobbying and testimony. Describes several organizations established by Nader including the Center for the Study of Responsive Law and the Public Interest Research Group.

206 "Nader's Conglomerate." *Time* 101 (11 June 1973): 82.

A report on the new consumer groups organized by Ralph Nader. Briefly discusses the work of the Center for the Study of Responsive Law, Public Citizen, Corporate Accountability Research Group, Congress Watch, and the independent public interest research groups (PIRGs).

207 "Ralph Nader Becomes an Organization." *Business Week*, 28 November 1970, 86-88.

A report on the consumer organizations Ralph Nader has begun to build. Describes the Center for the Study of Responsive Law, Public Interest Research Group, Center for Auto Safety, and Project on Corporate Responsibility. Discusses Nader's life-style, activities, and policy goals which, if achieved, "would amount to a revolution in traditional business practices."

208 SHAFER, RONALD G. "Nader & Co.: Empire of the Consumer Crusader Blossoms." *Wall Street Journal*, 19 November 1970, 40.

A lengthy article on Ralph Nader's growing network of groups in Washington and at the grass roots. Provides limited information on how these groups are structured and relate to Nader. Reports a consensus that the groups are having an impact, chiefly by forcing greater disclosure from federal agencies.

209 STEWART, THOMAS A. "The Resurrection of Ralph Nader." *Fortune* 119 (22 May 1989): 106+.

An article on the comeback of Ralph Nader, as suggested by the passage of Proposition 103 in California and the defeat of the congressional pay raise. Briefly discusses Nader's declining influence in the late 1970s and 1980s. Notes his personal crises in 1986. Describes the issues on which his groups are working – auto insurance, auto safety (Center for Auto Safety), government reform, entrepreneurship (Buyers

Up), and health care (Health Research Group). Suggests that the best defense against Nader is to "leave him with little or nothing to complain about."

210 TALBOTT, BASIL. "Nader Planted Seeds of Consumer Activism." *Chicago Sun-Times*, 20 February 1989, 45.

Treats the network of some fourteen public interest groups Ralph Nader founded such as the Center for Study of Responsive Law, Public Citizen, and Center for Science in the Public Interest (CSPI). Notes that Nader's long hours, low compensation, and Spartan life-style have influenced the subculture of all these groups.

211 WARK, LOIS G. "Nader Campaigns for Funds to Expand Activities of His Consumer Action Complex." *National Journal* 3 (18 September 1971): 1904-16.

A detailed article on the network of organizations that Nader has founded or helped create. Contains sections on fund-raising, credibility, institutional presence, contacts with government, working for Nader, and outlook, as well as a chart of "the Ralph Nader organization." Suggests that Nader has been instrumental in passing at least six major pieces of legislation. Observes that he wants to spin off many autonomous groups but that he is "tightening up" his groups in Washington. Includes lengthy sidebars on the Center for the Study of Responsive Law, Nader satellite organizations such as the Corporate Accountability Research Group, the Center for Auto Safety, and public interest research groups (PIRGs), with shorter ones on the Clearing House for Professional Responsibility, the study group reports, and Robert Fellmeth, a Harvard-trained lawyer who wrote three of these reports.

212 WARNE, COLSTON E. "The Nader Network for Consumer Impact." In *Consumer Activists: They Made a Difference*, edited by Erma Angevine, 554-68. Mount Vernon, N.Y.: Consumers Union Foundation, 1982.

An article by a leading consumerist on Ralph Nader's advocacy and his impacts. Summarizes his contributions. Lists the organizations he has founded. Recounts a Nader speech he heard that ended at 2:00 a.m. Discusses Nader's relation to Consumers Union, including his resignation from the board in 1975. Outlines his efforts to promote research and set up organizations in the late 1960s and early 1970s. Notes his recent interest in organizing consumer cooperatives. Reviews his successes and failures. Concludes that consumers "owe him an immense debt of gratitude." Although not systematic or carefully

Nader Network

researched, this essay incorporates the perceptive analysis of an economist and prominent consumer leader.

NADER RAIDERS

213 COLLIER, BARNARD LAW. "The Story of a Teen-Age Nader Raider." *New York Times Magazine*, 14 March 1971, 30+.

A moving article about six prep school girls who worked for Ralph Nader one summer on an exposé of nursing homes. Focuses on one, Claire Townsend, the leader of the group and the daughter of a major contributor to Nader. Includes descriptions of their work in nursing homes and their relation to Nader.

214 CONROY, SARAH BOOTH. "Rallying the Raiders." *Washington Post*, 28 October 1989, sec. C, p. 1.

A style-section article on the twentieth anniversary dinner of Nader Raiders. Reports Ralph Nader's remarks. Lists many of the Raiders who attended.

215 DASCHA, JULIUS. "Stop! In the Public Interest." *New York Times Magazine*, 21 March 1971, 4+.

An article on Nader's Raiders that suggests Ralph Nader "has become an institution at least as formidable as General Motors." Discusses the organizations he has created–Center for the Study of Responsive Law, Public Interest Research Group, Center for Law and Social Policy, and Center for Auto Safety. Briefly profiles some of the leaders of these organizations. Discusses Nader's relation to his Raiders, his relation to Congress, and his goals.

216 KINSLEY, MICHAEL E. "My Life and Hard Times with Nader's Raiders." *Seventeen*, September 1971, 148+.

An article written by a Nader Raider, who later became a prominent columnist, on his experience as a Raider. Depicts a summer of isolated research, frustration at accomplishing little, guilt at not meeting Nader's expectations, and satisfaction when some of his research was reported on by the press. Suggests that Nader is greatly admired not just because of his accomplishments but also because of his asceticism.

217 LEVENTHAL, PAUL L. "Political Reaction Overshadows Reform Aim of Massive Congressional Study." *National Journal* 4 (9 September 1972): 1483-95.

Nader Raiders

Long article on Ralph Nader's Congress Project, a study of Congress prepared by some 1,000 volunteers and 250 summer staffers. Describes the intended products of the study including separate studies of each representative, of key congressional committees, and of eleven issues. Notes congressional apprehension and criticism. Discusses in detail how the research was conducted. Includes sidebars on Nader and Congress, *Who Runs Congress?*, the eleven issue studies, and thirteen congressional committee studies.

218 MUELLER, MARTI. "Nader: From Auto Safety to a Permanent Crusade." *Science*, 21 November 1969, 979-83.

A complimentary article on Ralph Nader the person and his advocacy of the public interest. Describes the work of some 100 Nader Raiders who researched the relationship between government and industry. Discusses Nader's personal style, his impact on Congress, and his views of scientists, whom he believes react "too little and too late" to problems such as underground atomic testing, the military's use of nerve gas, and pollution from deep-well drilling. Credits much of his success to extensive research and his care with facts. Contains comments about Nader from Congress and from his own Raiders.

219 "Nader's Raiders: Older and Bolder." *Marketing Magazine*, 15 March 1970, 27-28.

Discusses the work of Nader's Raiders. Notes the impact of their critique of the Federal Trade Commission and six studies that will soon be published. Indicates that the newly created Center for the Study of Responsive Law has filed six lawsuits accusing federal agencies of failing to comply with the Freedom of Information Act. Suggests that the principal goal of the Raiders is not to pass new laws but to force regulatory agencies to act in the public interest. Describes the offices of the center.

220 NEWFIELD, JACK. "Nader's Raiders: The Lone Ranger Gets a Posse." *Life*, 3 October 1969, 56A+.

An article on Ralph Nader and his Raiders. Suggests that he has had a profound impact including the "spawning of a movement," persuading U.S. senators to advocate consumer protections, and opening up a new career path for law students. Provides information about Nader's work and personal life. Describes some of the research of his Raiders and how it was conducted.

221 WHITESIDE, THOMAS. "A Countervailing Force." *New Yorker* 49 (8 October 1973): 50+; (15 October 1973): 46+.

Nader **Raiders**

A lengthy two-part article on Ralph Nader and his organizations based largely on interviews and time spent with Nader and on interviews with Nader's lieutenants. Part 1 discusses Nader groups such as the Center for the Study of Responsive Law and Public Citizen; Nader's view of society as dominated by large corporations that strongly influence government; his auto safety advocacy; the work of Nader Raiders; profiles of Sidney Wolfe, Bob Fellmeth, and Harrison Wellford; descriptions of public interest research groups (PIRGs) and citizen action groups (CAGs) and their lead organizer, Don Ross; and litigation initiated by Nader groups. Part 2 describes time the author spent with Nader while traveling and giving speeches; what it is like to work for Nader; Nader's influence in Congress; the campaign for a consumer protection agency; business criticisms; and Nader's views of and relation to lawyers. A perceptive and fairly objective portrait written at a time when much of the press and the public enthusiastically supported Nader.

NATIONAL ASSOCIATION OF RAILROAD PASSENGERS

222 HENRY, LYELL DEWEL, Jr. "The National Association of Railroad Passengers: A Case Study of the Formation, Organization, and Political Effectiveness of a Consumer Interest Group." Ph.D. dissertation, University of Iowa, 1973. 310 pp.

Examines the establishment, finances, leadership, membership, leader-member relations, decision making, and political activities of the National Association of Railroad Passengers (NARP), a consumer interest group founded in 1967 to advocate the preservation, expansion, and modernization of intercity rail passenger service. Demonstrates that the NARP had a substantial impact on public policy through litigation, lobbying, coalition building, and public relations. Suggests that "exchange theory," which features an "entrepreneur/organizer" who offers benefits to potential group members in return for benefits to himself, provides a better explanation of the formation, persistence, and effectiveness of NARP than do traditional interest-group theories. For a more detailed summary, see the *DAI* 34 (1973): 3487A.

NATIONAL CONSUMERS LEAGUE

Established in 1899 mainly to improve working conditions for women and children. Also supported food and drug safety legislation in this period. Recently has sought to represent both consumer and worker interests before government

National Consumers League

and business. Includes consumer, government, labor, and corporate representatives on its board of directors. Directed by Linda Golodner. Based in Washington, D.C. Nearly 70 linear feet of records of NCL for the period 1881-1972 are held by the Library of Congress.

223 ATHEY, LOUIS LEE. "The Consumers' Leagues and Social Reform, 1890-1923." Ph.D. dissertation, University of Delaware, 1965. 355 pp.
      See entry 85 for annotation.

224 KEYSERLING, MARY DUBLIN. "The First National Consumers Organization: The National Consumers League." In *Consumer Activists: They Made a Difference*, edited by Erma Angevine, 343-60. Mount Vernon, N.Y.: Consumers Union Foundation, 1982.
      See entry 75 for annotation.

225 MORRIS, BAILEY. "Consumer 'Gadflies' Gaining Recognition." *Washington Star*, 20 January 1978, sec. B, p. 5+.
      A profile of Sandra Willett, head of the National Consumers League. Discusses the personal challenges of her job, the growth of National Consumers League under her direction, and her education and training.

226 NATIONAL CONSUMERS LEAGUE. *National Consumers League Bulletin*. Washington, D.C.
      See entry 10 for annotation.

PUBLIC CITIZEN

Established by Ralph Nader in 1971 to raise funds for several of his other organizations. Now serves as an umbrella group for Buyers Up, Congress Watch, Critical Mass Energy Projects, Health Research Group, and the Litigation Group. Since 1982, has been directed by Joan Claybrook. Based in Washington, D.C.

227 ALLEN, HENRY. "Nader's New Dream." *Washington Post*, 28 September 1981, sec. B, p. 1+.
      A style-section article on Public Citizen's tenth anniversary celebration and conference. Emphasizes that Nader made no effort to rouse his audience and that they appeared to lack enthusiasm. Notes the presence of celebrities and the absence of political leaders.

Public Citizen

228 BROWN, MERRILL, and HAMILTON, MARTHA M. "Ralph Nader Resigns from Consumer Post." *Washington Post*, 28 October 1980, sec. E, p. 1+.

A short article on Ralph Nader's resignation as head of Public Citizen and replacement by Sidney Wolfe, head of the Health Research Group. Indicates that Nader desired to be free of administrative duties and to be able to spend more time building an endowment for Public Citizen, organizing new single-issue groups, and working with consumer groups in other countries.

229 DENTON, HERBERT H. "Claybrook Rejoins Nader as Head of Public Citizen." *Washington Post*, 17 February 1982, sec. A, p. 2.

An article on Joan Claybrook's appointment as president of Public Citizen. Notes the organization's increasing contributions. Reports Claybrook and Ralph Nader's comments on the dispute between the two when she headed the National Highway Traffic Safety Administration.

230 MAYER, CAROLINE E. "Nader, Imitating Fat Cats, to Hold Big Fund-Raiser." *Washington Post*, 1 September 1981, 1+.

An article on Public Citizen's plan to hold a big fund-raiser on its tenth anniversary. For the first time, the organization sought $1,000 contributions and even solicited corporations who supported the consumer protection agency.

231 MAYER, CAROLINE E. "Nader of the Lost Bark." *Washington Post*, 13 September 1981, sec. F, p. 1+.

A lengthy article on the past successes and waning influence of Public Citizen and Ralph Nader. Attributes the latter to rising public concern about the cost of regulation, the loss of leading advocates to the Carter administration, and Nader's "vitriolic attacks" on opponents. Notes that Public Citizen's direct-mail fund-raising netted less than $1,000 last year and is being turned over to professional fund-raisers. Discusses Nader's campaign to organize citizen utility boards (CUBs) in many states.

232 "Nader Forms Unit to Aid Crusaders for Public." *Washington Post*, 2 June 1971, sec. A, p. 2.

A short article on the creation of Public Citizen by Ralph Nader to raise funds for consumer and environmental research and advocacy.

233 PUBLIC CITIZEN. *Public Citizen*. Washington, D.C. *Public Interest Perspectives: The Next Four Years*. Proceedings from the first major

gathering of public interest advocates. Washington, D.C.: Public Citizen, 1977. 218 pp.
    See entry 11 for annotation.

234 SINCLAIR, MOLLY. "Nader Forms Local Group to Sell Heating Oil at Bargain Prices." *Washington Post*, 8 December 1983, sec. C, p. 3.
    An article about Public Citizen's establishment of a new organization, Buyers Up, that will bargain for low-priced heating oil for its members. Notes that similar groups exist in Boston and New York City.

235 "Six Hundred Forty Two Thousand and Forty Dollars Given to Nader Unit." *Washington Post*, 19 March 1972, sec. A, p. 12.
    A report on the funds raised by Public Citizen and how they will be spent on litigation, health, and tax reform units.

PUBLIC CITIZEN LITIGATION GROUP

Organized in 1971 by Ralph Nader and Alan Morrison to litigate on behalf of the interests of consumers, workers, and citizens. In the 1980s, mounted challenges to the legislative veto and the Gramm-Rudman budget act. Also litigates for organizations outside the Public Citizen umbrella on a broad array of economic, product safety, and governmental issues. Directed by Alan Morrison. Based in Washington, D.C.

236 COHEN, RICHARD E. "A Constitutional Gadfly Who's Hard to Brush Off." *National Journal* 3 (May 1988): 611.
    A profile of Alan B. Morrison, director of the Public Citizen Litigation Group. Discusses his legal role as "catalyst" and his work on separation of powers issues.

237 SHAPIRO, MARGARET. "Big League Litigator Aims to Throw Out Budget Act." *Washington Post*, 15 January 1986.
    An article on Alan Morrison's legal challenge to the Gramm-Rudman law that also profiles this head of the Public Citizen Litigation Group. Describes his earlier cases, views of the constitution, education, and previous work.

238 WITT, ELDER. "Attorney Morrison: Constitutional Gadfly." *Congressional Quarterly*, 19 April 1986, 875.
    A profile of Alan Morrison, head of the Public Citizen Litigation Group and the consumer movement's most active litigator. Describes

Public Citizen Litigation Group

his education, career, political views, organization, and accomplishments.

PUBLIC CITIZEN'S HEALTH RESEARCH GROUP

Founded by Ralph Nader and Sidney Wolfe in 1971, seeks to promote the nation's health by monitoring the Food and Drug Administration, the drug industry, and the medical establishment. As well as undertaking advocacy, prepares publications that have netted millions of dollars in income for Public Citizen, its umbrella organization. Directed by Sidney Wolfe. Based in Washington, D.C.

239 ALLEN, HENRY. "The Wolfe among Watchdogs." *Washington Post,* 5 December 1978, sec. B, p. 1.
    A style-section profile of Sidney Wolfe, head of Health Research Group. Reports on his background and his life-style.

240 SCHORR, BURT, and CONTE, CHRISTOPHER. "Coming of Age: Public-Interest Groups Achieve Higher Status and Some Permanence." *Wall Street Journal,* 27 August 1984, 1+.
    See entry 130 for annotation.

241 SPERLING, DAN. "Sidney Wolfe." *USA Today,* 19 March 1986, sec. d, p. 4.
    Discusses Sidney Wolfe and the organization he heads, Health Research Group (HRG). Gives information on his background, his work at HRG, and his personal life. Notes the impact of HRG on the Food and Drug Administration.

242 "Valuable Gadfly." *Time* 112 (20 November 1978): 71.
    An article on Sidney Wolfe, director of the Health Research Group. Characterizes him as a gadfly who "buzzes around federal agencies urging them to take action on health issues." Briefly explains why he became a consumer advocate. Notes his impacts on federal agencies.

243 "Waste Not, Want Not." *Wall Street Journal,* 22 April 1988, 30R.
    An interview with Sidney Wolfe, head of the Public Citizen Health Research Group. Focuses on solutions to rising health care costs.

Public Voice for Food and Health Policy

PUBLIC VOICE FOR FOOD AND HEALTH POLICY

An organization established by Ellen Haas in 1982 to protect the consumer interest in federal food and health policies. Has worked on issues such as dairy and sugar price supports, nutritional labeling, and fish inspection. Directed by Ellen Haas. Based in Washington, D.C.

244 SINCLAIR, WARD. "Ellen Haas: Bringing a New Approach to the Consumer Movement." *Washington Post*, 18 August 1986, sec. A, p. 15.

A profile of Ellen Haas, head of Public Voice for Food and Health Policy. Outlines her progress from a student activist to consumer leader. Describes Public Voice. Discusses its legislative role and its impact on Congress.

USPIRG

A Washington-based lobbying organization organized in 1983 by public interest research groups (PIRGs). Works on environmental and consumer issues. Directed by Gene Karpinski.

245 COOPER, ANN. "On Active Duty for the Public." *National Journal* 17 (14 September 1985): 2062.

A profile of Gene Karpinski and the organization he directs, USPIRG. Discusses Karpinski's education, earlier public interest work, and motivations. Describes the organization's origins, staffing, and activities.

WHITE HOUSE CONSUMER OFFICE

246 "Can Betty Furness Help the Consumer?" *Consumer Reports* 32 (May 1967): 256-58.

A skeptical article on the replacement of Esther Peterson by Betty Furness as the president's special assistant for consumer affairs. Lauds Peterson for her accomplishments. Suggests several problems she faced and the reason for her replacement. Questions the qualifications of Furness for the position. Urges her to resist any attempts to appoint business representatives either to the President's Committee on Consumer Interests or to the Consumer Advisory Council.

247 DEMKOVICH, LINDA E. "Esther Peterson – The Consumer Advocate with the President's Ear." *National Journal* 10 (5 August 1978): 1242-44.

White House Consumer Office

See entry 488 for annotation.

248 "Has Reagan Forgotten the Consumer? Interview with Virginia Knauer, White House Adviser on Consumer Affairs." *U.S. News and World Report* 91 (5 October 1981): 58.

An interview with Virginia Knauer, the president's adviser on consumer affairs. She suggests that the administration is focusing on the number one consumer complaint, inflation, and on deregulation (e.g., of airlines) that lowers prices.

249 HERMAN, THOMAS. "Betty Furness on Consumer Firing Line." *Wall Street Journal*, 20 September 1967, 18.

A lengthy article on consumer representation in the executive branch of the federal government. Explains that Esther Peterson was relieved of her position of consumer adviser to President Johnson after taking positions that aroused industry opposition. Reports criticism from Congress and nonprofit consumer advocates of her successor, Betty Furness. Describes several proposals to increase the clout of consumers in the executive branch.

250 JANSSEN, RICHARD F. "Consumer Defender: New Presidential Aide Shuns War on Business As She Helps Shoppers, but Mrs. Peterson Criticizes Some Packaging Practices, Alerts Unwary Housewives." *Wall Street Journal*, 26 May 1964, 1+.

A feature article on the first special assistant to the president for consumer affairs, Esther Peterson. Suggests Peterson will stress consumer education, smart shopping, and improved communication between sellers and buyers. Reports that business leaders, after initial apprehension, are "feeling reassured."

251 "The Lady with a Sympathetic Ear: Betty Furness, the President's New Adviser on Consumer Affairs, Hears a Lot of Complaints – Especially about Repair and Service Problems." *Business Week*, 23 September 1967, 68+.

A profile of Betty Furness, the president's new adviser on consumer affairs. Indicates that she plans to proceed more cautiously than her predecessor, Esther Peterson, who provoked strong business opposition on several occasions.

252 LUCCO, JOAN. "Roles of Interest Group Representatives at the White House: Consumer Units in the Modern Presidency from John F. Kennedy to Jimmy Carter." Ph.D. dissertation, Johns Hopkins University, 1986. 607 pp.

White House Consumer Office

Investigates the role of White House consumer representatives in presidential administrations from Kennedy to Carter. Separate chapters on these five administrations examine not only the position but also its advantages and disadvantages for presidents, for consumer groups, and for the public. Concludes that the consumer representatives were beneficial to all three groups: they helped presidents govern more effectively and win election; by giving advocates access to the White House, they heightened their visibility and legitimacy; and they helped make the public aware of unmet consumer needs. For a more detailed summary, see *DAI* 47 (1986): 1469A.

253 McLAUGHLIN, FRANK E. "Problems Encountered by the President's Committee on Consumer Interests." In *Consumerism – Viewpoints from Business, Government, and the Public Interest*, edited by Ralph M. Gaedeke and Warren W. Etcheson, 220-26. San Francisco: Canfield Press, 1972.

A former staffer reviews problems experienced by the office of the president's special assistant for consumer affairs. These include too few resources to meet too many demands, business opposition to protection proposals, the absence of government-business dialogue except during crises, and inadequate consumer representation in policy-making.

254 MORRIS, JOHN D. "Nixon's Consumer Affairs Aide Off to Fast Start." *New York Times*, 26 May 1969, 24.

An article on the initial efforts, and praise they received, of Virginia Knauer, President Nixon's consumer adviser. Notes she testified in favor of strong credit-reporting legislation and product safety standards.

255 "Mrs. Consumer." *Newsweek* 30 (2 November 1964): 78+.

An article on adverse business reaction to Esther Peterson, President Johnson's consumer adviser. Discusses criticism from advisers and from other businessmen who fear increased government regulation. This criticism led to Peterson's replacement by Betty Furness after the presidential election.

256 PETERSON, ESTHER. "Consumer Representation in the White House." In *Consumer Activists: They Made a Difference*, edited by Erma Angevine, 198-212. Mount Vernon, N.Y.: Consumers Union Foundation, 1982.

A personal account of Peterson's selection and work as consumer advisor to presidents Johnson and Carter. Provides insight into her selection to this position, her relations with White House officials, and her work on specific issues.

257 PETERSON, ESTHER. "Representing the Consumer Interest in the Federal Government." *Michigan Law Review* 64 (May 1966): 1323-28.
See entry 104 for annotation.

258 SCHOENFELD, ANDREA F. "Mrs. Knauer, Consumer Envoy–Both for and to the White House." *National Journal* (10 January 1970): 90-98.
A detailed analysis of the office of special assistant for consumer affairs to President Nixon, which is headed by Virginia Knauer. Outlines limitations on the influence of the office. Discusses in depth Knauer's relations with the president, Congress, federal agencies and departments, the public, consumer organizations, and industry. Concludes that if legislation before Congress is passed, the office will gain influence and stature. Includes sidebars on Knauer, on her key staffers, on national consumer organizations, and on the kinds of mail Knauer receives.

259 SHAFER, RONALD G. "Knauer Power: Nixon's Consumer Aide Wins Praise of Public, but Clout Is Uncertain." *Wall Street Journal*, 26 August 1969, 1+.
A feature article reporting consumerist and business views on the president's special assistant for consumer affairs, Virginia Knauer, four months after she assumed the position. Almost all assessments are positive. Consumer advocates praise her for advocating legislation allowing class-action suits and limiting fat content in hot dogs. Business representatives are pleased with her emphasis on consumer education and communication with companies.

260 "Virginia Knauer Talks Business." *Pacific Business* 61 (July-August 1971): 33-36.
An interview with President Nixon's special assistant for consumer affairs in which she explains her views of consumerism, business, and her office to a business audience.

261 "Will Virginia Knauer Use Her Consumer Power?" *Consumer Reports* 34 (June 1969): 326-27.
Discusses President Nixon's new special assistant for consumer affairs, Virginia Knauer. Evaluates her performance as director of Pennsylvania's state consumer agency. Urges Knauer to try to convince Nixon to support the creation of a federal consumer protection agency.

262 WITCOVER, JULES. "The GOP Discovers the Consumer." *Progressive* 34 (March 1970): 32-35.

Discusses the consumer advocacy of Virginia Knauer, special assistant to the president for consumer affairs, and its restraint by the administration. Describes disagreements between the administration and advocates on class-action suits and on consumer protection agency legislation. Notes the intention of some Republicans to compete with Democrats for consumer support.

6. State and Local Organizations

263 BOYTE, HARRY C. *The Backyard Revolution: Understanding the New Citizen Movement*. Philadelphia: Temple University Press, 1980. 271 pp.

The only comprehensive description and evaluation of grass-roots citizen action groups in the 1970s. Written by an enthusiastic supporter, the book argues that this new social movement is fundamentally populist in character. Locates the origins of this movement in corporate abuses, the social movements of the 1960s, and neighborhood organizing initiated by Saul Alinsky. Examines a number of organizations that are fighting for consumer, citizen, worker, and environmental protection. In a chapter on citizen activists, focuses on Massachusetts Fair Share, senior groups, antinuclear activists, Ralph Nader and the PIRGs, the Citizens Action League, ACORN, and the new Citizen Action coalition. Concludes that the citizen movement is growing not only in the United States, but also in other countries. Although highly optimistic and sympathetic, the book contains valuable information about and insight into citizen organizations and the thinking of their leaders.

264 BROBECK, STEPHEN, and NISHIMURA, GLENN. "Statistical Report on the Grassroots Consumer Movement." Unpublished report. Washington, D.C.: Consumer Federation of America, 1983.

A report on grass-roots consumer advocacy based on analysis of the Consumer Federation of America's *1983 Directory of State and Local Organizations*. Located in all regions of the United States, the 391 groups reported more than two million individual members. The large majority were established in the 1960s or 1970s, and 60 percent are at least eight years old. Most belong to national networks such as ACORN, Citizen Action, PIRG, or Gray Panthers. The top three priority issues are utilities, health, and housing.

265 CARLEY, WILLIAM M. "Fraud Fighters: States Step Up Drive to Protect Consumers against Business Gyps." *Wall Street Journal*, 10 October 1963, 1+.

Discusses recent state efforts to set up task forces to investigate consumer fraud. Identifies the most serious types of abuses. The revelation of these abuses gave impetus to grass-roots consumer activism.

266 "Consumers Battle at the Grass Roots." *Business Week*, 26 February 1972, 86+.

Discusses the growth of grass-roots consumer activism and protection. Reports that dozens of new protection units have been established at the state or local level. Focuses on new groups in Maryland, New York, California, Pennsylvania, Massachusetts, and Texas.

267 CONSUMERS UNION. *Consumer Protection: A Roster of State and Local Organizations ... A Listing of Consumer Protection Activities.* Mount Vernon, N.Y.: Consumers Union, 1966. 202 pp.

A state-by-state analysis of consumer protections and consumer activities. Includes listings of some twenty-five nonprofit groups working at the state or local level. Almost all are run by volunteers and have no paid staff. Many emphasize consumer education.

268 FRIEDMAN, MONROE P[ETER]. "Local Consumer Organizations: Their Problems, Prospects, and a Proposal." *Journal of Consumer Affairs* 2 (Winter 1968): 205-11.

A prescient article that seeks to explain the absence of local consumer groups and that suggests specific services such organizations could offer. Hypothesizes that activists, especially younger ones, are far more interested in working for groups addressing the problems of the poor and minorities than for groups focused on serving the middle class. Urges consumerists to establish local groups that assist individual consumers in shopping and complaint resolution and that seek to document unfair business practices. Interestingly, many of the hundreds of grass-roots groups and protection agencies established in the 1970s incorporated one or more of these functions.

269 MIROW, DEENA. "Frenzy Gone: Activist Groups Here Take a Calmer Tack in Consumer Crusade." *Plain Dealer*, 19 September 1976, 24+.

A lengthy feature article on the consumer movement in Cleveland. Suggests that the movement has been "accepted by society" and "institutionalized." Discusses the priorities of Cleveland Consumer Action, Consumer Protection Association, and the Citizens League. Quotes consumer leaders Solomon Harge, Jay Seaton, Bob Weaver, and Stephen Brobeck.

270 NELSON, HELEN. *A Guide to Consumer Action*. Report issued by the Office of Education, U.S. Department of Health, Education, and Welfare, Washington, D.C., n.d.

A report prepared in the late 1970s by a longtime educator/activist on organizing consumer activities. Chapter 2 includes case studies of the Concerned Consumers League (Wis.), Virginia Citizens Consumer Council, Michigan Public Interest Research Group (PIRGIM), Texas Consumer Association, Utility Consumers Council of Missouri, Northeastern Minnesota Consumers League, and Consumers Against High Prices (Fla.). In 1990, the first four groups were still active.

271 SORENSON, PHILIP C. "Report to Consumers Union Regarding State and Local Consumer Organizations." Unpublished report to Consumers Union, Mount Vernon, N.Y.: Consumers Union, 1972. 44 pp.

A brief report of grass-roots consumer groups based on on-site visits to twenty-one state or local organizations, interviews with national leaders, and examination of files of Consumers Union and the Consumer Federation of America. Prepared for Consumers Union to assist it in deciding how to support these groups. Discusses the consumer movement in general, and analyzes the characteristics of grass-roots organizations–their leadership, membership, size, purposes, staff, financial status, militancy, accomplishments, and weaknesses. Concludes that, although there is no unified consumer movement, there are a number of "surprisingly effective" state and local groups that enjoy "relatively easy access to the media and policymakers" but lack funding and other resources. Although sketchy, the study represents a unique source of information on these organizations in the early 1970s.

272 "U.S. Consumer Groups: Livelier Than Ever." *U.S. News and World Report* 81 (6 December 1976): 90-91.

A report on the growing strength of grass-roots consumer groups throughout the nation. Briefly describes the work of some organizations

General

in the Midwest (Chicago Consumers Coalition, Michigan Citizens Lobby, PIRGIM, Illinois Public Action Council), the Far West (Consumer Advocates, CAUSE), the South (Carolina Action, Georgia PIRG, Louisiana Consumers League, and others), and the Northeast, which "probably has the highest concentration" of such groups.

273 WARNE, COLSTON E. *Consumer Protective Movements on the State and Local Levels – 1964.* Amherst, Mass.: Colston E. Warne, 1964. 27 pp.

A paper (held by Consumers Union's library) on ten nonprofit consumer groups and thirteen government agencies or advisory councils that were seeking to protect consumers in 1963. The nonprofit organizations are the Association of California Consumers, Consumer Conference of Greater Cincinnati, Maryland Consumers Council, Massachusetts Consumer Association, St. Louis Consumer Federation, Metropolitan New York Consumer Council, Consumers League of New Jersey, Centre Consumer Association (Pa.), Consumer Information Clearinghouse (Vt.), and Center for Consumer Affairs (Wis.). Each organization is described in several paragraphs.

ACORN

274 KOPKIND, ANDREW. "ACORN Calling: Door-to-Door Organizing in Arkansas." *Working Papers for a New Society,* Summer 1975, 13-20.

An informative article on one of the most successful statewide grass-roots organizations, Arkansas Community Organizations for Reform Now (ACORN), which later expanded to dozens of states. Explains how the some seventy neighborhood ACORN groups organize around local issues, then combine to mount statewide campaigns on issues such as utility rate reform and property tax reform. Describes the founding of the organization by Wade Rathke, its expansion, its organizing methods, its current activities, and its successes.

ALLIANCE FOR CONSUMER PROTECTION

275 HENNESSY, TOM. "Forum Interview – David Pittle: The Pittsburgh Nader." *Pittsburgh Forum,* 29 June 1973, 6+.

An interview with David Pittle, president of the Alliance for Consumer Protection. Pittle discusses consumer protection in Pittsburgh and the alliance's complaint-resolution experience, consumer deputy corps, and press coverage.

Alliance for Consumer Protection

276 PATTERSON, MAGGIE. "Consumers Unite for More Clout." *Pittsburgh Press*, 15 November 1971.

An article on the Alliance for Consumer Protection. Discusses its work resolving individual complaints and its plans to address public policy issues. Quotes its chairman, David Pittle.

CENTER FOR COMMUNITY CHANGE

277 LAUTENSCHLAGER, SCOTT. "Louise Trubek." *Wisconsin State Journal*, 23 July 1989, sec. G, p. 2.

A profile of Louise Trubek and the Center for Public Representation she heads. Describes Trubek's education and her founding and leadership of CPR, which provides legal representation and education for disadvantaged groups.

278 STOCKINGER, JACOB. "Legal Center Looks Upscale after Its Move." *Capital Times*, 4 October 1989, 27.

An article on the Center for Public Representation based in Madison, Wisconsin. Discusses the organization's accomplishments since its founding in 1974, its priorities, its budget, its new Milwaukee branch, and its new Madison offices.

CITIZEN ENERGY CORPORATION

279 STONE, PETER. "Joe Kennedy vs. the Gang of Seven." *Working Papers for a New Society*, January-February 1981, 12-14.

Discusses Joe Kennedy's organization of a Citizen Energy Corporation to purchase and sell heating oil to citizens at low rates. Reports on its success and the hope of organizers to expand to other states.

CITIZEN UTILITY BOARDS

280 "Citizen Boards Battle the Utilities." *New York Times*, 25 October 1987, 34.

Discusses citizen utility boards (CUBs) that were created to ensure a consumer voice in public policy decisions made on utility issues by public service commissions and state legislatures. Dependent on access to utility mailings, CUBs were proposed by Ralph Nader as a way for citizens to support directly and participate in a utility watchdog

Citizen Utility Boards

group. Focuses particular attention on Illinois CUB, which claims credit for lower utility rates and reform of the state public utilities act. Includes utility responses. Notes a recent court decision restricting CUB access to utility mailings that jeopardizes the future of this institution.

281 DUKE, PAUL, Jr. "Consumer Groups View Bill Inserts as a Potent Force against Utilities." *Wall Street Journal*, 23 October 1985, 57.
Examines the controversy about whether citizen utility boards (CUBs) should be allowed to solicit members and funds using utility bill inserts. The Supreme Court is reviewing a California Public Utilities Commission decision requiring utilities to mail the inserts. Summarizes arguments of both the CUBs and utilities on the issue. Indicates that, in their present form, CUBs depend on access to the utility bills.

282 KOHN, ALFIE. "Citizen Utility Boards: People Power vs. Power Companies." *Nation*, 29 December 1984, 710-12.
Describes the emergence of citizen utility boards (CUBs) that represent consumers at utility rate hearings. Conceived of by Ralph Nader, these organizations exist in Wisconsin and Oregon. Discusses reasons for their growing popularity. Notes that activists are planning to establish similar organizations to represent consumers on banking and insurance issues.

CLEVELAND CONSUMER ACTION

Records of the organization and other relevant sources from the 1970s are held by the Western Reserve Historical Society.

283 "Conversation with Steve Brobeck, Consumer Advocate." *Cleveland Magazine*, July 1975, 21+.
An interview with the cofounder and coordinator of Consumer Action Movement (later, Cleveland Consumer Action) in which he discusses grass-roots consumer action, other local consumer agencies, and the role of federal consumer laws.

284 "Energy Keeps Consumer Action Hopping." *Cleveland Press*, 21 September 1981.
An article about Cleveland Consumer Action's complaint-referral and complaint-handling services. The latter are based on those of the Consumer Education and Protective Association.

285 MYLER, KATHLEEN. "Activist Trades Signs for Briefcase." *Houston Chronicle*, 21 February 1988.
See entry 159 for annotation.

286 SKOCH, TOM. "Consumer Groups Merge for Action." *Cleveland Press*, 1 June 1976, sec. A, p. 5.
An article on the merger of Consumer Action Movement and Citizen Action to form Cleveland Consumer Action. Discusses the group's activities, new structure, local reputation, legislative accomplishments, complaint-resolution record, and plans to expand.

CONNECTICUT CITIZEN ACTION GROUP

287 CAPLAN, MARC. *A Citizen's Guide to Lobbying*. New York: Dembner Books, 1983. 288 pp.
A manual for citizen groups that wish to lobby state legislatures. Written by advocates working for the Connecticut Citizen Action Group (CCAG). In separate chapters, discusses groundwork, forces, organizing public support, the press, fund-raising, legislative committees, public hearings, negotiations, lobbying the floor, and floor debate. Liberally illustrated from the CCAG experiences of the writer.

CONSUMER EDUCATION AND PROTECTIVE ASSOCIATION

288 COLIMORE, EDWARD. "Weiner's Influence Is Yet to Be Stilled." *Philadelphia Inquirer*, 23 February 1987, 6+.
A lengthy profile of Max Weiner, head of the Consumer Education and Protective Association, who is characterized as "Philadelphia's Ralph Nader." Describes his youth, Depression and war years, early career as an accountant, organization of CEPA, and current activism. Includes a sidebar listing CEPA's ten biggest battles.

289 HAAS, AL. "Consumed with Consumerism." *Philadelphia Inquirer*, 2 January 1986, sec. E, p. 1+.
A lengthy feature article on Max Weiner, founder and head of the Consumer Education and Protective Association. Describes CEPA's recent lawsuits and other protests; Weiner's personality and life-style; his early career as a labor organizer, accountant, and realtor; his founding of CEPA with Garland Dempsey; and the organization's accomplishments.

Consumer Education and Protective Association

290 ITTIG, KATHLEEN BROWNE. "Consumer Collective Action: A Study of Consumers Education and Protective Association International, Inc." M.S. thesis, Cornell University, 1973. 231 pp.

An analysis of the Consumer Education and Protective Association (CEPA), which developed a unique method of resolving individual consumer grievances using collective action, to determine whether the organization uses individual and/or family resources effectively and efficiently. Chapter 1 provides an overview of the consumer movement, past and present, including the history of CEPA, which was organized and led by Max Weiner. Chapter 2 discusses the economics of collective action as developed mainly by John R. Commons and Mancur Olson. Chapter 3 uses the results of a survey of consumer members to assess the effectiveness of CEPA in "facilitating the growth of consumer sophistication." Although only 102 of 966 members completed usable questionnaires, these respondents were found to have "a high level of consumer sophistication." Chapter 4 evaluates CEPA in terms of the history of the consumer movement, economic theory, and the membership survey. Finds similarities in the development of the consumer and labor movements. Learns that CEPA members strongly support the organization but do not necessarily participate in meetings with merchants and picketing, though acknowledges that, because of the uniqueness of the group, there is no basis for comparison. Useful principally for its description of CEPA and the views of some of its members.

291 ROSENBERG, AMY. "Crusader Max Weiner Dies at 77." *Philadelphia Inquirer*, 23 October 1989, sec. A, p. 1+.

An obituary for Max Weiner, head of the Consumer Education and Protective Association and the Consumer party, who is described by Ralph Nader as "the most persistent and effective consumer advocate at the community level in the country." Describes his life and work for CEPA and the Consumer party.

CONSUMER PROTECTION ASSOCIATION

292 "Harge Is Director of Consumer Group." *Plain Dealer*, 19 June 1968.

An article on Solomon Harge, who was just appointed head of the new Consumer Protection Association. Discusses his past accomplishments and his new organization.

293 TAYLOR, MARGARET. "Shield against Sharks." *Plain Dealer Sunday Magazine*, 25 October 1970, 18+.

Consumer Protection Association

An article on the new Consumer Protection Association, headed by Solomon Harge, that handles consumer complaints, undertakes consumer education, and establishes new sources of credit for individuals.

COUNCIL TO ADVOCATE PUBLIC UTILITY RESPONSIBILITY

294 "Consumerists Claim a Seat on Northern States Power Board." *Wall Street Journal*, 13 September 1973, 12.
A short article reporting on the possible election of a consumer advocate to the board of Northern States Power Company. Discusses the proxy fight waged by the Council to Advocate Public Utility Responsibility (CAPUR).

295 SMABY, ALPHA. "The CAPUR Crusade." *Progressive* 38 (July 1974): 19-23.
An article by a Minnesota citizen activist on a campaign by the Coalition to Advocate Public Utility Responsibility (CAPUR) to place a citizen activist on the board of Northern States Power Company. Discusses the campaign's initiation, development, and conclusion with the defeat of the activist by NSP shareholders. Assesses reasons for this defeat. Evaluates the impact of the campaign.

MASSACHUSETTS FAIR SHARE

296 KOPKIND, ANDREW. "Fair Share's Ballot Box Blues." *Working Papers for a New Society*, Winter 1977, 26-32.
An insightful analysis of Massachusetts Fair Share's unsuccessful ballot campaign to reform utility rates. Traces the history of the organization. Describes the utility reform campaign in some detail. Develops an explanation as to why it lost. Reports the heavy cost to the organization in terms of lost credibility and resources.

NEW JERSEY CONSUMERS LEAGUE

297 COURTNEY, MARIAN. "Consumers League: A Spry 87." *New York Times*, 2 August 1987, NJ-1.
A lengthy article on the New Jersey Consumers League that was established eighty-seven years ago. Emphasizes the league's concern for the welfare of workers as well as that of consumers throughout its history. Discusses its budget and some 500 members, all of whom are

New Jersey Consumers League

volunteers. Briefly profiles several members and identifies banking, consumer education, and child labor as issues of greatest concern.

PUBLIC INTEREST RESEARCH GROUPS

298 ANDERSON, JACK. "Student Activism: 'Idealism Is Not Dead.'" *Washington Post*, 9 September 1974, sec. B, p. 7.
   An article by a prominent syndicated columnist on public interest research groups (PIRGs). Reports that they exist on 135 campuses in nineteen states. Describes activities of a number of PIRGs. Discusses opposition from politicians and college trustees. Notes that PIRGs try to keep an arms-length distance from radical groups.

299 ANDERSON, JACK, and SPEAR, JOSEPH. "Student Activists Keep Naderism Alive." *Washington Post*, 16 June 1987, sec. B, p. 10.
   A syndicated column on the growth of public interest research groups (PIRGs), which, despite conservative attacks, now exist on 115 campuses in twenty-five states.

300 GRIFFIN, KELLEY. *More Action for Change*. New York: Dembner Books, 1987. 226 pp.
   A book on the successes of public interest research groups (PIRGs). In separate chapters, treats their history, research, and advocacy, and profiles New York PIRG, Colorado PIRG, and seven student activists. Concluding chapters summarize the contributions of PIRGs and discuss their future. A rich source of information on PIRGs written from their perspective.

301 LYONS, RICHARD D. "Public Interest Groups on 138 Campuses Set to Fight Local Problems." *New York Times*, 5 September 1973, 22.
   A lengthy article on public interest research groups (PIRGs), inspired by Ralph Nader, that have been established on more than 100 college campuses. Outlines many of their proposed reforms. Discusses their controversial checkoff funding mechanism.

302 MINTZ, MORTON. "Students Forming Nader-Type Units." *Washington Post*, 7 December 1972, sec. K, p. 3.
   An article on public interest research groups (PIRGs) that have been established at more than fifty colleges and universities. Explains their funding by student activity fees, their staffing, and some of their accomplishments.

Public Interest Research Groups

303 SILBER, JOHN R. "Nader's Campus Protégés Mix Coercion and Consumerism." *Wall Street Journal*, 23 August 1984, 22.

An op-ed essay by the controversial president of Boston University criticizing public interest research groups (PIRGs). While its central point is the unfairness of the "negative checkoff" method of funding PIRGs through student activity fees, the article also finds fault with the liberal politics of the organizations.

304 TREASTER, JOSEPH B. "College Republicans Open a Drive against Student Activist Groups." *New York Times*, 13 March 1983, 28.

A report on a campaign initiated by the College Republican National Committee against public interest research groups (PIRGs) based on college and university campuses. The committee claims that such groups promote leftist political ideas and are anti-Reagan. It distributed an information packet to state chairs with suggested strategies for weakening the PIRGs or preventing new groups from organizing. These strategies emphasize attacking those student activity fees that fund the groups. Ralph Nader, who helped organize the PIRGs, and PIRG leaders respond that each group is autonomous and that students approve the funding.

SAN FRANCISCO CONSUMER ACTION

305 DUNGAN, ELOISE. "Out to Stop the Ripoff." *San Francisco Examiner*, 7 April 1972, 22+.

An article on the new San Francisco Consumer Action and its leader Kathryn Pachtner. Discusses the organization's origins, structure, dependence on volunteers, and focus on complaint resolution.

306 NAVARRO, MIREYA. "Consumer Action: Grass Roots to Big Time." *San Francisco Examiner*, 18 June 1986, sec. B, p. 1+.

An article on San Francisco Consumer Action that describes its origins, past accomplishments, current priorities, and staff, including executive director Ken McEldowney.

307 WEINSTEIN, HENRY. "Inside a Consumer Group." *New York Times*, 9 February 1975, sec. III, p. 7.

An article on San Francisco Consumer Action, which it characterizes as "the most effective consumer interest group in the West." Reviews its growth and accomplishments since it was founded in 1971. Indicates that its activities range from research to lobbying to complaint resolution. Identifies its "principal problem" as raising funds.

San Francisco Consumer Action

308 WILSON, GREGORY, and BRYDOFF, ELIZABETH. "Grass Roots Solutions: San Francisco Consumer Action." In *No Access to Law: Alternatives to the American Judicial System*, edited by Laura Nader, 417-59. New York: Academic Press, 1980.

An informative article on one of the most successful local consumer groups in the 1970s, San Francisco Consumer Action. Concentrates on its complaint handling, but also treats its leaders (Kathryn Pachtner and Neil Gendell), founding, staffing, activities, and funding. Includes a discussion of the organization's self-help complaint committees and those maintained by Cleveland Consumer Action, both based on complaint methods developed by the Consumer Education and Protective Association. Incorrectly identifies the date of inception of the San Francisco complaint committees (it should be 1975, not 1974) and fails to point out that they were established by two Cleveland Consumer Action organizers.

VIRGINIA CITIZENS CONSUMER COUNCIL

309 ANDERSON, BELINDA. "Consumer Group Fights Never-Ending Battle." *Roanoke Times & World-News*, 6 April 1987, sec. B, p. 2+.

A lengthy article about the Virginia Citizens Consumer Council, which is twenty years old but is now becoming more active under the leadership of Jean Ann Fox. Discusses the group's dependence on volunteers, its lack of resources and influence with legislators, and its priorities. Since 1987, VCCC has become far more active and influential in Richmond.

7. Movement Relationships

WITH ACADEMICS

310 BROBECK, STEPHEN. "Academics and Advocates: The Role of Consumer Researchers in Public Policy-Making." *Journal of Consumer Affairs* 22 (Winter 1988): 187-200.

A revised version of a Colston E. Warne lecture that addresses the relationships between consumer advocates and consumer academics. First, reviews current relations between academics and advocates. Concludes that relations are good yet not as close as desirable, and suggests reasons why. Second, explains why there should be closer cooperation, particularly involvement of academics in consumer policy-making. Suggests that need, opportunity, and morality all justify the latter. Third, suggests a specific role for researchers in this policy-making: namely, conducting socially relevant research and communicating research results to policymakers. Fourth, proposes a number of specific measures that allow more participation of academics in the policy-making process. Concludes that the need for such participation will grow in the future if the marketplace becomes even more complex.

WITH BUSINESS

311 BELKIN, LISA. "Consumerism and Business Learn Together." *New York Times*, 13 April 1985, 48.

An article on the current status of consumerism – not only consumer advocacy groups but also government protection agencies and

With Business

consumer affairs offices in business. Suggests that advocates "have learned from business and become as sophisticated." Indicates that businesses are responding to consumer concerns by creating their own consumer programs. Notes that many of the earlier problems have been solved and consumers have become better able to protect themselves. Reports some disagreements among consumerists over the relation of regulators and advocates to business.

312 DONOHUE, GERRY. "The Consumer's Best Friend." *Professional Agent*, January 1980, 25-27.

Focuses on Esther Peterson, consumer adviser to presidents Johnson and Carter, who is now serving as the national consumer adviser to the Professional Insurance Agents (PIA). Summarizes her career over the past fifty years. Quotes Peterson as explaining why she was willing to advise PIA and what she hopes to accomplish. Describes the Consumer Insurance Interest Group (CIIG) Peterson created to work as a partner with PIA on strengthening state insurance departments.

313 DONOHUE, GERRY. "The New Spirit of Cooperation." *Professional Agent*, January 1988, 22-24.

Discusses the Consumer Insurance Interest Group (CIIG) and its cooperation with the Professional Insurance Agents (PIA). CIIG is an organization consisting of Esther Peterson, Public Citizen's Joan Claybrook, National Insurance Consumer Organization's Robert Hunter, and Consumer Federation of America's Stephen Brobeck that will work with PIA to strengthen state insurance departments. Its principal activities will be conducting research and making policy recommendations, then seeking to build coalitions of insurance agents and grass-roots consumer activists to implement these policies.

314 KRAMER, LARRY. "Chamber Suit Hits Consumer Funding." *Washington Post*, 16 August 1978, sec. E, p. 5.

See entry 154 for annotation.

315 LEVY, CLAUDIA. "Counting on Esther Peterson." *Washington Post*, 12 May 1974, sec. L, p. 1+.

An article on Esther Peterson's work as consumer adviser to Giant Food. Discusses her varied activities there and the changes she has effected.

316 MAYER, ROBERT N. "When Businesses Oppose Businesses in Support of Consumerist Goals." *Journal of Consumer Policy* 11 (December 1988): 375-94.

The first academic study to examine political coalitions linking consumer and business representatives that are opposed by other businesses. Classifies these coalitions in terms of political cleavages within the business community. Identifies two major types – those with divisions between sellers of the same goods and those with divisions between sellers of different goods – and subtypes of each. Suggests future research on the causes and efforts of these consumer-business coalitions. Discusses briefly the costs and benefits to consumer participants. Relies on reports from advocates describing specific coalitions. Misreads the significance of one consumer-business collaboration: The Credit Union National Association joined with the Consumer Federation of America on savings disclosures, not to advance legislation but to convince Congress that its members were already voluntarily disclosing adequate information and therefore should be exempted from any "truth in savings" requirements.

317 MORRIS, BETTY. "Peterson, Inside, Looks Out." *Supermarket News*, 21 September 1970, 1+.

An article based on an interview with Esther Peterson, who just began working as consumer adviser to Giant Food, where she will develop and present recommendations for more proconsumer policies and practices. Suggests she will recommend open dating, unit pricing, better labeling of chemicals in foods, and environmentally sound practices. Identifies a number of valid complaints from consumer groups, including confusing practices, rising prices, higher prices for the poor, and costly trading stamps.

318 SHAFER, RONALD G. "The House Critic: A Food Chain Recruits a Consumer Advocate to Shape Its Policies." *Wall Street Journal*, 13 January 1972, 1+.

A feature article on Esther Peterson's first year as consumer adviser to Giant Food. Indicates that she has persuaded the supermarket chain to become an industry leader in consumerism through adoption of open dating, unit pricing on thousands of products, ingredient disclosure on house-brand products, and sale of recycled-paper products and nonpolluting laundry soap. Reports that the new policies have contributed to record sales and have earned plaudits from advocates. Develops an explanation for Peterson's success.

With the Civil Rights Movement

WITH THE CIVIL RIGHTS MOVEMENT

319 SIMMONS, HERBERT, Jr. "The Consumer Movement and the Civil Rights Movement." In *Proceedings, 27th Annual Conference of the American Council on Consumer Interests*, edited by Carol B. Meeks, 180-85. Columbia, Mo.: American Council on Consumer Interests, 1981.

A comparison of the consumer and civil rights movements by an activist who has participated in both. Considers the goals, scope, dynamics and constituencies, focus and impetus, and futures of the two movements. Suggests that both have "proceeded along a lengthy continuum" and have achieved gains for their constituencies. Argues that both are in need of a revival and outlines a "prescription for curing [their] ills."

WITH ENVIRONMENTALISTS

320 MAGNUSON, WARREN G. "Consumerism and the Emerging Goals of a New Society." In *Consumerism: Viewpoints from Business, Government, and the Public Interest*, edited by Ralph M. Gaedeke and Warren W. Etcheson, 3-7. San Francisco: Canfield Press, 1972.

See entry 554 for annotation.

321 MITCHELL, ROBERT CAMERON. "Consumerism and Environmentalism in the 1980s: Competitive or Companionable Social Movements?" In *The Future of Consumerism*, edited by Paul N. Bloom and Ruth Belk Smith, 23-36. Lexington, Mass.: Lexington Books, 1985.

Addresses the question whether consumerism and environmentalism will work against or with each other in the 1980s. Outlines the general similarities between them. Discusses their potential for conflict. Argues that this conflict is unlikely to materialize because of shared ideology, common constituencies, broad public support, a common enemy, and agreement on many potentially divisive energy issues. Concludes that the two movements will continue to cooperate and be mutually supportive.

WITH GOVERNMENT

322 FRIEDMAN, ROBERT S. "Representation in Regulatory Decision Making: Scientific, Industrial, and Consumer Inputs to the F.D.A." *Public Administration Review* (May-June 1978): 205-14.

An evaluation of the Food and Drug Administration's advisory committee system based on responses to questionnaires and interviews with committee members, FDA staff, congressional staff, industry, and consumer groups. Reports favorable assessments by scientists and professionals on the committees and by FDA staffers. Finds that most participants viewed consumer inputs as "qualitatively inferior." Notes that consumer leaders believe that this problem reflects their lack of compensation and political or ideological differences with other committee members. But suggests that the central difficulty is that the consumer representatives lack relevant professional training. Recommends the continuation of the advisory committees.

323 KARR, ALBERT R. "Inside View: Former Consumerists Now in Agencies Find New Jobs Frustrating." *Wall Street Journal*, 15 December 1977, 1+.

A feature article about former advocates working as top officials in the Carter administration. Focuses most attention on Joan Claybrook, head of the National Highway Traffic Safety Administration. Reports Ralph Nader's criticism, the Department of Transportation's nervousness, and her own frustrations as well as her accomplishments. Briefly discusses Carol Foreman of the U.S. Department of Agriculture and Gus Speth of the President's Council on Environmental Quality.

324 KRAMER, LARRY. "Consumer Activists – How Many Needed." *Washington Post*, 18 January 1979, sec. D, p. 1.

An article on a Public Citizen survey revealing that only 4 percent of higher-level appointees in the Carter administration are former consumer advocates. These eight persons are listed.

325 McPHERSON, MYRA. "Former Consumer Activist Doing Job from Inside." *Washington Post*, 17 November 1977, sec. A, p. 2.

An article on former Consumer Federation of America executive director Carol Foreman, who is now an assistant secretary at the U.S. Department of Agriculture. Characterizes her as outspoken but pragmatic. Describes opposition to her demands on nitrites and nitrates. Also reports Ralph Nader's criticism of former advocates in government such as Foreman, Harrison Wellford, Peter Schuck, and Joan Claybrook.

326 MAYER, CAROLINE E. "A Rude Awakening for Activists in Government." *U.S. News & World Report* 84 (6 March 1978): 52+.

Reports criticisms by activists such as Ralph Nader of former advocates who now run federal agencies, including Mike Pertschuk,

With Government

Joan Claybrook, Carol Foreman, and Sam Brown. Discusses accomplishments of these officials. Also notes the constraints under which they operate.

327 MAYER, ROBERT N., and SCAMMON, DEBRA L. "Intervenor Funding at the FTC: Biopsy or Autopsy." *Policy Studies Review* 2 (February 1983): 506-15.

Evaluates the Federal Trade Commission's intervenor funding program, which reimbursed many advocacy groups for participating in the agency's regulatory proceedings. Describes the program. Reviews alleged benefits and costs. Reports the results of a survey of fund applicants that helps reveal the program's successes and limitations. Suggests different approaches for improving the program, which was shut down by the Reagan administration about the time this article was published.

328 MORONE, JAMES A., and MARMOR, THEODORE R. "Representing Consumer Interests: The Case of American Health Planning." *Ethics* 91 (April 1981): 431-50.

An evaluation of the national network of local health-planning institutions, called health systems agencies (HSAs), that was authorized by the National Health Planning and Resources Development Act of 1974. Discusses the intended purpose of requiring a consumer majority on each HSA governing board. Examines the competing ideas of representation, participation, and accountability. Finds that the consumer board members often lacked expertise and accountability. Recommends that HSA staff be assigned to these consumer representatives and that they be selected by consumer/community organizations.

329 O'BRIEN, TIM. "FEA Consumer Office Chief Quits, Cites Lack of Influence." *Washington Post*, 13 August 1974, sec. A, p. 1.

A front-page article on the resignation of Lee Richardson as director of the Federal Energy Administration's consumer office. Discusses Richardson's lengthy letter of resignation in which he charged FEA with ignoring his office.

330 "Professional Consumer Advocate: Eileen Hoats." *New York Times*, 1 February 1975, 52.

An article on Eileen Hoats, executive director of the New York Consumer Assembly and new president of the Consumer Federation of America. Focuses on her work for the assembly and discusses her refusal to sit on a federal advisory panel unless she was paid the per diem that other members received.

331 ROSENBAUM, DAVID E. "Public Affairs Groups, Now on the Outside, Expect Access to Power under Carter." *New York Times*, 1 December 1976, sec. II, p. 6.

A lengthy article on the roles of public interest advocates in the Carter administration. Suggests that it will present new opportunities (e.g., access to the executive branch) but also problems (e.g., fund-raising by critics of Carter). Discusses the roles several advocates see for themselves in the new era. Notes that some such as Carol Tucker Foreman are advising the transition team, while others such as Ralph Nader will not take a position in the new administration.

332 WARE, CAROLINE. "Consumer Participation at the Federal Level." In *Consumer Activists: They Made a Difference*, edited by Erma Angevine, 171-97. Mount Vernon, N.Y.: Consumers Union Foundation, 1982.

See entry 82 for annotation.

WITH LABOR

333 BARKIN, SOLOMON. "Trade Unions and Consumerism." *Journal of Economic Issues* 7 (June 1973): 317-21.

Discusses the relationship of U.S. trade unions to consumerism. Notes that many European unions have offered their members specific consumer services and have fought for consumer protections. Suggests that most such services initiated by U.S. unions have not been sustained. Points out that the AFL-CIO supports some national consumer groups and that member unions provide consumer information in their publications. Challenges unions to play a more active role in ensuring the quality, safety, and health of the products they produce.

334 BENNETT, JAMES T., and DiLORENZO, THOMAS J. "Tax-Funded Unionism III: Front Organizations." *Journal of Labor Research* 8 (Spring 1987): 179-89.

A conservative critique of the establishment by labor unions of public interest "front" groups that frequently receive federal government support. Focuses most attention on the National Council of Senior Citizens (NCSC), National Consumers League (NCL), and Citizen/Labor Energy Coalition (CLEC). Argues that NCSC has been supported mainly by federal grants, that NCL has received half its funds from the government, and that CLEC promotes anticorporate attitudes

With Labor

that help unions. It is significant that the article identifies only one "front" organization, NCSC, that receives substantial government monies, and it neglects to evaluate the funded programs of this group. Since the late nineteenth century, though NCL has carried a "consumer" label, it has functioned primarily as a labor support organization. Another consumer group mentioned in the article, Consumers Union, has had well-publicized differences with unions. Most importantly, the article fails to recognize the historical commitment of the labor movement, especially industrial unions, to consumer protections because they benefit union members as consumers.

335 "Connubial Consumerism." *Wall Street Journal*, 31 August 1976, 10.
    See entry 148 for annotation.

336 LOFTUS, JOSEPH A. "Nader Calls Union Leaders Lax in Protecting Safety of Members." *New York Times*, 3 July 1968, 15.
    A short article reporting congressional testimony on unsafe working conditions in which Ralph Nader criticized labor unions for not focusing enough attention on the issue.

337 WARNE, CLINTON L. "The Consumer Movement and the Labor Movement." *Journal of Economic Issues* 7 (June 1973): 307+.
    Discusses the recent growth of the consumer movement and labor's relation to it. Focuses most attention on the relatively new Consumer Federation of America, a coalition of consumer advocates, cooperatives, and trade unions. Describes CFA's program and structure. Indicates that trade unions historically have tried to establish consumer cooperatives (usually unsuccessfully), have supported local consumer groups like the Consumers League of Ohio, and have assisted initiatives to pass consumer legislation. Notes that trade issues sometimes strain the alliance between unions and consumer groups. Urges labor to participate even more actively in the consumer movement.

WITH SOCIAL WORKERS

338 ORLIN, MALINDA. "A Role for Social Workers in the Consumer Movement." *Social Work* 18 (January 1973): 60-65.
    Explores the role of social workers in the solution of consumer problems. Explains why these problems are relevant to the field of social welfare. Describes the U.S. Office of Economic Opportunity's consumer action programs. Suggests that social workers can assist individuals through consumer education, advocacy, and referral to community resources. Also argues that they can "make the environment

more sensitive to consumer needs" through lobbying, monitoring law enforcement, conducting research, and working with business. Concludes that the problem-solving, research, negotiation, and organizational skills of social workers equip them to perform these consumerist functions.

WITHIN THE MOVEMENT

339 BURROS, MARIAN. "Nader Talks, Claybrook Doesn't, about the Rift." *Washington Post*, 2 December 1977, sec. D, p. 6.
A short article on consumer movement reactions to Ralph Nader's criticism of former colleague Joan Claybrook, who now heads the National Highway Traffic Safety Administration. Quotes Nader on the incident.

340 "Consumer versus Advocate." *Wall Street Journal*, 2 February 1977, 16.
An editorial discussing the disagreement between Consumers Union and Ralph Nader's Health Research Group over the safety of ionization-type smoke detectors. Comments favorably on the Consumers Union position.

341 KARPATKIN, RHODA. "Memo to Members." *Consumer Reports* 40 (September 1975): 524.
See entry 174 for annotation.

342 "Nader Quits CU." *New York Times*, 23 August 1975, 10.
See entry 182 for annotation.

343 "Nader to Claybrook: What Have You Done for Us Lately?" *Consumer Reports* 43 (April 1978): 92+.
An article on Ralph Nader's demand that Joan Claybrook, a former associate, resign as head of the National Highway Traffic Safety Administration. Outlines Nader's criticisms of the agency. Explains that Claybrook took over a "moribund agency" and has been faced with severe constraints. Summarizes her priorities for the agency. Concludes that "if the Claybrooks can't get the job done, who can?"

344 "Reformers: Ralph's Wrath." *Newsweek* 90 (12 December 1977): 90+.
A short article on Ralph Nader's criticism of former associate Joan Claybrook, now head of the National Highway Traffic Safety Administration, and her response. Suggests that many activists who joined the Carter administration have disappointed Nader.

Within the Movement

345 SHERILL, ROBERT. "The Zany Sport of Liberal Fratricide." *Nation*
236 (15 January 1983): 44-46.

An article on the tendency of liberals to attack each other that
features Ralph Nader's quarrel with Toby Moffett, a proconsumer
member of Congress and former Nader associate. Nader's criticism may
have been instrumental in Moffet's close defeat in a U.S. Senate race.

8. Movement Leaders

GENERAL

346 BARKSDALE, HIRAM C., and FRENCH, WARREN A. "Response to Consumerism: How Change Is Perceived by Both Sides." *MSU Business Topics* 23 (Spring 1975): 55-67.

A description and analysis of the results of a nationwide survey of 597 marketing managers and 102 consumer advocates on such topics as product planning, advertising, physical distribution of products, pricing, and customer service. Finds remarkable agreement between the two groups on the impacts of consumer advocacy. Both see little conflict between the objectives of consumerism and those of marketing management. Both view the consumer movement as essentially a positive force. Both agree that consumerism has affected all aspects of marketing except physical distribution and has stimulated more government regulation.

347 FRIEDMAN, MONROE PETER. "The 1966 Consumer Protest As Seen by Its Leaders." *Journal of Consumer Affairs* 5 (Summer 1971): 1-23.

One of the first academic studies of modern consumer protest. Using survey data from leaders of sixty-four participating organizations, examines the characteristics and stated motivations of these leaders and the goals, actions, and impacts of their groups. Finds that the leaders tend to be young, well-educated, middle-class housewives affiliated with the Democratic party. Discovers that their goals are to reduce prices through the elimination of supermarket advertising expenditures and trading stamps. Learns that they believe their actions had a temporary

General

effect of lowering prices. Concludes that the study supports other research suggesting that citizen activism is increasing.

348 GAEDEKE, RALPH M[ORTIMER]. "What Business, Government, and Consumer Spokesmen Think about Consumerism." *Journal of Consumer Affairs* 4 (Summer 1970): 7-18.

Uses survey responses from twenty-five business spokespersons, seventeen consumer leaders, and thirteen government representatives to examine differences in perceptions about the nature and causes of consumerism and the desirability of proposed solutions to consumer problems. Finds that while all three groups believe the scope of consumerism is broadening, their views of consumerism often diverge, with greatest agreement between consumer and government representatives. Discovers both agreement and disagreement about the causes of consumerism. Learns that almost all consumer and government representatives, but only a small minority of business spokespersons, support additional consumer legislation. Yet, finds that a significant percentage of all three groups think "more cooperation among government, business, and consumers" is desirable. Samples are small, possibly unrepresentative, and not always clearly distinct: government respondents included advocates and educators from two advisory councils.

349 LICHTER, S. ROBERT, and ROTHMAN, STANLEY. "What Interests the Public and What Interests the Public Interests." *Public Opinion*, April-May 1983, 44-48.

An informative portrait of public interest leaders in Washington, D.C., and New York City based on a survey of 157 individuals from lobbying groups and related organizations. Reveals that these leaders are mainly well-educated white males from big cities on the East Coast with parents who are liberal and Democratic. Reports that they vote Democratic and have liberal views: they look to the government for solutions, support affirmative action, are prochoice on abortions, have dovish foreign policy views, and believe society is dominated by the business, military, government, and news media. Also, they have high regard for Ralph Nader, Senator Edward Kennedy, John K. Galbraith, Gloria Steinem, and Andrew Young. And despite a fairly affluent upbringing and good salaries, they are profoundly dissatisfied with the existing social and economic order. The results of this research were publicized by conservatives who suggested that public interest leaders do not represent the views of most Americans.

350 LOUIS HARRIS AND ASSOCIATES, INC. *A Survey of the Public, Community Leaders, and Consumer Activists on: Consumerism.* New York: Louis Harris and Associates, 1978. 73 pp.
See entry 121 for annotation.

351 MOLOTSKY, IRWIN. "Behind Nader, a Generation at the Ready." *New York Times*, 9 September 1985, 8.
Discusses younger advocates, those in their late twenties and thirties, working for consumer groups in Washington. Explores their backgrounds and motivations as well as their work.

BANZHAF, JOHN III

352 PAGE, JOSEPH A. "The Law Professor behind ASH, SOUP, PUMP, and CRASH." *New York Times Magazine*, 23 August 1970, sec. VI, p. 32+.
A profile of John Banzhaf III, a George Washington University law professor and public interest advocate. Discusses his background and his use of law students to prepare lawsuits against various abuses. Describes his efforts to establish the rights of nonsmokers. Reviews other public interest law practiced in Washington, D.C.

353 RINGLE, KEN. "Lone Ranger: Public Interest Lawyer John Banzhaf Takes on Other People's Fights." *Washington Post*, 15 May 1984, sec. B, p. 1+.
A short article on law professor John Banzhaf, a longtime consumer advocate. Summarizes his major cases. Quotes Banzhaf on why he has chosen a different career path from most other lawyers.

BROBECK, STEPHEN

Born 1944. Received B.A. from Wheaton (Ill.), Ph.D. from Pennsylvania. In the 1970s, cofounded and coordinated Cleveland Consumer Action while teaching at Case Western Reserve University. In the 1980s, directed the Consumer Federation of America. Has specialized in banking and insurance issues.

354 "Conversation with Steve Brobeck, Consumer Advocate." *Cleveland Magazine*, July 1975, 21+.
See entry 283 for annotation.

Brobeck

355 MIROW, DEENA. "Brobeck's Battle for Consumers Moves to Higher Level." *Plain Dealer*, 8 September 1982, sec. C, p. 4.
See entry 158 for annotation.

356 MYLER, KATHLEEN. "Activist Trades Signs for Briefcase." *Houston Chronicle*, 21 February 1988.
See entry 159 for annotation.

BROWN, ANN

357 SNIDER, KEN. "Business Profile: She Aims Arrows at Chains, FTC." *Washington Star*, 7 October 1975.
A profile of consumer advocate Ann Brown, chairman of the Consumer Affairs Committee of the Americans for Democratic Action. Discusses her criticism of the lack of competition among Washington-area food chains and of the Federal Trade Commission for refusing to intervene.

CHARREN, PEGGY

Born 1928. Received B.A. from Connecticut College. Founded Action for Children's Television, Inc., in 1968. Has served as its president since then. For two decades, has been the nation's foremost critic of the quality of the programming of children's television and of children's advertising.

358 "A Harsh Critic of Kids' TV." *Business Week*, 29 May 1978, 52.
See entry 126 for annotation.

359 WATERS, HARRY F. "The Ms. Fixit of Kidvid." *Newsweek* 111 (30 May 1988): 69.
An article about Peggy Charren, founder and head of Action for Children's Television. Describes an ACT twentieth anniversary dinner that was attended by television industry leaders and stars. Quotes Charren as blaming the Reagan administration for "everything rotten that's happened to children's television." Reports reforms that ACT has helped achieve. Discusses Charren's reasons for creating ACT and her hope that home video will eventually serve as a quality alternative.

CHOATE, ROBERT

360 LICHTENSTEIN, GRACE. "New Groups Are Serving as Watchdogs for Consumers." *New York Times*, 3 January 1972, 41+.
See entry 204 for annotation.

361 ROBBINS, MICHAEL. "The Advocate." *Washington Post Potomac Magazine*, 28 October 1973, 8+.
An article on Robert Choate, highly visible critic of the lack of nutritiousness and the marketing of breakfast cereals. Discusses his establishment background, his midcareer decision to become involved in liberal causes, his work on hunger problems, and the impacts of his criticism of cereals.

CLAYBROOK, JOAN

Born 1937. Received B.A. from Goucher, J.D. from Georgetown. Worked for the Social Security Administration, Congress, and U.S. Department of Transportation before joining Nader's Public Interest Research Group in 1970. In 1973, founded and directed Public Citizen's Congress Watch. From 1977 to 1981, served as administrator of the National Highway Traffic Safety Administration. Since 1982, has served as president of Public Citizen. Along with Ditlow, one of the nation's leading public interest advocates for improved auto safety.

362 DENTON, HERBERT H. "Claybrook Rejoins Nader as Head of Public Citizen." *Washington Post*, 17 February 1982, sec. A, p. 2.
See entry 229 for annotation.

363 KARR, ALBERT R. "Inside View: Former Consumerists Now in Agencies Find New Jobs Frustrating." *Wall Street Journal*, 15 December 1977, 1+.
See entry 323 for annotation.

364 "Nader to Claybrook: What Have You Done for Us Lately?" *Consumer Reports* 43 (April 1978): 92+.
See entry 343 for annotation.

365 "Reformers: Ralph's Wrath." *Newsweek* 90 (12 December 1977): 90+.
See entry 344 for annotation.

Denenberg

DENENBERG, HERBERT

366 GROTTA, DANIEL. "The Ralph Nader of Insurance." *Saturday Review* 55 (1 July 1972): 34-41.

A profile of Herbert Denenberg, Pennsylvania insurance commissioner, who in the 1970s was the nation's leading critic of the insurance industry. Describes his criticisms of the industry and the efforts of his department to reform it. Suggests that his impact reaches beyond Pennsylvania.

367 *"Populus Iamdudum Defutatus Est." Washington Post,* 9 September 1972, sec. B, p. 1+.

An interview with Herb Denenberg in which he discusses state insurance departments, price surveys, no-fault insurance, health insurance, auto insurer lack of support for safety improvements, and group auto coverage.

368 SHAPIRO, HOWARD S. *How to Keep Them Honest.* Emmaus, Pa.: Rodale Press, 1974. 231 pp.

A book based on Herbert Denenberg's advice about how to protect yourself against insurance rip-offs. The first chapter profiles the Pennsylvania insurance commissioner – his style, his work as commissioner, his family background and education, and his career.

369 "They Are All Afraid of Herb the Horrible." *Time* 100 (10 July 1972): 80+.

An article on Herbert Denenberg in which he discusses his criticisms of the industry and activities of his office such as publishing price surveys, publicly investigating complaints, and denying rate increases. Describes his qualifications as an insurance regulator, including his holding an insurance chair at the Wharton School.

DITLOW, CLARENCE

Born 1944. Received B.S. from Lehigh, LL.B. and M.A. from Harvard. From 1971 to 1976, worked for Public Interest Research Group. Since then, has directed the Center for Auto Safety. Considered, along with Claybrook, to be one of the nation's most effective consumer advocates on auto safety issues.

370 JENSEN, CHRISTOPHER. "This Man Gives the Auto Industry Nightmares." *Plain Dealer,* 24 July 1988, sec. D, p. 1+.
See entry 128 for annotation.

371 SCHORR, BURT, and CONTE, CHRISTOPHER. "Coming of Age: Public Interest Groups Achieve Higher Status and Some Permanence." *Wall Street Journal*, 27 August 1984, 1+.
See entry 130 for annotation.

EISENBERG, PABLO

Born 1932. Received A.B. from Princeton, B.Litt. from Oxford. Worked for the U.S. Information Agency, Operation Crossroads Africa, Office of Economic Opportunity, and National Urban Coalition. Consulted to, then became president of the Center for Community Change. Since 1975, has held this position. The nation's most effective fund-raiser for grass-roots consumer/community activism.

372 JOHNSTON, DAVID. "The Poor's Voice among Philanthropists." *Los Angeles Times*, 18 December 1986, 1+.
See entry 131 for annotation.

373 WILLIAMS, ROGER. "Centering on the Underdog." *Foundation News*, September-October 1987, 18-24.
See entry 132 for annotation.

FOREMAN, CAROL TUCKER

Born 1938. Received B.A. from Washington University (St. Louis). Worked for Congress, the Democratic Party, U.S. Department of Housing and Urban Development, Planned Parenthood, and the Citizens Committee on Population and American Future, which she directed, before serving as executive director of the Consumer Federation of America between 1973 and 1977. From 1977 to 1981, held the position of assistant secretary in the U.S. Department of Agriculture. Since then, has run a business consulting firm. Since the mid-1970s, has been a leading consumer advocate on food issues.

374 CERRA, FRANCES. "A Lobbyist for Consumers." *New York Times*, 31 November 1976, sec. III, p. 7.
See entry 147 for annotation.

375 LEONARD, MARY. "US 'Food Lady'–More Spice Than Sugar." *Detroit News*, 5 December 1977, sec. A, p. 1+.
See entry 155 for annotation.

Foreman

376 "Protecting the Consumer: Interview [with] Carol Foreman." *Challenge* 20 (September-October 1977): 24-28.

An interview with the past executive director of the Consumer Federation of America in which she discusses trends in consumer concerns, the rationale for regulation, the impact of the consumer movement, the need for greater consumer participation in policy-making, the relation between the consumer movement and consumers, the relation between farmer and consumer interests, and the relation between labor and consumer interests.

377 SCHORR, BURT. "Winning Friends: When Carol Foreman Talks Consumerism, Congressmen Listen." *Wall Street Journal,* 9 April 1975, 1+.

See entry 161 for annotation.

378 SOLOMON, GOODY C. "Carol Foreman: Status for the Consumer Movement." *Washington Star,* 12 March 1977, sec. C, p. 1+.

See entry 162 for annotation.

FURNESS, BETTY

Born 1916. Worked for radio and television in public affairs programming before being appointed White House consumer adviser in 1967. Later headed the New York State Consumer Protection Board and the New York City Department of Consumer Affairs. Since 1974, has worked as a reporter for WNBC-TV in New York. Regarded as the "dean" of TV consumer reporters.

379 "Can Betty Furness Help the Consumer?" *Consumer Reports* 32 (May 1967): 256-58.

See entry 246 for annotation.

380 "The Lady with a Sympathetic Ear: Betty Furness, the President's New Adviser on Consumer Affairs, Hears a Lot of Complaints – Especially about Repair and Service Problems." *Business Week,* 23 September 1967, 68+.

See entry 251 for annotation.

GREEN, MARK

Born 1945. Received B.A. from Cornell, J.D. from Harvard. Directed Nader's Corporate Accountability Research Group from 1970 to 1975 and Public

Citizen's Congress Watch from 1977 to 1980. In the 1980s, established and directed the Democracy Project. The consumer movement's most prolific author.

381 GROSS, SUSAN. "Mark Green: Nader's Most Prolific Raider." *Business and Society Review* 9 (Spring 1974): 38-39.

A profile of Mark Green, the Nader's Raider with the greatest impact. Discusses his background and his reasons for joining Nader. Describes the many books Green has written or is working on, and discusses the organization he and Nader set up, CARG, to monitor the government's antitrust enforcement.

HAAS, ELLEN

Received B.A. from Michigan. Founding president of the Maryland Citizens Consumer Council, staffer at a local consumer affairs office, and executive director of National Consumers League before joining the staff of the Community Nutrition Institute. In 1982, founded Public Voice for Food and Health Policy. Since then, has served as its executive director. One of the most influential consumer advocates with Congress.

382 SINCLAIR, WARD. "Ellen Haas: Bringing a New Approach to the Consumer Movement." *Washington Post*, 18 August 1986, sec. A, p. 15.
See entry 244 for annotation.

HARGE, SOLOMON

383 "Harge Is Director of Consumer Group." *Plain Dealer*, 19 June 1968.
See entry 292 for annotation.

384 KELLY, MICHAEL. "CPA Director Named to Consumer Group." *Plain Dealer*, 1 January 1977, sec. C, p. 7.

An article on the appointment of Solomon Harge, head of the Consumer Protection Association, as a member of the U.S. Department of Agriculture's consumer advisory committee. Describes the role he hopes to play on the committee and other boards and advisory committees on which he has served.

Jacobson

JACOBSON, MICHAEL

Received B.A. from Chicago, Ph.D. from MIT. Worked for the Salk Institute, then for Nader's Center for the Study of Responsive Law. In 1971, cofounded and, since then, has directed Center for Science in the Public Interest. Has built this organization into one of the largest and most influential consumer groups in the nation. Today, it is considered to be the nation's leading critic of the quality of our food supply.

385 MARTER, MARILYN. "A Hungry Watchdog." *Philadelphia Inquirer*, 11 May 1988, sec. F, p. 1+.
      See entry 134 for annotation.

386 VAN VYNCKT, VIRGINIA. "Consumer Advocate's Rage Turns to Resolve." *Chicago Sun-Times*, 1 March 1989.
      See entry 137 for annotation.

KARPATKIN, RHODA

Born 1930. Received B.A. from Brooklyn, LL.B. from Yale. From 1954 to 1974, practiced law. Since then, has served as executive director of Consumers Union. Since 1984, has served as president of the International Organization of Consumers Unions. Has supported strengthening of both Consumers Union's consumer information role and its advocacy activities. Next to Nader, probably the most influential U.S. consumerist in the international arena.

387 "Advocate's Advance." *Time* 103 (28 January 1974): 66.
      See entry 165 for annotation.

388 BAILEY, JEFF. "Altering the Product at *Consumer Reports*." *Wall Street Journal*, 5 June 1987, 29.
      See entry 166 for annotation.

389 GOLD, GERALD. "Consumers Union Picks Lawyer to Be Its First Woman Director." *New York Times*, 13 January 1974, 41.
      See entry 177 for annotation.

KARPINSKI, GENE

Born 1952. Received B.A. from Brown, LL.B. from Georgetown. Worked for Congress Watch, People for the American Way, and Colorado PIRG before setting up USPIRG in 1984. Has directed this organization since then.

390 COOPER, ANN. "On Active Duty for the Public." *National Journal* 17
(14 September 1985): 2062.
See entry 245 for annotation.

KNAUER, VIRGINIA

Born 1915. Received M.F.A. from Pennsylvania. Active for twenty years in Philadelphia politics and, between 1960 and 1969, was a city council member. Directed the Pennsylvania Consumer Protection Bureau in 1968-69 before being appointed White House consumer adviser. Held this position under three presidents – Nixon, Ford, and Reagan. In the late 1970s and today, has worked as a business consultant. For the past two decades, the most prominent Republican consumerist.

391 "The Consumer Revolution: Interview with Mrs. Virginia H. Knauer, Special Assistant to the President." *U.S. News and World Report* 63 (25 August 1969): 43-44.
An interview with Virginia Knauer, special assistant to the president for consumer affairs, which focuses on individual consumer problems and their solutions. Knauer emphasizes making appeals to manufacturers and improving consumer education before resorting to regulation.

392 "Consumers' Guardian." *New York Times*, 10 April 1969, 24.
An article on Virginia Knauer, President Nixon's new consumer adviser. Discusses her personal and professional life in the Philadelphia area, where she has been a consumerist and a leader in the Republican party.

393 "Has Reagan Forgotten the Consumer? Interview with Virginia Knauer, White House Adviser on Consumer Affairs." *U.S. News and World Report* 91 (5 October 1981): 58.
See entry 248 for annotation.

394 MORRIS, JOHN D. "Nixon's Consumer Affairs Aide Off to Fast Start." *New York Times*, 26 May 1969, 24.

Knauer

See entry 254 for annotation.

395 SCHOENFELD, ANDREA F. "Mrs. Knauer, Consumer Envoy–Both for and to the White House." *National Journal*, 10 January 1970, 90-98.
See entry 258 for annotation.

396 SHAFER, RONALD G. "Knauer Power: Nixon's Consumer Aide Wins Praise of Public, but Clout Is Uncertain." *Wall Street Journal*, 26 August 1969, 1+.
See entry 259 for annotation.

397 "Virginia Knauer Talks Business." *Pacific Business* 61 (July-August 1971): 33-36.
See entry 260 for annotation.

398 "Will Virginia Knauer Use Her Consumer Power?" *Consumer Reports* 34 (June 1969): 326-27.
See entry 261 for annotation.

399 WITCOVER, JULES. "The GOP Discovers the Consumer." *Progressive* 34 (March 1970): 32-35.
See entry 262 for annotation.

LIPSON, JUDY BRAIMAN-

400 WHISKEYMAN, DOLORES. "A Soldier in the War on Unsafe Products." *Rochester Business Journal*, 18-24 July 1988, 10.
A profile of product safety advocate Judy Braiman-Lipson, president of the Empire State Consumer Association. Describes Lipson's effective individual advocacy against potentially unsafe products ranging from hair spray to superabsorbent diapers.

MORRISON, ALAN

Born 1938. Received B.A. from Yale, LL.B. from Harvard. From 1968 to 1972, worked as assistant U.S. attorney. Since 1972, has directed the Public Citizen Litigation Group. Since 1986, has held the position of adjunct professor at New York University Law School. The most active and effective litigator in the consumer movement.

401 COHEN, RICHARD E. "A Constitutional Gadfly Who's Hard to Brush Off." *National Journal* 3 (May 1988): 611.
    See entry 236 for annotation.

402 SHAPIRO, MARGARET. "Big League Litigator Aims to Throw Out Budget Act." *Washington Post*, 15 January 1986.
    See entry 237 for annotation.

403 WITT, ELDER. "Attorney Morrison: Constitutional Gadfly." *Congressional Quarterly*, 19 April 1986, 875.
    See entry 238 for annotation.

MYERSON, BESS

404 PINKERTON, W. STEWART, Jr. "Curbing Fraud: New York City Fights Shady Merchandisers with New Legal Curbs." *Wall Street Journal*, 9 January 1970, 1+.
    A feature article on the New York City's Department of Consumer Affairs, headed by Bess Myerson Grant, that Ralph Nader claims could be a model for other cities to follow. Suggests Grant has taken far more initiative than many who initially criticized her appointment.

405 SINISI, J. S. "Face of an Angel." *Supermarket News*, 13 March 1972, 3-5.
    Discusses Bess Myerson's performance for three years as New York City's commissioner of consumer affairs. Suggests a number of specific accomplishments. Focuses on regulation of food markets, especially inspection for short-weighting violations. Quotes Myerson and the inspectors.

406 WINGO, HAL. "A Consumer Champion." *Life*, 16 July 1971, 23+.
    An uncritical article on Bess Myerson, New York's new commissioner of consumer affairs. Suggests she has "transformed" the consumer office into "one of the country's most effective champions of the consumer." Includes some information on her background and personal life.

NADER, RALPH

Born 1934. Received A.B. from Princeton, LL.B. from Harvard. Practiced law, taught history and government, worked as a reporter, and worked for Congress

Nader

before emerging as an independent consumer advocate in the mid-1960s. In the 1970s, set up or inspired dozens of public interest organizations. Probably, along with John L. Lewis and Martin Luther King, one of the nation's three most influential social reformers of this century.

407 ACTON, JAY, and Le MOND, ALAN. *Ralph Nader: A Man and a Movement*. Anderson, Ind.: Warner Publications, 1972. 239 pp.

A sympathetic, largely derivative book on Ralph Nader and the organizations he established. Covers the same ground as most Nader biographies – family background, education, early work, *Unsafe at Any Speed* and its aftermath, the Nader organizations and advocates, and their efforts to reform government and business. Apparently they interviewed Nader only once and spoke to few of his colleagues. Relied heavily on other sources such as McCarry's *Citizen Nader*.

408 ALLEN, HENRY. "Nader's New Dream." *Washington Post*, 28 September 1981, sec. B, p. 1+.

See entry 227 for annotation.

409 ANDERSON, PATRICK. "Ralph Nader, Crusader, or, the Rise of a Self-Appointed Lobbyist." *New York Times Magazine*, 29 October 1967, sec. VI, p. 25+.

An article on Ralph Nader's potent advocacy in Washington on issues involving the abuse of corporate power. Discusses his goals, motivation, congressional lobbying, views of his critics, background, and hope of setting up a public interest law firm. Suggests he not only has helped pass legislation but also has inspired many congressional staffers.

410 ARMSTRONG, RICHARD. "The Passion That Rules Nader." *Fortune* 83 (May 1971): 44+.

A lengthy article on Ralph Nader that suggests his real goal is not consumer protection but "smashing . . . corporate power." Credits Nader with creating consumerism, being instrumental in passing six major laws, reforming federal agencies, and saving lives. Reports his highly critical views of large corporations, their lawyers, and their advertising agencies. Suggests that Nader's power is still growing, in large part because of his access to the press. Describes the organizations he has created and the type of person who works for them. Comments on Nader's views on capitalism and how to improve it. Discusses his reports on federal regulatory agencies and their impacts. Speculates about his future.

411 AULETTA, KEN. "Ralph Nader, Public Eye." *Esquire*, December 1983, 480-87.

A sympathetic portrait of Ralph Nader that endows him with religious qualities. Discusses his personal views, life-style, and impact on society including legislation, regulatory reform, and network of organizations. Reports criticisms, mainly from conservatives. Concludes that, despite recent consumer defeats in Washington, Nader "is in no danger of disappearing."

412 BENDER, MARILYN. "Capitalism Lives–Even in Naderland." *New York Times*, 7 January 1973, 49+.

See entry 194 for annotation.

413 BROWN, MERRILL, and HAMILTON, MARTHA M. "Ralph Nader Resigns from Consumer Post." *Washington Post*, 28 October 1980, sec. E, p. 1+.

See entry 228 for annotation.

414 BUCKHORN, ROBERT F. *Nader: The People's Lawyer.* Englewood Cliffs, N.J.: Prentice-Hall, 1972. 310 pp.

An informative, sympathetic biography of Ralph Nader written by a reporter. Based on interviews with Nader, as well as over 200 current and past associates, and on Nader's writings and congressional testimony. Chapters discuss General Motors' investigation of Nader, his youth and college years, his views of and relation to the press, the Center for the Study of Responsive Law, other Nader-affiliated organizations and projects, Nader's views of Washington lawyers, his fund-raising, public interest research groups (PIRGs), whistle-blowing, the views of GM's chairman on Nader, his agreement with tire makers, his views of government and industry consumer offices, his letters from individual citizens, his relation to Congress, and his overall impact. Concludes that Nader has become a "folk hero," but this was written during the height of his popularity. Although positive in its assessment of Nader and his contributions, includes criticisms. Although this book focuses mainly on events and too often relies on the judgments of others, it represents an invaluable source of information about the views and recollections of Nader and his associates.

415 BURLINGHAM, BO. "Popular Politics: The Arrival of Ralph Nader." *Working Papers for a New Society*, Summer 1974, 5-14.

A New Left evaluation of Ralph Nader. Notes that New Leftists felt little kinship with Nader in the 1960s but realized in the 1970s that they both regarded the collision of American corporate power and

Nader

governmental power as the most dangerous force in the world. Examines Nader-inspired public interest research groups (PIRGs) and consumer action groups (CAGs). Criticizes them and Nader for not emphasizing citizen organizing.

416 BURNHAM, DAVID. "Nader Today: His Main Interest Is in Getting Others Organized." *New York Times*, 13 June 1976, sec. IV, p. 20.
An article on Ralph Nader and the organizations he established that suggests they have great influence but do not always prevail. Indicates they have become one of the two or three "leading forces against nuclear power in the world."

417 BURROS, MARIAN. "Nader Talks, Claybrook Doesn't, about the Rift." *Washington Post*, 2 December 1977, sec. D, p. 6.
See entry 339 for annotation.

418 "Car Safety Crusader: Ralph Nader." *New York Times*, 23 March 1966, 32.
An article on Ralph Nader's background and interest in auto safety. Notes disadvantages he overcame as a student.

419 CHARLTON, LINDA. "Ralph Nader's Conglomerate Is Big Business." *New York Times*, 29 January 1978, sec. IV, p. 2.
See entry 197 for annotation.

420 CONROY, SARAH BOOTH. "Rallying the Raiders." *Washington Post*, 28 October 1989, sec. C, p. 1.
See entry 214 for annotation.

421 "Consumerism: Is Nader Fading?" *Newsweek* 87 (28 June 1976): 60.
An article on the current status and future of Ralph Nader. Reports criticisms of his single-mindedness, failure to involve citizens, and refusal to run for public office. But concludes that the "sun is [not] about to set on the Nader empire."

422 "Crusader Widens Range of His Ire." *Business Week*, 25 January 1969, 128-30.
A feature article on Ralph Nader before he established a network of organizations. Discusses his background, life-style, goals, and activities. Views him primarily as an investigative reporter.

423 DASCHA, JULIUS. "Stop! In the Public Interest." *New York Times Magazine*, 21 March 1971, 4+.

See entry 215 for annotation.

424 De TOLEDANO, RALPH. *Hit and Run*. New Rochelle, N.Y.: Arlington House, 1975. 160 pp.

An unrelentingly harsh critique of Ralph Nader based largely on secondary sources that it fails to identify. Examples of its extremism abound: On the second page of text, it asserts that Nader's theories are the same as Benito Mussolini's. On the third, it suggests he was a CIA agent. On the fourth, it quotes from an unidentified biography that Nader is "blind to all that is human." On the fifth, it calls him a "revolutionist." While Nader has his well-documented faults, these can be researched more usefully in primary and more reliable secondary materials.

425 DICKSON, PAUL. "What Makes Ralph Run? The Nader Story." *Progressive* 34 (January 1970): 28-32.

See entry 199 for annotation.

426 DREIFUS, CLAUDIA. "The World According to Nader." *Progressive* 48 (July 1984): 58-61.

An interview with Ralph Nader in which he comments on the sources of his concern for justice, his accomplishments, the Reagan administration, his goal of a consumer-controlled economy, and his lack of a personal life.

427 EASTERBROOK, GREGG. "Saint Ralph's New Crusade." *Best of Business Quarterly* 8 (Winter 1986): 9-11, 13-15.

An interview with Ralph Nader that focuses mainly on his views of the corporate CEOs interviewed for *The Big Boys*. Explains he wrote the book to understand how corporate leaders use, abuse, or do not use power. Includes his views of Roger Smith, David Roderick, Paul Oreffice, Felix Rohatyn, T. Boone Pickens, William McGowan, and William Norris, among others. Indicates opposition to industrial policy. Identifies emerging issues.

428 "A Fading Ralph Nader Rewrites His Strategy." *Business Week*, 9 April 1979, 72.

Discusses the apparent loss of influence of the consumer movement and Ralph Nader, as evidenced by the congressional refusal to create a consumer protection agency. Reports that Nader is seeking to build citizen groups in congressional districts to encourage legislators to be more responsive to citizen concerns. Indicates that he is still highly regarded by most of the public and has clout at the grass roots.

Nader

429 FISHER, MARC. "Ralph Nader's Paradise Lost." *Washington Post Magazine*, 23 July 1989, 13+.

A lengthy article on Ralph Nader that suggests he has not changed much in the past twenty years. Describes the town of Winsted, Connecticut, where he grew up and where a Nader organizer now works. Punctures several myths about his life-style and confirms others. Discusses a personal crisis in 1986. Reports his popularity with local press. Describes his recent victories passing Proposition 103 in California and defeating a proposed congressional pay raise. Suggests that his early life in Winsted helps explain what he is today.

430 FISK, MARY. "Nader Advocates Greater Social Activism." *Trial* 13 (September 1977): 6.

A report on a speech by Ralph Nader to the annual convention of the Association of Trial Lawyers. He recommends the establishment of a national sabbatical law firm, the creation of a nationwide bank of incidents of defective products, and increased access to information on defective products collected by federal agencies. He also criticizes the insurance industry's tort reform efforts.

431 GATES, DAVID. "Nader the Raider Marches On." *Newsweek* 103 (20 February 1984): 9+.

An article on Ralph Nader at fifty that credits him with helping pass dozens of laws that the Reagan administration is now watering down and failing to enforce. Reports that he is seeking to organize individual consumers at the grass roots.

432 GOREY, HAYS. *Nader and the Power of Everyman*. New York: Grosset & Dunlap, 1975. 320 pp.

A sympathetic, uncritical portrait of Ralph Nader by a *Time* reporter. Based largely on several hundred interviews with Nader, his parents, his associates, and those he has worked with and against, and on personal observations of Nader at work. Discusses his philosophy, personal values and life-style, economic ideas, views of politics, public interest research groups (PIRGs), involvement in selected issues, litigation, the Congress Project, and overall impact. Focuses much attention on Nader's relation to the times. Lacks systematic analysis of his impacts on the consumer movement, public policy, and public attitudes.

433 GRIEDER, WILLIAM. "A 'Raider' Rating of Nader: Ineffective." *Washington Post*, 6 December 1971, sec. A, p. 1+.

A lengthy, provocative article on Ralph Nader's impact and goals. Suggests that his solutions are "ineffective" because they have added to government bureaucracy and raised prices while accomplishing only part of their intended aims. Indicates that auto safety is the exception to this rule. Reports that Nader's response to this criticism is that regulation will be effective only when "the leverage of citizens action is applied." Points out similarities between Nader and the muckrakers of the Progressive period. Suggests, however, that Nader is "progressing from single-issue attacks ... toward a broader concentration of what's wrong." Discusses whether he will run for public office and the priority he assigns to involving citizens in the political process. Reports Nader's three criteria for a model society. The article neglects to examine Nader's considerable influence on "consumer consciousness" and on public policy at the state and local levels.

434 HARBRECHT, DOUGLAS A. "The Second Coming of Ralph Nader." *Business Week*, 6 March 1989, 28.
Discusses the revival of Ralph Nader's influence as evidenced by the defeat of the congressional pay raise and passage of an insurance reform initiative in California. Notes that he is more powerful at the state than the federal level. Suggests he has changed little since the early 1970s, though he now praises some corporations.

435 HENTOFF, NAT. "Ralph Nader vs. the First Amendment." *Washington Post*, 21 February 1982, sec. D, p. 7.
An article by a weekly columnist on Ralph Nader's lawsuit against a conservative critic, Ralph de Toledano, who claimed that Nader had "falsified and distorted evidence" in *Unsafe at Any Speed*. Indicates that de Toledano lost his life savings defending himself. Faults Nader for being able to make but not take criticism.

436 HINDS, MICHAEL deCOURCY. "Nader Expanding Consumer Efforts." *New York Times*, 27 September 1979, sec. I, p. 31.
A report on a conference organized by Ralph Nader that revealed his new emphasis on setting up citizen utility boards (CUBs) in states and on supporting citizen control of publicly owned resources such as broadcast airwaves, public lands, and pension funds. Suggests that success in these efforts will not be easy.

437 HINDS, MICHAEL deCOURCY. "A Subdued Nader Works to Organize Consumers." *New York Times*, 27 April 1982, 20.
Discusses Ralph Nader's advocacy two years after President Reagan took office. Notes that he has focused on building state and

Nader

local organizations, using checkoff mechanisms, to counter business opposition to consumer protections. Includes conservative and consumerist (Esther Peterson) criticism of Nader and his response.

438 HOFFER, WILLIAM. "Nader: Consumer Champion or Sorehead?" *Best of Business Quarterly* 8, no. 4 (Winter 1986): 12+.

A report on assessments of Ralph Nader by a variety of persons including an early biographer and a former Raider. Most agree that in the 1960s and 1970s he forced major changes in business, yet today has less influence.

439 IGNATIUS, DAVID. "Stages of Nader." *New York Times Magazine*, 19 January 1976, 8-9+.

See entry 210 for annotation.

440 "Interview with Ralph Nader: A Progress Report on Consumers Issues." *U.S. News and World Report* 79 (27 October 1975): 26-29.

An interview with Ralph Nader on a wide range of topics. He stresses the following themes: A federal consumer advocacy agency is needed to give consumers a voice in regulatory decision making. The main limitation of consumer groups is lack of funding. Big business has too much economic and political power and is insufficiently competitive. We are moving toward a form of corporate socialism in which the interests of big business and big government merge. Government must toughen antitrust policy and enforcement and should deregulate cartelized industries. Small business tends to be more responsive to consumers. There is a corporate crime wave in the country. Yet, in several areas there have been improvements for consumers.

441 "Is Nader Losing His Clout?" *U.S. News & World Report* 83 (19 December 1977): 18.

An article provoked by Ralph Nader's criticism of former colleague Joan Claybrook, head of the National Highway Traffic Safety Administration, and of three "friendly" members of Congress. Reports criticism of Nader as a "dogmatic ideologue" who is unable to compromise. Discusses Nader's efforts to win approval for a federal consumer protection agency.

442 JOSEPH, GERI. "Time for a Vacation, Ralph." *Washington Post*, 28 June 1976, sec. A, p. 19.

An op-ed essay by a Minneapolis newspaper editor that commends Ralph Nader for improving the lives of consumers but urges him to take a break because his relentless criticisms are beginning to wear people out and erode his support.

443 KINSLEY, MICHAEL [E.]. "Saint Ralph." *New Republic*, 9 December 1985, 4.

A tribute to Ralph Nader from a columnist who used to work for him. Suggests that "no living American is responsible for more concrete improvements" in our society than Nader. Credits him with reforms that even conservative business executives have grown to appreciate. Attributes his strength of purpose in part to the "classic zealot's worldview, paranoid and humorless." Faults him for overlooking the benefits that accompany risks and for relying too heavily on legal remedies.

444 LAZARUS, SIMON. "Ralph Nader, the Last New Dealer." *Washington Monthly*, January 1974, 32-37.

Principally a critique of Ralph Nader's proposal for "federal chartering" of corporations. Suggests that Nader is trying to create another New Deal and that he sees antitrust lawsuits as a way to reduce the economic and political power of corporations.

445 LEE, JOHN M. "Doubts Voiced in Britain As Nader Airs His Views." *New York Times*, 21 October 1971, 17.

An article on reaction in Britain to Ralph Nader's challenge to organize a consumer movement. Indicates Nader is seeking to establish an advocacy group. Notes the difficulties of doing so in a society with greater government secrecy and less acceptance of one-sided advocacy than the United States.

446 LELYVELD, JOSEPH. "Nader Undaunted by Setbacks to Consumer Drive." *New York Times*, 24 November 1975, 1+.

See entry 203 for annotation.

447 LOFTUS, JOSEPH A. "Nader Calls Union Leaders Lax in Protecting Safety of Members." *New York Times*, 3 July 1968, 15.

See entry 336 for annotation.

448 McCARRY, CHARLES. *Citizen Nader*. New York: Saturday Review Press, 1972. 335 pp.

An informative biography of Ralph Nader based largely on interviews with some 300 persons, including Nader. The first chapter describes Nader's emergence as a public figure in congressional hearings on auto safety. The second and third outline his life before

Nader

moving to Washington in 1964. The fourth discusses his critique of highway and auto safety prepared for the Labor Department. The fifth focuses on the experiences of William Haddon, the first head of the National Traffic Safety Agency, with Nader. The sixth discusses his relation to and use of the press. The seventh examines his life-style. The eighth treats his advocacy of federal legislation, especially the Wholesome Meat Act. The ninth discusses his relations to members of Congress and their staffers. The tenth and eleventh focus on the Raiders and the Center for the Study of Responsive Law. The twelfth examines his involvement in the United Mine Workers. The thirteenth treats his involvement in West Virginia protests against Union Carbide. The fourteenth reports on a speaking tour. The fifteenth discusses Nader's vision for America, which is called "revolutionary." This book ignores Nader's human qualities, documented in other sources, and fails to assess his impact on society. Still, the experiences and observations recounted represent the most valuable source of information on Nader.

449 McROBERT, ROSEMARY. "Nader's British Raiders." *New Statesman*, 29 October 1971, 581.

A short, opinionated article on Ralph Nader's attempt to stimulate consumer advocacy in Britain. Suggests that Nader's emphasis on structural reform is at odds with the priority British consumers give to problem resolution.

450 MARSHALL, ELIOT. "St. Nader and His Evangelists." *New Republic*, 23 October 1971, 13-14.

See entry 205 for annotation.

451 MAYER, CAROLINE E. "Nader of the Lost Bark." *Washington Post*, 13 September 1981, sec. F, p. 1+.

See entry 231 for annotation.

452 "Meet Ralph Nader." *Newsweek* 71 (22 January 1968): 65+.

A sympathetic cover story on Ralph Nader that describes him as the "mainspring of the consumer movement." Discusses his influence in Washington, his work, his background, and his future. Written before he set up a network of organizations.

453 MUELLER, MARTI. "Nader: From Auto Safety to a Permanent Crusade." *Science*, 21 November 1969, 979-83.

See entry 218 for annotation.

454 "Nader." *Nation* 213 (13 September 1971): 197-98.

A short article on the significance and philosophy of Ralph Nader. Identifies Nader's central goal as redistributing power from large corporations and institutions to the people. Explains that he is seeking to establish "a new form of citizen and community action." Calls him a radical reformer who is effective.

455 "Naderism Spread Its Wings." *Economist* 239 (29 May 1971): 49-51.
   Reports on the great influence of Ralph Nader and his efforts to "internationalize" the consumer movement. Notes that he addresses environmental and worker as well as consumer issues.

456 "Nader Quits CU." *New York Times*, 23 August 1975, 10.
   See entry 182 for annotation.

457 "Nader: Success or Excess?" *Time* 110 (14 November 1977): 76+.
   An article suggesting that Ralph Nader is "losing momentum" because he has spread himself too thin and has alienated people by being abrasive. Briefly describes five of his organizations. Notes the defeat of the consumer protection agency legislation and the lack of progress of other proconsumer bills.

458 "Nader the Raider." *Economist*, 22 August 1970, 40.
   A short article on Ralph Nader's early efforts to expand his advocacy. The subject is covered more thoroughly by other sources.

459 "Nader to Claybrook: What Have You Done for Us Lately?" *Consumer Reports* 43 (April 1978): 92+.
   See entry 343 for annotation.

460 NEWFIELD, JACK. "Nader's Raiders: The Lone Ranger Gets a Posse." *Life*, 3 October 1969, 56A+.
   See entry 220 for annotation.

461 O'BRIEN, TIM. "A New Director at Consumers Union." *Washington Post*, 14 January 1974, sec. B, p. 3.
   See entry 557 for annotation.

462 PERL, PETER. "Editors Claim Firing by Nader Based on Unionization Attempt." *Washington Post*, 28 June 1984, sec. B, p. 3.
   An article on the complaints of three editors of *Multinational Monitor*, who were fired by Ralph Nader for neglecting to clear with him a controversial article before publication. Suggests these disputes reflect in part the intensity of public interest work and the low salaries.

Nader

Notes that there was a recent move for unionization of Public Citizen employees.

463 "Ralph Nader: A Cause Too Far." *Economist*, 24 December 1977, 30-31.
   A critical article about Ralph Nader. Suggests his influence with legislators has waned. Faults him for creating a new organization to represent the interests of sports fans and for demanding the resignation of former associate Joan Claybrook, administrator of the National Highway Traffic Safety Administration.

464 "Ralph Nader Assesses Consumer Movement's Future." *Washington Post*, 5 August 1979, sec. F, p. 1.
   An interview with Ralph Nader in which he discusses the Carter administration, consumer organizing, regulation, and the next presidential election.

465 "Ralph Nader Becomes an Organization." *Business Week*, 28 November 1970, 86-88.
   See entry 207 for annotation.

466 "Ralph Nader on the Public Interest Movement: An Interview." *National Journal* 5 (9 June 1973): 842.
   Excerpts from a 90-minute interview with Ralph Nader in which he discusses the goals and accomplishments of public interest groups. Emphasizes the "modest dimension" of the public interest movement compared with the large number of corporate lobbyists and support groups.

467 "Ralph Nader Takes on Congress As Well As Big Business." *National Journal* 10 (11 March 1978): 388-90.
   An interview with Ralph Nader in which he discusses the defeat of the consumer protection agency bill, business influence in Congress, the need for campaign finance reform, the performance of consumerists in the federal government, and the strength of the consumer movement.

468 "Reformers: Ralph's Wrath." *Newsweek* 90 (12 December 1977): 90+.
   See entry 365 for annotation.

469 ROWE, JONATHAN. "Ralph Nader Reconsidered." *Washington Monthly* 17 (March 1985): 12-21.
   A perceptive reappraisal of Ralph Nader at a time when he had relatively little public visibility. Goes beyond a description of appearance and style to reveal Nader's values and philosophy, which stress citizens

banding together to work for a more democratic and humane society. Discusses his current focus on "empowerment" projects like Buyers Up and citizen utility boards (CUBs). Reports that in speeches Nader is still able to appeal to the idealism of listeners and motivate them to action. Correctly predicts that his star is "going to rise again on the national scene."

470 SAMUELSON, ROBERT J. "The Aging of Ralph Nader." *Newsweek* 106 (16 December 1985): 57.

An assessment of Ralph Nader written at a time when his "luster had faded." Explains the latter in terms of his successes and "the arrogant excesses and obvious inconsistencies" of his crusade. Yet, concludes that he is a reformer, not a radical, who "has improved America" by insisting on "the accountability of large institutions."

471 SANFORD, DAVID. *Me & Ralph*. Washington, D.C.: New Republic Books, 1976. 135 pp.

An attempt by a *New Republic* editor to demonstrate that Ralph Nader has human faults and motives. Accuses Nader of being furtive, insensitive to employees, manipulative, sexist, and thin-skinned. Based largely on rumors and reports from disaffected employees. Of limited use because it contains little information on Nader's life not found in earlier biographies and because it does not carefully examine Nader's role in and impact on society.

472 SHAFER, RONALD G. "Nader & Co.: Empire of the Consumer Crusader Blossoms." *Wall Street Journal,* 19 November 1970, 40.

See entry 208 for annotation.

473 SHANNON, WILLIAM K. "The Man Who Beat the System." *New York Times*, 23 August 1970, sec. IV, p. 12.

An editorial-page essay comparing Ralph Nader with radical activists that argues it is Nader who "could bring about a kind of revolution" through his "commitment to lawful, orderly methods" and "his skills as a lawyer and his mastery of facts."

474 SHENON, PHILIP. "Nader, after Eight Years, Is Back on the Inside." *New York Times*, 10 May 1989, sec. II, p. 6.

An article on the recent successes of Ralph Nader, including California insurance reform, defeat of a congressional pay raise, and the introduction of air bags. Suggests that he has mellowed little over the years.

Nader

475 SHERILL, ROBERT. "The Zany Sport of Liberal Fratricide." *Nation* 236 (15 January 1983): 44-46.
    See entry 345 for annotation.

476 STEWART, THOMAS A. "The Resurrection of Ralph Nader." *Fortune* 119 (22 May 1989): 106+.
    See entry 209 for annotation.

477 TALBOTT, BASIL. "Nader Again Rides into the Spotlight." *Chicago Sun-Times*, 19 February 1989, 75.
    Discusses the revival of Ralph Nader's influence and visibility on issues such as the proposed congressional pay raise and the California insurance reform initiative. Contains criticism by Nader of the *New York Times*, *Washington Post*, and *Wall Street Journal*.

478 "The U.S.'s Toughest Customer." *Time* 94 (12 December 1969): 89+.
    A cover story on the growing consumer movement. Devotes most attention to Ralph Nader and his work. Credits him with forcing the Department of Transportation to issue stricter safety standards, persuading Congress to pass five major laws, and increasing public awareness of consumer problems among other impacts. Quotes him as saying, "My job is to bring issues out in the open where they cannot be ignored." Discusses the reports of his Raiders that are critical of federal regulatory agencies. Notes criticism of Nader from both the Left and the Right. Explains the rise of consumerism in terms of higher expectations, greater distrust of authority, and problems in the marketplace such as deceptive promotion, hidden charges, sloppy service, and unsafe or impure products. Describes the efforts of other consumerists including Consumers Union and state and local protection agencies. Discusses the current priorities of Nader and other Washington-based advocates. Outlines and illustrates his advocacy methods. Includes a sidebar on Nader's background, life-style, and personality.

479 WHITESIDE, THOMAS. "A Countervailing Force." *New Yorker* 49 (8 October 1973): 50+; (15 October 1973): 46+.
    See entry 221 for annotation.

480 WHITESIDE, THOMAS. *The Investigation of Ralph Nader*. New York: Arbor House, 1977.
    An engaging account by a journalist of General Motors' investigation of Ralph Nader and its aftermath. Primarily a narrative description based on congressional hearing transcripts and interviews.

481 WILLIAMS, JUAN. "Return from the Nadir." *Washington Post Magazine*, 23 May 1982, 6+.

A lengthy article on Ralph Nader. Notes the 167 public interest research groups (PIRGs) and Washington organizations he has established. Reports on a speaking tour on Michigan college campuses. Discusses briefly his life-style including books he has read recently. Examines his relation to Congress. Describes a number of his critics. Suggests his harsh attacks have alienated many policymakers and opinion leaders. Reports Nader's emphasis on citizen involvement in the political process.

NELSON, HELEN

482 NELSON, HELEN EWING. "Consumer Representation at the State Level." In *Consumer Activists: They Made a Difference*, edited by Erma Angevine, 228-46. Mount Vernon, N.Y.: Consumers Union Foundation, 1982.

An account by a leading advocate of her work as California consumer counsel between 1959 and 1966. Discusses her role in passing laws and in promulgating regulations.

PERTSCHUK, MICHAEL

Born 1933. Received B.A. and LL.B. from Yale. After practicing law, worked as a congressional staffer. As chief counsel and staff director of the Senate Commerce Committee, helped initiate and guide to enactment numerous consumer bills. From 1977 to 1981, chaired the Federal Trade Commission; from 1981 to 1984, served as a commissioner. In 1984, cofounded the Advocacy Institute, and since then, served as codirector. Considered, along with Peterson, to be one of the most influential consumer advocates within the federal government in the past quarter-century.

483 BURNHAM, DAVID. "Caught in a Crossfire of Praise at F.T.C." *New York Times*, 20 March 1977, sec. III, p. 3.

An article on the Federal Trade Commission and the person, Michael Pertschuk, whom President Carter is likely to nominate as chairman. Outlines "possible developments" at the FTC under his leadership. Discusses the Nader Raider critique of the agency. Describes Pertschuk's background and his work as a staff member of the Senate Commerce Committee.

Pertschuk

484 COHEN, STANLEY E. "Pertschuk Rides into the Sunset–Maybe."
Advertising Age, 17 September 1984, 28+.
A tribute to Michael Pertschuk, who was appointed chairman of
the Federal Trade Commission in 1977 and had just finished his term as
a commissioner. Credits him with transforming Nader's message from
exposé to law. As chief counsel of the Senate Commerce Committee in
the early 1970s, Pertschuk "was the pivotal strategist forming coalitions
behind an awesome list of legislation." As FTC chairman, he insisted
that his agency crack down on false and deceptive advertising.
Summarizes Pertschuk's critique of the FTC in the Reagan
administration.

485 OLDENBERG, DON. "Advocates for Activism." *Washington Post*, 9
January 1990, sec. D, p. 5+.
A lengthy style-section article on Michael Pertschuk and David
Cohen, who head the Advocacy Institute. Explains how they assist
public interest groups in their advocacy. Pertschuk was formerly
chairman of the Federal Trade Commission.

486 "Pertschuk, Michael." In *Current Biography Yearbook, 1986*, edited by
Charles Moritz, 427-30. New York: H. W. Wilson Co., 1986.
An informative biographical sketch of Michael Pertschuk that
draws upon interviews with Pertschuk, Ralph Nader, and others as well
as on articles, book reviews, and other published works.

PETERSON, ESTHER

*Born 1906. Received B.A. from Brigham Young, M.A. from Columbia Teachers
College. Worked in the labor movement before being appointed assistant
secretary in the U.S. Department of Labor in 1961, a position held until 1969.
Between 1964 and 1967, also served as White House consumer adviser. Worked
as consumer adviser to Giant Food between 1970 and 1977, when was
appointed the president's consumer adviser. Since 1981, led U.S. efforts for
strong UN consumer protections. During the past twenty-five years, except for
Nader, the nation's most visible and inspirational consumer leader. Most of her
personal papers are held by the Schlesinger Library at Harvard University.*

487 "Can Betty Furness Help the Consumer?" *Consumer Reports* 32 (May
1967): 256-58.
See entry 246 for annotation.

488 DEMKOVICH, LINDA E. "Esther Peterson – The Consumer Advocate with the President's Ear." *National Journal* 10 (5 August 1978): 1242-44.
Profiles Esther Peterson, President Carter's special assistant for consumer affairs, and her staff. Identifies her priorities, the most important of which is ensuring consumer input in administration decision making. Discusses her influence in the White House. Includes a sidebar describing her background and her staffers.

489 DONOHUE, GERRY. "The Consumer's Best Friend." *Professional Agent*, January 1980, 25-27.
See entry 312 for annotation.

490 JANSSEN, RICHARD F. "Consumer Defender: New Presidential Aide Shuns War on Business As She Helps Shoppers, but Mrs. Peterson Criticizes Some Packaging Practices, Alerts Unwary Housewives." *Wall Street Journal*, 26 May 1964, 1+.
See entry 250 for annotation.

491 LEVY, CLAUDIA. "Counting on Esther Peterson." *Washington Post*, 12 May 1974, sec. L, p. 1+.
See entry 315 for annotation.

492 MOLOTSKY, IRWIN. "Every Man's Advocate." *New York Times*, 8 December 1986, sec. II, p. 40.
An article on longtime activist Esther Peterson on the occasion of her eightieth birthday. Discusses her many contributions to the public interest. Notes that she is still active in the public interest movement.

493 MORRIS, BETTY. "Peterson, Inside, Looks Out." *Supermarket News*, 21 September 1970, 1+.
See entry 317 for annotation.

494 "Mrs. Consumer." *Newsweek* 30 (2 November 1964): 78+.
See entry 255 for annotation.

495 NEGIN, ELLIOT. "Esther Peterson: The Grande Dame of Consumerism." *Public Citizen* 5 (Winter 1985): 17-21.
A profile of Esther Peterson. Reports on her life as an advocate for consumers, workers, and women. Discusses her current work with the International Organization of Consumers Unions (IOCU) in support of UN consumer protection guidelines.

Peterson

496 PETERSON, ESTHER. "Consumer Specialist." *Annals of New York Academy of Science* 208 (15 March 1973): 57-59.
An autobiographical sketch by Peterson.

497 RICHBURG, KEITH B. "Esther Peterson, Foreign Agent?" *Washington Post*, 1 November 1984, sec. A, p. 23.
Discusses the controversy over whether Esther Peterson, who was representing the Netherlands-based International Organization of Consumers Unions (IOCU), should be required to register as a foreign agent before meeting with President Reagan's consumer adviser, Virginia Knauer. Peterson wants to urge the administration to support the proposed UN guidelines on consumer protection, which the administration opposes.

498 SHAFER, RONALD G. "The House Critic: A Food Chain Recruits a Consumer Advocate to Shape Its Policies." *Wall Street Journal*, 13 January 1972, 1+.
See entry 318 for annotation.

PITTLE, R. DAVID

Born 1938. Received B.S. from Maryland, M.S. and Ph.D. from Wisconsin. Taught at Wisconsin and Carnegie-Mellon. In Pittsburgh, helped found and lead the Alliance for Consumer Protection. From 1973 to 1982, served as a commissioner on the Consumer Product Safety Commission. Since then, has held the position of technical director of Consumers Union. The consumer movement's leading expert on home product safety.

499 CIMONS, MARLENE. "Consumerist Crying in the Wilderness." *Los Angeles Times*, 29 August 1977, 1+.
A lengthy article on Consumer Product Safety Commission member R. David Pittle, who, in the early 1970s, helped organize and lead the Alliance for Consumer Protection in Pittsburgh. Discusses his critical role in a conservative commission and the possibility he will not be reappointed. Notes that several congressional and consumer leaders have urged the White House to make this reappointment. Explains the origins of his interest in the commission and President Nixon's appointment of him.

500 HENNESSY, TOM. "Forum Interview–David Pittle: The Pittsburgh Nader." *Pittsburgh Forum*, 29 June 1973, 6+.
See entry 275 for annotation.

RICE, FLORENCE

501 BRIGGINS, ANGELA. "Out There All by Herself." *City Sun*, 22-28 November 1989, 26.

A profile of Florence Rice, founder and president of the Harlem Consumer Education Council. Focuses on her consumer education activities and quotes her extensively about the need among low-income consumers for this education.

502 COX, CLINTON. "How to Fight Unfair Bills." *Daily News*, 14 December 1975.

A lengthy article on consumer advocate Florence Rice, who has headed the Harlem Consumer Education Council for the past twelve years. Describes her background as an orphan and high school dropout who now is New York City's leading advocate for low-income consumers. Discusses her advocacy in opposition to utility rate hikes.

503 MURDOCK, STEVE. "Fighting for Harlem: Florence Rice vs. the Utilities." *Nation* 215 (25 December 1972): 659-60.

A profile on Harlem consumer advocate Florence Rice. Discusses her background and her work complaining about rising phone and electricity rates and teaching low-income consumers how to comparison shop.

RICHARDSON, LEE

504 GAPAY, LES. "Energy Office Aide Quits, Criticizes Unit for Ignoring Public, Favoring Oil Firms." *Wall Street Journal*, 13 August 1974, 5.

Reports the resignation of Lee Richardson, director of the Federal Energy Administration's Office of Consumer Affairs, because of the department's anticonsumer policies and failure to listen to the consumer office. Outlines Richardson's criticism and the FEA response.

505 McCULLY, CARRIE. "Consumer Advocate Eyes Cable TV: He Makes Mountains of Molehills." *Columbia Flier*, 10 February 1983, 16.

An article on longtime consumer advocate and educator Lee Richardson, who helped found the Louisiana Consumers League and now heads the Maryland Citizens Consumer Council. Discusses his involvement in 1966 protests against rising food prices, resignation from the Federal Energy Office, his advisory role with a local Maryland protection agency, and his views on cable TV.

Richardson

506 O'BRIEN, TIM. "FEA Consumer Office Chief Quits, Cites Lack of Influence." *Washington Post*, 13 August 1974, sec. A, p. 1.
See entry 557 for annotation.

SANDBACH, WALKER

507 LEVY, ROBERT. "The Other Ralph Nader." *Dun's Review*, December 1971, 42-43.
See entry 178 for annotation.

SILBERGELD, MARK

Born 1940. Received B.A. from Indiana, LL.B. from Washington University (St. Louis). From 1965 to 1971, worked for the Federal Trade Commission. In 1972, began working for Consumers Union's Washington office. Since 1977, has served as its director. Has worked most extensively on advertising, product safety, consumer credit, and trade issues.

508 SOLOMON, BURT. "A Consumer Advocate Who Isn't a Shouter." *National Journal* 19 (18 April 1987): 956.
A profile of Mark Silbergeld, who has headed Consumers Union's Washington office since the mid-1970s. Emphasizes his thoughtfulness and the careful work of his office. Quotes Michael Pertschuk as calling Silbergeld "the Plato of the consumer movement."

TRUBEK, LOUISE

509 LAUTENSCHLAGER, SCOTT. "Louise Trubek." *Wisconsin State Journal*, 23 July 1989, sec. G, p. 2.
See entry 277 for annotation.

WARNE, COLSTON

Born 1900. Received B.A. and M.A. in economics from Cornell in 1921, Ph.D. from Chicago in 1925. Taught at Pittsburgh, Denver, and Amherst. Helped found Consumers Union in 1936 and served as its president until 1980. In the latter capacity, helped establish the International Organization of Consumers Unions, American Council on Consumer Interests, and state consumer associations. Served on numerous federal and state consumer advisory bodies.

Warne

Next to Nader, the most influential consumer leader in the movement's history. Warne's papers are held by Consumers Union's Center for the Study of the Consumer Movement. The 50 linear feet of materials include correspondence, writings, clippings, personal material, and scrapbooks. The center has prepared an excellent ninety-five-page index of the materials.

510 CIMONS, MARLENE. "A Slow Move to Activism." *Washington Post*, 2 January 1980, sec. D, p. 14.
See entry 168 for annotation.

511 "Colston Warne Retires as Consumers Union's President." *Consumer Reports* 45 (February 1980): 68-69.
An article on the career of Colston Warne, who just retired as president of Consumers Union.

512 GOLD, GERALD. "A Longtime Champion of the Consumer." *New York Times*, 30 June 1970, 43.
An article on Colston Warne, president of Consumers Union and a self-described "rebel, a disturber of convention." Describes a lifetime of activism.

513 GORDON, LELAND J. "Colston Estey Warne: Mr. Consumer." *Journal of Consumer Affairs* 4 (Winter 1970): 89-92.
A tribute to Colston Warne that describes his activity as an economist, innovator, public servant, and rebel. Credits Warne with essential contributions to Consumers Union, American Council on Consumer Interests, International Organization of Consumers Unions, and state consumer associations. Identifies his participation on federal and state consumer advisory committees. Discusses his commitment to civil liberties.

514 NEWELL, BARBARA WARNE. "Tribute to Colston E. Warne." *Journal of Consumer Affairs* 14 (Summer 1980): 1-8.
A Colston E. Warne lecture in which the daughter of Warne pays tribute to her father. Discusses Warne's family background, intellectual development, role at Consumers Union including the encouragement of new organizations such as the American Council on Consumer Interests, and role creating an international consumer movement.

515 PETERSON, ESTHER. "The Colston Warne Legacy." *Journal of Consumer Affairs* 23 (Winter 1989): 213-25.
A Colston E. Warne lecture on a broad range of topics, especially the growth of an international consumer movement to protect Third

Warne

World consumers. Based on decades of personal experience, it includes comments on Warne, the consumer movement's historical accomplishments, and misplaced national priorities. Urges consumer educators to become activists.

516 "Protecting the Consumer: Colston E. Warne, President, Consumers Union." *Challenge* 9 (November 1960): 22-27.
A lengthy interview with Colston Warne, president of Consumers Union and the leading consumerist of his time. Includes comments on a proposed consumer protection agency, the consumer movement, the need for product standards, consumer education, consumer credit, and the work of Consumers Union.

WEINER, MAX

517 COLIMORE, EDWARD. "Weiner's Influence Is Yet to Be Stilled." *Philadelphia Inquirer*, 23 February 1987, 6+.
See entry 288 for annotation.

518 HAAS, AL. "Consumed with Consumerism." *Philadelphia Inquirer*, 2 January 1986, sec. E, p. 1+.
See entry 289 for annotation.

519 ROSENBERG, AMY. "Crusader Max Weiner Dies at 77." *Philadelphia Inquirer*, 23 October 1989, sec. A, p. 1+.
See entry 291 for annotation.

WILLETT, SANDRA

520 MORRIS, BAILEY. "Consumer 'Gadflies' Gaining Recognition." *Washington Star*, 20 January 1978, sec. B, p. 5+.
See entry 225 for annotation.

WOLFE, SIDNEY

Born 1937. Received B.S. and M.D. from Case Western Reserve University. Worked for the National Institutes of Health before creating and directing the Health Research Group, now part of Public Citizen. Recognized as the nation's foremost consumer advocate in the area of health.

521 ALLEN, HENRY. "The Wolfe among Watchdogs." *Washington Post*, 5 December 1978, sec. B, p. 1.
    See entry 239 for annotation.

522 SPERLING, DAN. "Sidney Wolfe." *USA Today*, 19 March 1986, sec. d, p. 4.
    See entry 241 for annotation.

523 "Valuable Gadfly." *Time* 112 (20 November 1978): 71.
    See entry 242 for annotation.

524 "Waste Not, Want Not." *Wall Street Journal*, 22 April 1988, 30R.
    See entry 243 for annotation.

9. Movement Perspectives

GENERAL

525 KARPATKIN, RHODA H. "Changing Issues, Changing Agendas: Winning for the Consumer in the Next 50 Years." In *Proceedings, 32nd Annual Conference of the American Council on Consumer Interests*, edited by Karen P. Schnittgrund, 1-7. Columbia, Mo.: American Council on Consumer Interests, 1986.

A Colston E. Warne lecture by the head of Consumers Union that identifies pressing issues needing attention such as hazardous technologies, corporate crime, and poverty. Suggests that these issues are international in scope and that they should be a high priority for consumerists over the next fifty years.

526 NADER, RALPH, ed. *The Consumer and Corporate Accountability*. New York: Harcourt Brace Jovanovich, 1973. 390 pp.

An anthology of thirty-one articles on corporate abuses and an "agenda for action." Most articles are grouped in sections that treat abuses related to health and safety, advertising, consumer waste and frustration, compulsory consumption, low-income consumers, and the failure of regulatory agencies to correct them. Profiles two examples of whistle-blowing. Includes several articles on proposed reforms such as federal chartering of corporations. Seven of the articles are by Nader.

527 SANFORD, DAVID. *Hot War on the Consumer*. New York: Pitman Publishing Corp., 1969. 280 pp.

A collection of sixty-four articles reprinted from the *New Republic*, mainly on corporate threats to consumer health, safety, and pocketbooks. Focuses particular attention on food safety, drug safety,

General

air travel, automotive safety, and insurance. Ironically, assembled by a *New Republic* staffer who later wrote critically of Ralph Nader (entry 471), yet includes nine articles by this advocate.

BUSINESS

528 CLAYBROOK, JOAN. White-Collar Crime." *Trial*, April 1986, 35-36.
    A reprint of a *Public Citizen* article that argues corporate crimes exact a huge toll on society, persist largely because of mild government penalties, and can be reduced only through safety standards and stiffer criminal penalties.

529 GREEN, MARK [J.], ed. *The Big Business Reader*. New York: Pilgrim Press, 1983. 514 pp.
    Fifty articles on the harmful impact of corporate power on citizens. The first four, which make up "The Corporation and the Consumer" section, examine the food, oil, pharmaceutical, and auto industries. Contributors include Ralph Nader and Mark Green.

530 GREEN, MARK [J.], and BERRY, JOHN S. "Corporate Crime." *Nation* 8 (June 1985): 697, 704-707; (15 June 1985): 731-34.
    A two-part essay on white collar crime and ways to curb it. Discusses the recent rash of corporate crime and its social price. Identifies seven "walls" law enforcement officials must scale to apprehend corporate criminals. Proposes a number of remedies that companies could voluntarily adopt or Congress could require.

531 KNAUER, VIRGINIA. "Presidential Adviser Urges More Self Regulation." *Association Management* 22 (October 1970): 71-75.
    A speech by Virginia Knauer to the American Society of Association Executives on current consumerism and business responses. Reports substantial disagreement between consumer and business leaders on the significance of consumerism. Explains that consumer advocacy is supported by dissatisfied consumers. Urges businesses to resolve and prevent complaints and to regulate themselves.

532 NADER, RALPH. "A Citizen's Guide to the American Economy." *New York Review of Books*, 2 September 1971, 14-18.
    A critique of "the institutionalized abuses of unchecked corporate power." Discovers four major types of abuses or "subeconomies" – involuntary, transfer, controlled market, and corporate socialism.

533 NADER, RALPH. "Corporate Power in America." *Nation*, 29 March 1980, 365-67.

An essay discussing the dominance of corporations in American society. Outlines the historical development of this influence. Notes the modest goals of today's reformers.

534 NADER, RALPH. "The Great American Gyp." In *Consumerism*, edited by David A. Aaker and George S. Day, 39-52. New York: Free Press, 1984.

Argues that consumers are being "manipulated, defrauded, and injured not just by marginal business ... but by ... U.S. blue-chip business firms." Attributes the failure to recognize this malpractice to the myth of the omniscient consumer, the myth of only a few bad apples in the business barrel, and the myth of the effectiveness of regulatory agencies. Briefly discusses the growing support for reform. Suggests ten types of consumer reforms needed – better product disclosures, greater use of recalls and refunds, a greater role for the courts, more product standards, adequate government research on product safety, more real competition, more socially responsible scientists, engineers, and professionals; stronger individual remedies, new government institutions with responsibility for protecting the consumer, and public interest firms of professionals. Reprinted from the *New York Review of Books*.

535 NADER, RALPH, and GREEN, MARK J., eds. *Corporate Power in America*. New York: Grossman, 1973. 319 pp.

An anthology of papers given at a conference on corporate accountability sponsored by Nader and Green. Organized in sections on the problems of corporate power, federal incorporation as a solution, and other restraints on corporate power including citizen action, law enforcement, regulation, and public enterprise. Most contributors are academics.

536 PETERSON, ESTHER. "Consumer Affairs: The Case for Joint Enterprise." *Michigan Business Review* 19 (May 1967): 9-14.

An article by a past special assistant to the president for consumer affairs which emphasizes the areas of agreement and the potential for cooperation between government and business. Describes changes in the marketplace that have increased consumer information needs. Urges government-business partnerships to meet these needs.

Competition and Economic Regulation

COMPETITION AND ECONOMIC REGULATION

537 CAIN, CLARISSA, and WEINER, MAX. "Consumers and the Oligopoly Problem: Agenda for a Reformed FTC." *Antitrust Law and Economics* 3 (Spring 1970): 9-20.

A position paper prepared by two leaders of the Consumer Education and Protective Association proposing specific reforms of the Federal Trade Commission. These include measures such as a study of oligopoly, annual reports to Congress on the competitive and regulated sectors of the economy, public disclosure of whether consumer pricing is competitive, and effective antitrust enforcement. Includes an introduction which discusses internal differences within the Consumer Federation of America.

538 FELLMETH, ROBERT C. *The Interstate Commerce Omission: Ralph Nader's Study Group Report on the Interstate Commerce Commission and Transportation.* New York: Grossman, 1970. 423 pp.

A critique by Nader Raiders of the Interstate Commerce Commission that accuses it of shielding inefficient shippers from the discipline of the marketplace. Specifically faults the commission for ignoring the public interest, for having an incestuous relationship with the industry, and for failing to regulate adequately industry concentration, rates, trucker safety, home mover abuses, preferences to large shippers, boxcar shortages, and the phasing out of passenger train service. Proposes abolition of both the ICC and anticompetitive regulations so as to allow the marketplace to discipline shippers.

539 GREEN, MARK J. "Appropriateness and Responsiveness: Can the Government Protect the Consumer?" *Journal of Economic Issues* 8 (June 1974): 309-28.

Addresses the questions of the appropriateness and effectiveness of government regulation. Criticizes the pro-free-market work of the Chicago School as "theories in search of a reality." Distinguishes between economic regulation, which mainly protects business, and health and safety regulation, which is intended to protect consumers. Discusses four areas where government regulation seems warranted – product hazards, nonmarket externalities, enabling regulation, and yardstick enterprise. Evaluates the performance of federal regulatory agencies. Recommends the encouragement of public interest law firms, the establishment of a consumer protection agency, the facilitation of class-action suits, and the disclosure of more information by government agencies.

Competition and Economic Regulation

540 GREEN, MARK [J.]. "The Case for Corporate Democracy." *Regulation* 4 (May-June 1980): 20-25.

Argues that the political agenda of the 1980s should focus on the size and abuses of big business. Suggests that federal legislation is needed because of the failure of state chartering, the extensiveness of corporate illegality, and the power of large corporations. Proposes the Corporate Democracy Act as a remedy for this failure, and discusses its implications for directors and shareholders, for corporate disclosures, for communities, for employee rights, and for enforcement. Maintains the passage of this act would reduce autocracy and increase democracy.

541 GREEN, MARK J., ed. *The Monopoly Makers: Ralph Nader's Study Group Report on Regulation and Competition*. New York: Grossman, 1973. 400 pp.

A collection of critiques of economic regulation in communications, shipping, railroads, airlines, electricity, pharmaceuticals, defense, patents, and foreign trade by Nader Raiders. Faults economic regulation for promoting monopoly and oligopoly. Distinguishes this regulation from regulation to promote competition, ensure product safety, reduce pollution, and subsidize needed products that industry refuses to produce.

542 GREEN, MARK J.; MOORE, BEVERLY C., Jr.; and WASSERSTEIN, BRUCE. *The Closed Enterprise System: Ralph Nader's Study Group Report on Antitrust Enforcement*. New York: Grossman, 1972. 488 pp.

A report of Ralph Nader's study group on antitrust enforcement. Focuses on the Department of Justice and the Federal Trade Commission. Reveals how corporations engage in price-fixing, collusion, and oligopolistic behavior, and how the Department of Justice and the FTC are unable or unwilling to correct these illegal practices. Recommends reforms for improving antitrust enforcement at the two agencies.

543 GREEN, MARK [J.], and NADER, RALPH. "Economic Regulation vs. Competition: Uncle Sam, the Monopoly Man." *Yale Law Journal* 82 (April 1973): 871-89.

An article that argues current economic regulation undermines competition and entrenches monopoly at the public's expense. Criticizes the design and process of this regulation for producing inefficient rate regulation, entry restrictions, mergers, and "technological lethargy." Estimates the total economic loss due to regulation just in transportation and communications at $16-24 billion annually. Proposes

Competition and Economic Regulation

deregulation as a solution with the caveat that several types of regulation must be retained. Suggests several intermediate reforms.

544 McELDOWNEY, KEN. "Living with Deregulation: The Role of Consumer Action Groups." In *Proceedings, 33rd Annual Conference of the American Council on Consumer Interests*, edited by Vickie L. Hampton, 49-54. Columbia, Mo.: American Council on Consumer Interests, 1987.

A speech by the executive director of Consumer Action of San Francisco that describes the priorities and activities of his organization. Identifies the key activity as price surveys of banking and telephone services that not only provide shoppers with useful information but also identify problems needing government attention.

545 NADER, RALPH; GREEN, MARK [J.]; and SELIGMAN, JOEL. *Taming the Giant Corporation.* New York: Norton, 1976. 312 pp.

An argument and proposal for federal chartering of large corporations. Chapters examine the harmful effects of these companies, the failure of state corporation law to remedy these problems, the federal chartering alternative, the content of such chartering (e.g., disclosure, guarantees of employee rights, deconcentration), the enforcement of chartering, and the inadequacy of the case against chartering.

CONGRESS

546 GREEN, MARK [J.]. *Who Runs Congress?* New York: Dell Publishing Co., 1982. 428 pp.

The fourth edition of a critical analysis of how Congress really works. Separate chapters discuss money (congressional needs, corporate contributions, needed reforms), lobbyists, organization and leaders, relation to the executive and judiciary branches, lawbreakers, rituals, activities, and elections. An epilogue explains how individual citizens can influence Congress. A perceptive introduction by Ralph Nader discusses how this institution has changed in the last decade.

547 GREEN, MARK [J.]. "Why the Consumer Bill Went Down." *Nation*, 25 February 1978, 198-201.

A leading advocate for a federal consumer protection agency offers an explanation for its defeat in Congress. Cites business lobbying, an "antigovernment mood," defections among moderates, lack of Democratic party cohesion, business campaign contributions, and poor timing as factors. Recommends that advocates devote more attention to local organizing and to public funding of elections.

CONSUMER EDUCATION

548 WILLETT, SANDRA L. "Consumer Education or Advocacy ... or Both?" *Social Policy* 8 (November-December 1977): 10-17.

An analysis of the relation between consumer advocacy and education that argues they are mutually supportive. Briefly describes the efforts of several individuals to link the two. Identifies three models of consumer education – as a change agent, as a means of enforcement, and as a channel to consumer representation. Makes recommendations for strengthening consumer education.

CONSUMER MOVEMENT

549 ANGEVINE, ERMA, ed. *Consumer Activists: They Made a Difference.* Mount Vernon, N.Y.: Consumers Union Foundation, 1982. 365 pp.

See entry 22 for annotation.

550 BOLLIER, DAVID. *Citizen Action and Other Big Ideas: A History of Ralph Nader and the Modern Consumer Movement.* Washington, D.C.: Center for Study of Responsive Law, 1989. 111 pp.

See entry 195 for annotation.

551 BROBECK, STEPHEN. "Academics and Advocates: The Role of Consumer Researchers in Public Policy-Making." *Journal of Consumer Affairs* 22 (Winter 1988): 187-200.

See entry 310 for annotation.

552 GREEN, MARK [J.]. "Where Is Consumerism Going?" In *Consumerism*, edited by Mary Gardiner Jones and David M. Gardner, 81-88. Lexington, Mass.: Lexington Books, 1976.

An assessment of the future of consumerism by a leading advocate. Suggests that this will be determined by five factors: First, the extent to which consumerism focuses on processes as well as product and on the structure of industry. Second, the extent to which it becomes political. Third, the extent to which it deals not only with the passage of laws but also with their enforcement. Fourth, the extent to which it focuses its efforts on government rather than business. Fifth, the extent

Consumer Movement

to which consumer groups continually monitor and pressure government agencies.

553 KASS, BENNY L. "Consumer Activist." In *Protecting the Consumer Interest: Private Initiative and Public Response*, edited by Robert N. Katz, 175-81. Cambridge: Ballinger Publishing Co., 1976.

An evaluation of consumerism by a Washington lawyer/activist. Attributes failures of the consumer movement partly to internal conflicts between consumers and within the movement. Discusses five responses to consumer problems–no action, complaint agencies, legislation, litigation, and arbitration. Proposes solutions to enhance the consumer protection role of the legal profession.

554 MAGNUSON, WARREN G. "Consumerism and the Emerging Goals of a New Society." In *Consumerism: Viewpoints from Business, Government, and the Public Interest*, edited by Ralph M. Gaedeke and Warren W. Etcheson, 3-7. San Francisco: Canfield Press, 1972.

A brief discussion by a leading U.S. senator of where consumerism and environmentalism are headed. Suggests that they are "institutionalizing their concerns and broadening their base of support." Predicts that in the future corporations will be required to undergo "social audits."

555 MORSE, RICHARD L. D. "The Consumer Movement: A Middle Class Movement." In *Proceedings of the 27th Annual Conference, American Council on Consumer Interests*, edited by Carol B. Meeks, 160-164. Columbia, Mo.: American Council on Consumer Interests, 1981.

A provocative paper by a longtime activist and academic that argues for consumerism's compatibility with conservatism. Begins by noting predictions that voter rejection of liberal government would lead to the consumer movement's demise. Discusses a 1934 pamphlet, "A Positive Program for Laissez-Faire," by a conservative University of Chicago professor that supported a strong Federal Trade Commission to ensure competition, federal chartering of corporations, establishment of consumer cooperatives, extension of public services, limiting waste in marketing, and product-testing organizations. Locates support for Consumers Union mainly in the middle class and predicts that consumerists responsive to the needs and ethical values of this class will survive. Predicts that in the future the consumer movement will focus greater attention on conservative issues–"consumer sovereignty and the fundamental right of consumers to direct the allocation of productive resources with their dollar votes." Correctly predicts declining consumer support for liberal solutions, but fails to anticipate growing emphasis of consumer organizations on the problems of the least affluent.

556 NADER, RALPH. "The Consumer Movement Looks Ahead." In *Beyond Reagan*, edited by Alan Gartner, Colin Greer, and Frank Riessman, 271-85. New York: Harper and Row, 1984.

An article by Nader which reveals his current thinking about the goals of the consumer movement. Criticizes regulatory and antitrust approaches to consumer protection. Advocates instead consumer initiation of direct private actions for negotiating the conditions of buying. These actions include banding together for group buying (e.g., American Association of Retired Persons), complaint handling (e.g., Consumers Against General Motors), and negotiating (e.g., citizen utility boards). Suggests that these groups can "broaden and metabolize the community quest for economic justice." In retrospect, Nader failed to anticipate legal and social impediments to such organizations.

557 O'BRIEN, DAVID, ed. *Conference Proceedings: Ninth Annual Mid-American Consumer Conference.* Oklahoma State University, 1985.

A record of speeches given at an annual conference attracting largely a regional audience but featuring nationally known speakers. The keynote speeches by Mary Gardiner Jones, Carol Tucker Foreman, and Stephen Brobeck provide different but interesting perspectives on the current consumer movement.

558 PEI, MARIO. *The Consumer's Manifesto.* New York: Crown Publishers, 1960. 111 pp.

A visionary book arguing that business and labor have conspired to exploit consumers and that a new consumers organization must be established to represent consumers in labor-management negotiations. In the first section, discusses the development and mechanisms of this "conspiracy." In the second section, outlines a proposal for a new consumer group called the United Consumers of America. Outlines the structure, membership, educational and informational role, participation in labor negotiations, and enforcement ability of such a new organization.

559 PERTSCHUK, MICHAEL. "The Case for Consumerism." *New York Times Magazine*, 29 May 1983, 16+.

An article assessing the current condition of the consumer movement and its future role, written by a leading regulator and advocate. Argues that, by attacking existing consumer protections, President Reagan has revived it. Suggests, however, that the movement

Consumer Movement

has been and continues to be weak at the grass roots. Characterizes the consumer movement as driven by individual citizens striving for "the betterment of community and society." Urges consumer advocates to be sensitive to the needs of workers threatened with unemployment. Identifies the future role of the movement as insisting that the consumer interest be represented in economic policy-making.

560 PERTSCHUK, MICHAEL. "The Politics of Consumer Regulation: The Public Restraint of Private Greed." In *Proceedings, 29th Annual Conference of the American Council on Consumer Interests*, edited by Karen P. Goebel, 158-62. Columbia, Mo.: American Council on Consumer Interests, 1983.

A speech to the American Council on Consumer Interests on the revival of consumerism two years after President Reagan took office. Reports opinion surveys implying that public support for consumer groups has grown. Suggests that the results of recent congressional elections also indicate rising support. Attributes this public reaction to the Reagan administration's "poisonous admixture of crude free market ideology and corporate sycophancy." Urges consumerists to make campaign finance reform a top priority. Expresses sympathy for victims of high unemployment rates, but argues that advocates must insist on "a place at the bargaining table with business and labor."

561 PERTSCHUK, MICHAEL. "The Role of Public Interest Groups in Setting the Public Agenda for the '90s." *Journal of Consumer Affairs* 21 (Winter 1987): 171-82.

A Colston E. Warne lecture by a leading advocate on influencing the public agenda in the 1990s. Draws lessons from case studies of five victories won by public interest groups. These lessons include seizing the middle ground and being willing to compromise. Discusses three types of lobbyists – "apocalyptic," "bureaucratic," and "movement." Urges public interest groups to make campaign finance reform the top priority.

562 PETERSON, ESTHER. "The Colston Warne Legacy." *Journal of Consumer Affairs* 23 (Winter 1989): 213-25.

See entry 515 for annotation.

563 SCHLINK, F. J. "The Free Market and the Consumer." *Consumers Research*, February 1988, 16-19.

An excerpt from an article written by a founder of Consumers Research that criticizes a Consumers Union film on the history of the consumer movement, "America at Risk: A History of Consumer

Protest." Faults the film for neglecting the contributions of business to our society and for presenting a negative view of corporations. Suggests that consumerists are biased against business and in favor of government regulation.

564 TURNER, JAMES S. "Consumerism: Now to the Year 2000." In *Proceedings, 28th Annual Conference of the American Council on Consumer Interests*, 286-88. Columbia, Mo.: American Council on Consumer Interests, 1982.

A speech to the American Council on Consumer Interests that argues that consumerists are increasingly seeking to reconcile the structural split between production and consumption resulting from industrialism. Suggests that, now that "managed economic mercantilism" and "supply-side economics" have been discredited, demand-side economics should be developed and tested. Challenges consumer economists to "develop the details of content essential to making this economic theory actually work."

565 "Whither Consumerism?" *At Home with Consumers*. Washington, D.C.: Direct Selling Education Foundation, December 1984. 13 pp.

An issue of the "quarterly consumer information journal," published by the Direct Selling Education Foundation, on the future of consumerism. The six contributions include articles on consumerism in Japan, Europe, and the United States. Contributors include Stewart Lee, James Turner, and Stephen Brobeck.

CONSUMER PROTECTION

566 CAMPBELL, PERSIA. "State Protection for Consumers." *American Association of University Women Journal* 55 (March 1962): 144-48.

An article addressed to American Association of University Women (AAUW) members on the role of state consumer protection and the need for more effective consumer education. Illustrates points from her experience in New York State. Urges AAUW members to study consumer protection in their state.

567 KNAUER, VIRGINIA. "Let the Buyer Not Despair." *AAUW Journal* 64 (April 1971): 7-8.

A short article on consumerism by Virginia Knauer addressed to university women. Discusses "tragedies of the marketplace." Urges participation in local consumer groups.

Consumer Protection

568 MAGNUSON, WARREN G., and CARPER, JEAN. *The Dark Side of the Marketplace*. Englewood Cliffs, N.J.: Prentice-Hall, 1968. 176 pp.

Coauthored by the chair of the Senate Commerce Committee, one of the first influential critiques of abuses of consumers in the marketplace in the post-World War II period. Focuses on deceptive and fraudulent selling practices, unfair contracts, unconscionable debt collection practices, and unsafe products including drugs and cigarettes. In chapter 2, discusses the Consumer Education and Protective Association and how it targeted the practice of selling homes to collect debts.

ENERGY AND ENVIRONMENT

569 CARSON, RACHEL. *The Silent Spring*. Boston: Houghton Mifflin, 1962. 368 pp.

A critique of extensive pesticide use that represents one of the first and most influential exposés published in the upsurge of consumerism during the 1960s and 1970s. Draws from dozens of scientific studies to argue that pesticides have so contaminated the total environment that they threaten both nature and man. Concludes that the indiscriminate use of these chemicals must be stopped until scientists have had the opportunity to assess their risks and the public has had the chance to decide which of these risks are acceptable.

570 FRITSCH, ALBERT J. *The Contraconsumers: A Citizen's Guide to Resource Conservation*. New York: Praeger Publishers, 1974. 182 pp.

A critique of excessive consumption and recommendations for resource conservation by staffers at the Center for Science in the Public Interest. Blames corporate commercialism in large part for this consumption. Advocates a "radical environmentalism" that includes actions ranging from talking with friends to "lying in front of bulldozers." The appendixes include a "life-style index" to help readers compare their energy use and standard of living with those of people living in other countries.

571 LOWER, ANN K. "Natural Gas Pricing: Market Outcome or Industrial Policy?" *Journal of Economic Issues* 17 (June 1983): 423-32.

An analysis by a Consumer Federation of America staffer of the pricing of natural gas that focuses on the proposed deregulation of "old gas" prices. Cites research demonstrating that large oil companies will reap a windfall from price decontrol. Defends the policies mandated by the Natural Gas Policy Act.

572 BROWN, JAMES L. "Problems in Defining and Representing the Consumer Interest." *Journal of Retail Banking* 8 (Fall 1986): 53-58.

A perceptive discussion of the pursuit by consumerists of two goals that are "in substantial tension" – improving the efficiency of retail banking markets and increasing quality of access to these markets. Explains how change driven by technology and deregulation has heightened this tension. This change has decreased the availability of "single-function products" such as passbook savings accounts, encouraged the expansion of high-cost substitutes such as check-cashing outlets, promoted the use of explicit pricing of services that favors the affluent, and increased consumer information needs. Argues that the financial services industry should work with consumer groups to seek a balance between efficiency and access.

573 FERNSTROM, MEREDITH. *Consumerism: Implications and Opportunities for Financial Services*. Report published by the American Express Company in 1984.

A report on the consumer movement's concerns, policies, and strategies on financial services issues. Also discusses the implications of this consumerism for financial services providers.

574 LEINSDORF, DAVID, and ETRA, DONALD. *Citibank*. New York: Grossman Publishers, 1973.

A report on First National City Bank (Citibank) by a Ralph Nader Study Group. Separate sections treat retail banking, wholesale banking, banking for government, trust fund management, and regulation. Chapters on retail banking charge Citibank with poor service, irresponsible extension of credit, and violation of laws.

575 "Life Insurance and the Consumer." *Best's Review: Life/Health Insurance Edition* 88 (July 1987): 27+.

A section on life insurance and the consumer. Includes articles by an academic, an insurance regulator, and a Consumer Federation of America researcher that criticize the industry for deception and failure to disclosure important information. Also includes two industry responses to the CFA critique.

576 MITCHELL, JEREMY, ed. *Money and the Consumer: An International Consumer View of the Revolution in Financial Services*. London: Money Management Council, 1988. 210 pp.

Financial Services

A collection of papers on financial services topics presented mainly by U.S. and European advocates at an international conference held in Britain. Subjects addressed include access, choice, borrowing, payment, and redress. U.S. advocates with contributions are Allen Fishbein, Ken McEldowney, Helen Nelson, James Brown, and Stephen Brobeck.

577 NADER, RALPH. "Nader and No-Fault." *New Republic*, 9 September 1972, 13-14.

A response by Ralph Nader to Leah Young's criticism of his stance on no-fault auto insurance legislation (entry 861). Points out that he opposes the legislation because it does not go nearly far enough in overhauling the insurance system. Notes that criticism of the legislation has resulted in its improvement. Indicates that the trial lawyers' contribution to which Young refers was refused by the Center for Auto Safety. Suggests that Young and David Sanford, a *New Republic* editor who has written critically of Nader, conspired to produce a hatchet job that fails to meet standards of good journalism.

FUNERALS

578 MITFORD, JESSICA. *The American Way of Death*. New York: Simon and Schuster, 1963. 333 pp.

A highly critical evaluation of the funeral industry that represents one of the first consumer exposés in the post-World War II period. Examines funeral transactions, costs, service, allied industries, interment, and cremation. Compares American and English funerals. Explains how funeral directors are trying to establish themselves as a profession and how they resent clerical "interference" and a critical press. Briefly discusses efforts to reform the industry.

HEALTH AND SAFETY REGULATION

579 BOLLIER, DAVID, and CLAYBROOK, JOAN. *Freedom from Harm: The Civilizing Influence of Health, Safety, and Environmental Regulation*. Washington, D.C.: Public Citizen and Democracy Project, 1986. 302 pp.

A well-documented defense of health, safety, and environmental regulation by a journalist and an advocate. Discusses the historic purposes of regulation and the corporate attack on it. In separate chapters, investigates regulation of food, drugs, and cosmetics; meat and poultry; automobiles; the environment; workplaces; and household products. Examines the obstacles that regulators must overcome, particularly efforts by corporations to deny information on hazards and accurate cost estimates of regulations.

580 CLAYBROOK, JOAN. "Crying Wolf." *Regulation* 2 (November-December 1978): 14-16.

Argues that there is a growing corporate assault on government regulation, especially health and safety regulation. Illustrates this point by examining the auto industry's response to motor vehicle safety regulation. Maintains that the industry has overstated related costs and failed to acknowledge substantial economic benefits.

581 CLAYBROOK, JOAN, and THE STAFF OF PUBLIC CITIZEN. *Retreat from Safety: Reagan's Attack on America's Health.* New York: Pantheon, 1984. 270 pp.

A critique of the Reagan administration's attack on regulations and regulatory agencies protecting consumers and workers. Describes the administration's strategy of centralizing regulatory decisions in the White House and Office of Management and Budget, substituting cost-benefit analysis and voluntary guidelines for scientific research as the basis for decision making, and reducing public access to government information and the regulatory process. In separate chapters, examines infant formula, food and nutrition, drugs, product safety, worker health and safety, environmental protection, transportation safety, and energy.

582 GREEN, MARK [J.], and WAITZMAN, NORMAN. *Business War on the Law: An Analysis of the Benefits of Federal Health/Safety Enforcement.* Washington, D.C.: Corporate Accountability Research Group, 1981. 203 pp.

A critique of the conservative critique of government regulation. Develops a "rationale for regulation." Criticizes cost-benefit analysis. Addresses several presumed costs of regulation. Examines the flaws of alternatives to regulation. Estimates the benefits of regulation by five federal agencies. Includes an "ethical critique" of cost-benefit analysis by Steven Kelman.

583 GREEN, MARK [J.], and WAITZMAN, NORMAN. "Cost, Benefit, and Class." *Working Papers for a New Society* 7 (May-June 1980): 39-51.

A critique of cost-benefit analysis. Faults cost-benefit studies of federal regulation by Murray Weidenbaum and by Arthur Anderson, Inc., for ignoring benefits. Argues that cost-benefit analyses using the "discounted future earnings" or "willingness to pay" methods encounter unsolvable distributional, ethical, and measurement problems. Discusses

Health and Safety Regulation

several examples of industries that use cost-benefit analyses to try to escape socially beneficial regulations. Concludes that these analyses invariably overstate costs and understate benefits.

584 HUGHES, KATHLEEN. *Return to the Jungle*. Washington, D.C.: Center for the Study of Responsive Law, 1983. 63 pp.
A critical evaluation of the federal meat and poultry inspection program by a Ralph Nader staffer. Based largely on interviews with government inspectors and other Department of Agriculture officials. Argues that the Reagan administration is jeopardizing the integrity of these inspections by reducing their frequency, speeding up the work of the inspectors, relaxing enforcement standards and sanctions, and increasing the secrecy of the inspection reports.

585 NADER, RALPH. *Unsafe at Any Speed*. New York: Grossman, 1965. 365 pp.
A critique of unsafe cars and the industry producing them that represents the most important consumer exposé in the post-World War II period. In part because it provoked an investigation of Ralph Nader by General Motors, this book catapulted him into leadership of the consumer movement. Known primarily for its contention that the Corvair is dangerous, the report also examines other unsafe models, hazards in auto compartments, pollution, industry engineers, industry stylists, and the "traffic safety establishment" that has refused to address the most important safety problems.

586 PITTLE, R. DAVID. "The Restricted Regulator." *Trial*, May 1976, 17+.
An explanation and defense of the work of the Consumer Product Safety Commission in its first three years written by a commissioner.

587 TURNER, JAMES S. *The Chemical Feast*. New York: Grossman, 1970. 273 pp.
A critique of the Food and Drug Administration's regulation of the food industry as researched by Nader Raiders. Concludes that "in the face of the $125 billion food industry . . . the FDA is unable to exert any meaningful influence" on behalf of consumers. Explains this lack of influence in terms not only of the enormous size and power of the industry but also of an agency with insufficient resources and an ineffectual bureaucracy. Individual chapters treat specific issues such as cyclamates, hidden ingredients, and food-borne disease.

588 TURNER, JAMES S. "Corporate Responsibility and Product Safety." *San Diego Law Review* 8 (February 1971): 15-29.

An article by a consultant to Ralph Nader's Center for the Study of Responsive Law on what must be done to improve product safety. Argues that further improvements must deal with three "fundamental realities" – massive economic control exercised by large corporations, the subservience of science and technology to these corporations, and the resulting technological tragedy of unsafe products. Urges the creation of new mechanisms to generate unbiased, scientific information on product safety. Concludes that the proposed Consumer Product Safety Act would not accomplish this goal.

589 WELLFORD, HARRISON, ed. *Sowing the Wind: The Nader Summer Study Group Report on Food, Pesticides, and the Poor As Affected by the Department of Agriculture*. New York: Grossman, 1970. 384 pp.

A study by Nader Raiders of hazardous food-related technologies and the political and economic processes that shaped them. Examines meat and poultry inspection, chemicals in foods, pesticide use, and federal regulation. Finds that the influence of agri-business on regulatory agencies has jeopardized the food-related interests of consumers, workers, small farmers, and all those concerned about the environment.

INTERNATIONAL CONSUMERISM

590 PETERSON, ESTHER. "The Case against 'The Case against the UN Guidelines for Consumer Protection.'" *Journal of Consumer Policy* 10 (December 1987): 433-39.

A response to Weidenbaum's critique of the UN consumer protection guidelines (entry 892). Defends the role of government consumer protection policies and their compatibility with legitimate business practices. Emphasizes that the guidelines are just that – they cannot be imposed on individual nations. Suggests that their implementation will benefit legitimate businesses.

591 PETERSON, ESTHER. "Consumerism and International Markets." In *The Future of Consumerism*, edited by Paul N. Bloom and Ruth Belk Smith, 179-87. Lexington, Mass.: Lexington Books, 1986.

A critique of the Reagan administration's opposition to UN hazardous-product lists and international consumer guidelines. Argues that this opposition is shortsighted and irrational: the lists and guidelines would not increase the U.S. trade deficit and in fact could be used by technologically advanced U.S. companies to compete more successfully in international markets.

International Consumerism

592 PETERSON, ESTHER. "International Consumer Guidelines." In
*Proceedings of the 31st Annual Conference, American Council on
Consumer Interests*, edited by Karen P. Schnittgrund, 305-309.
Columbia, Mo.: American Council on Consumer Interests, 1985.

A paper on the proposed international consumer guidelines being
considered by the UN's General Assembly. Argues that these guidelines
will help consumers, especially those in the Third World, and that it is
appropriate for the UN to adopt them. Discusses the development and
character of the guidelines. Addresses objections to their adoption.
Briefly describes other initiatives intended to protect consumers
throughout the world.

593 PETERSON, ESTHER. "International Perspective: Consumer Issues in
Mainland China." In *Proceedings, 33rd Annual Conference of the
American Council on Consumer Interests*, edited by Vickie L. Hampton,
321-24. Columbia, Mo.: American Council on Consumer Interests, 1987.

A speech by a leading consumerist that describes the Chinese
Consumer Council in the People's Republic of China. Indicates that this
organization, established in 1984 by the government, attempts to
provide Chinese consumers with both protection and
education/information. It includes a staff of sixty-five persons in Beijing
and eighty-eight offices throughout the country. Suggests that since it is
a unique organization in the world, the CCC cannot look to other
organizations as a model. Also comments briefly on recent UN-related
developments with consumer implications.

LEGAL PROFESSION

594 GREEN, MARK J. *The Other Government: The Unseen Power of
Washington Lawyers*. New York: Grossman, 1975. 318 pp.

An analysis of the political influence of Washington lawyers that
focuses on Covington & Burling and its dominant lawyer, Lloyd Cutler.
Based primarily on interviews with 300 persons, including 90 past or
present lawyers with the firm. After an introductory chapter on
Washington law firms, examines the Covington culture, Cutler,
Covington's antitrust work, and its representation of pharmaceutical
firms, the food industry, the tobacco industry, auto manufacturers,
transportation companies, and the media. Discusses the pros, cons, and
insufficiency of *pro bono publico* work of the large firms. Examines the
ethical decisions Washington lawyers face and the pressures for ignoring
morality in these choices.

Legal Profession

595 NADER, RALPH. "Consumerism and Legal Services: The Merging of
Movements." *Law and Society Review* 11 (Special Issue 1976): 247-56.
A proposal for the merging of consumerism and legal services.
Criticizes the traditional legal emphasis on the solution of individual
problems and "access" to the legal system as insufficient. Maintains that
there must be a redistribution of power to ensure a balance between
consumers and large institutions. Advances a checkoff system as a
means of organizing consumers to achieve this balance of power.
Suggests that group-legal-service lawyers can assist these new
organizations by advocating reform of the procedural restraints on class
actions. Recommends that law schools reevaluate their curriculum,
especially their clinical education.

LOBBYING

596 CAPLAN, MARC. *A Citizen's Guide to Lobbying.* New York: Dembner
Books, 1983. 288 pp.
See entry 287 for annotation.

597 NADER, RALPH, and ROSS, DONALD. *Action for a Change: A
Student's Manual for Public Interest Organizing.* New York: Grossman,
1972. 184 pp.
A manual on organizing public interest research groups (PIRGs)
on college/university campuses and in high schools. In separate
chapters, discusses the role of students in an "initiatory democracy" and
the concept, funding, structure, history, method of organizing, and
issues of PIRGs. This revised edition contains a new chapter on
organizing PIRGs in high schools. A concluding chapter proposes
expanding the PIRG concept.

598 O'NEILL, BARBARA, and WHITNER, CATHARINE. "Shaping
Public Policy to Enhance Family Well-Being: Lobbying for a County
Consumer Affairs Office." *Journal of Home Economics*, Fall 1986, 17-
21.
See entry 738 for annotation.

599 OSHIRO, CARL, and SNYDER, HARRY. *Getting Action: How to
Petition State Government.* Mount Vernon, N.Y.: Consumers Union,
1980. 111 pp.
A useful handbook on effective methods of petitioning state
agencies. Part 1 describes the administrative petitioning process and
outlines how to petition a state agency. Part 2 is a case study of how the

Lobbying

petitioning process was used to effect reforms in the California real
estate industry. Part 3 explains what to do at each stage of this process.
Part 4 is a petitioner's manual, complete with a checklist of tasks,
worksheets, and sample petition form. Part 5 includes appendices on
how specific agencies regulate petitioning, additional sources on
petitioning, and a model petitioning law.

600 ROSS, DONALD. *A Public Citizen's Action Manual: Tools for Change.*
New York: Grossman, 1973. 237 pp.

A book by the key organizer of the public interest research groups
(PIRGs) on how citizens can take action to improve society. In separate
chapters, discusses several dozen projects to protect the consumer,
improve health, fight discrimination, reform taxes, and make
government more responsive to citizen concerns. Describes four types
of groups that could be organized – citizen action clubs, specialized
citizen action groups, PIRGs, and large citizen action groups.

601 SKINNER, MARY JUST. "Power Is the Issue." *Working Papers for a
New Society*, Summer 1976, 42-47.

Examines the use of utility rate reform as an issue for organizing
citizens. Describes successful efforts of public interest research groups
(PIRGs) and citizen action groups around the country to win lifeline
reforms. Points out the limitations of this reform as an organizing issue,
but concludes that it has "created and vitalized community action groups
throughout the country."

POVERTY

602 CAPLOVITZ, DAVID. *The Poor Pay More.* New York: Free Press of
Glencoe, 1963. 225 pp.

The first comprehensive study of low-income consumption.
Examines the finances, purchases, use of credit, relations to merchants,
and consumer problems of those residing in four low-income housing
projects in New York City, most of whom are black or Puerto Rican.
Introduces the concept of "compensatory consumption." The book
stimulated efforts to assist low-income consumers including the
Consumer Education and Protective Association and the groups it
inspired.

603 "Consumer Legislation and the Poor." *Yale Law Journal* 76 (March
1967): 745-92.

Examines consumer problems of the poor and the ability of
specific laws to solve them. Concludes that informational statutes will be

Poverty

of little help because the laws presuppose values, motivation, and knowledge that these consumers do not have. Discusses problems of the poor with prices, quality, sales methods, credit, and complaint resolution. Suggests that the most promising solution to these problems is consumer pressure on sellers through community action. Proposes a model statute that would protect low-income consumers.

PRODUCT QUALITY

604 PITTLE, R. DAVID. "Product Quality: Who Decides It?" In *Proceedings, 30th Annual Conference of the American Council on Consumer Interests*, edited by Karen P. Goebel, 80-84. Columbia, Mo.: American Council on Consumer Interests, 1984.

A speech by the technical director of Consumers Union to the American Council on Consumer Interests on product quality. Discusses the factors influencing product designs, including safety, new technologies, consumer demand, and *Consumer Reports*. Describes the problems Consumers Union faces in developing its product reports. Explains why these reports take the form they do. Emphasizes that Consumers Union must incorporate its own judgments in these reports because "consumers don't have the resources to judge for themselves."

10. Movement Advocacy

605 FRIEDMAN, MONROE. "Consumer Boycotts in the United States, 1970-1980: Contemporary Events in Historical Perspective." *Journal of Consumer Affairs* 19 (Summer 1985): 96-117.

A unique source of information and analysis about consumer boycotts that reports the results of a study of ninety boycotts in the United States between 1970 and 1980. Relies heavily on newspaper articles for data. Finds that boycotts have most often been national campaigns, sponsored by racial minorities or labor against producers or processors, over grievances about treatment of minorities or workers, respectively. Discovers that they increased in frequency throughout the decade. Learns that successful campaigns were more often national than local in scope, and were more often directed against the offending party than against a surrogate (e.g., retailer who sold products of a targeted producer). Concludes that in the 1970s boycotts affected many aspects of American life, that they represent an important part of the American political tradition, and that increasingly the precipitating grievances lie outside the workplace or marketplace (e.g., involve gay or abortion rights). A table listing the ninety boycotts and their most important characteristics would have been a useful addition.

606 HAPGOOD, DAVID, and HALL, RICHARD. *The Average Man Fights Back*. Garden City, N.Y.: Doubleday & Co., 1977. 280 pp.

An informative book on how consumers and citizens have been challenging the corporate and political establishment. In three early chapters, discusses challenges to professional and craft

General

"guilds" – lawyers, doctors, and others. In three subsequent chapters, examines those who are advocating reform of insurance, senior services (including American Association of Retired Persons), and property taxes. In other chapters, reports on the "Nader conglomerate" including public interest research groups (PIRGs); grass-roots advocacy organizations such as ACORN, Citizens League of Minneapolis and St. Paul, Northern Rockies Action Group, and Bay Area Citizens Action League; reform-minded public officials such as Herb Denenberg; and media-sponsored complaint and information services. Concludes that so far there have been only "promising beginnings," but in the future there will be significant improvements for ordinary citizens.

607 HERRMANN, ROBERT O., and WARLAND, REX H. "Does Consumerism Have a Future?" In *Proceedings of the 26th Annual Conference*, edited by Norleen M. Ackerman, 12-17. Columbia, Missouri: American Council on Consumer Interests, 1980.

A perceptive and generally well-researched paper on the recent decline of the consumer movement and its future. Begins by outlining a life cycle for social movements, proposed by Mauss, with five stages – incipiency, coalescence, institutionalization, fragmentation, and demise. Then cites evidence on co-option, leadership disagreement, loss of public support, and decline in media coverage that suggests the consumer movement is in the final two stages. Discusses the legacy of recent consumerism, including the strengthening of consumer consciousness, the shift from *caveat emptor* to *caveat venditor*, the strengthening of consumer protection institutions, and the creation of corporate consumer programs. Concludes that this structure of institutions, laws, norms, and attitudes will survive and become the foundation for future consumerist efforts. Fails to demonstrate that media coverage has declined and that the lack of consensus among consumer activists reflects more than issue specialization. Yet marshals convincing evidence that support for and influence of the consumer movement has waned.

608 MAYER, ROBERT N. "Consumerism in the 70's: The Emergence of New Issues." *Journal of Consumer Affairs* 15 (Winter 1981): 375-91.

Examines issues treated by the consumer movement in the 1970s to help assess its prospects in the 1980s. Operationally defines the consumer movement as the activities of major national organizations. Reports that in the 1970s this movement expanded the scope of its issues beyond traditional consumer concerns to include the welfare of workers, Third World consumers, and taxpayers, among others. Predicts that in the 1980s consumer groups will not continue to broaden their goals. Correctly identifies the broad definition of consumer issues by national groups. Yet, by failing to compare these issues with those advanced by consumer organizations in earlier periods, exaggerates the extent to which the wide range of issues in the 1970s represented a departure from past practice. For example, because its leaders were driven by commitments to social reform, in the 1930s Consumers Union saw itself as serving the interests of workers as well as consumers. Similarly, throughout its history, the National Consumers League has seen itself mainly as a labor support group. Yet, these two organizations were more narrowly focused on traditional consumer issues in the 1970s than in earlier periods.

609 NADEL, MARK V[ICTOR]. *The Politics of Consumer Protection*. Indianapolis: Bobbs-Merrill, 1971. 257 pp.

An important study of the making and significance of federal consumer protection policies, especially those adopted in the late 1960s. Includes a history of consumer protection policy, a description of the emergence of current interest in consumer issues, an analysis of the role of Congress and regulatory agencies in consumer protection, an examination of the role of the press and consumer advocates in the policy process, a discussion of the costs and benefits of consumer policies, and an exploration of problems of ensuring consumer representation in the policy process. Contains case studies of the Pure Food and Drug Act amendments, the truth in lending law, and the major automotive safety law. Chapter 5 contains a particularly informative analysis of the participation of National Consumers League, Consumer Federation of America, Consumers Union, the AFL-CIO, and Ralph Nader in congressional and regulatory consumer policy-making. It concludes that their main function was to broaden public awareness of consumer problems and thus build public support for government interventions. The study's principal and unavoidable limitation is that it was conducted before the proliferation of Washington-based consumer advocacy groups in the 1970s and only shortly after the laws on which it focuses were enacted. Nevertheless, it represents the best general analysis of how national consumer groups influence federal consumer policy-making. Based on a doctoral dissertation (entry 610).

610 NADEL, MARK VICTOR. "The Unorganized Interests: Consumers in the Policy Process." Ph.D. dissertation, John Hopkins University, 1971. 372 pp.

Analyzes the activities of several governmental and nongovernmental groups to understand better how certain consumer

General

problems are expressed as political demands and then become federal public policy. Looks at the President's Committee on Consumer Interests, the Federal Trade Commission, the Food and Drug Administration, and several departmental consumer advisers in the executive branch; at "consumer activists" in Congress; and at a national consumer group, the consumer press, and Ralph Nader. Finds that there is no permanent consumer coalition, only a small number of governmental and nongovernmental activists who work independently or in ad hoc coalitions. Discovers that Nader and the press are especially effective in their ability to broaden public support for consumer reforms. Concludes, however, that activists have mainly succeeded in winning health and safety legislation whose costs could be passed on to consumers. Legislative proposals intended to benefit the poor have not passed. Also, consumer legislation has not changed "existing power relationships" between major producers and consumers. For a more detailed summary, see *DAI* 31 (1970): 3614A.

611 PERTSCHUK, MICHAEL. *Revolt against Regulation*. Berkeley: University of California, 1982. 165 pp.
   A wise and witty analysis of the rise and decline of consumer advocacy for federal consumer regulation in the late 1960s and 1970s. Based on personal experiences and research, this book represents the revised version of five lectures given at the Graduate School of Business Administration at Berkeley by a former chairman of the Federal Trade Commission who earlier had worked on consumer issues as a Senate staffer. The first chapter explains the increasing interest of Congress in passing consumer protection laws in terms of "entrepreneurial politics" in a "uniquely benign political environment." The entrepreneurs were senators and representatives such as Warren Magnuson, congressional committee staffers, nonprofit advocates such as Ralph Nader, labor lobbyists, and sympathetic journalists. The analysis is illustrated by references to consideration of flammable fabrics, auto safety, warranty, and consumer product safety legislation. The second chapter analyzes the growing political influence of business in terms of its increasing solidarity, its mobilization of grass-roots pressure, rising popularity of free-enterprise economics, decline of the consumer entrepreneurs, and increasing public preoccupation with job security and disillusionment with the effectiveness of the federal government. Chapter 3 chronicles in detail rising business and congressional criticism of the Federal Trade Commission and the battle over proposed curbs on this agency. It includes, with illustrations, descriptions of the five most common business complaints. It describes the efforts of the FTC, and its consumer and labor allies, to defend the commission. It concludes that,

because of these efforts, the most severe restrictions proposed by business were moderated. Chapter 4 discusses "consumer strategies for the 1980s." It finds grounds for optimism about the revival of the consumer movement, but fails to anticipate President Reagan's enduring personal popularity and the lengthy period of economic growth after the 1982 recession. It identifies "inherent limits to entrepreneurial politics," including the unreliability of public outrage, the abstractness of many proposed reforms, ideological constraints on these reforms, and a Washington environment "calculated to dull and defuse outrage." It reflects on the growth of populist protest at the grass roots, which is the major hope of advocates such as Nader, but cautions that it is difficult to sustain. Chapter 5 reflects on what the author has learned about regulation–in brief, greater humility because of the imperfections of regulatory interventions. It frames seven questions that regulators should address before pushing these interventions. A brief epilogue reveals the author's shifting moods that influence the chapters. It finds "fragmentary evidence of a resurgent populism" and argues that this populism can succeed only if public confidence in the integrity and effectiveness of government is restored. This book is not, nor does it claim to be, a comprehensive history of the consumer movement during the late 1960s and 1970s. Yet, it represents a remarkably perceptive, well-informed, and, considering the position of the author, objective examination of the ebb and flow of consumer advocacy and regulation during this period. It is unlikely that the richness of its analysis, which reflects penetrating insights into personal experiences, will be equaled.

612 SAPOLSKY, HARVEY, ed. *Consuming Fears: The Politics of Product Risks*. New York: Basic Books, 1986. 241 pp.
      A book of seven papers and an introduction written by a professor and several graduate students at MIT on the growth and interaction of product fears. These chapters reflect the view that the maintenance needs of interested organizations and the interaction of these organizations strongly influence product risk controversies. Credits Ralph Nader with sparking the growth of public interest organizations that have initiated many of these controversies. Includes case studies on cigarettes, dairy and meat products, salt, artificial sweeteners, tampons, and urea-formaldehyde insulation. Discusses the role of Center for Science in the Public Interest, Public Citizen Litigation Group, and the Group Against Smokers Pollution (GASP) in specific controversies.

613 SMITH, DARLENE BRANNIGAN, and BLOOM, PAUL N. "Using Content Analysis to Understand the Consumer Movement." *Journal of Consumer Affairs* 23 (Winter 1989): 301-328.

General

A revealing analysis of changes in consumer activism between 1969 and 1982 using content analysis of issues of the *New York Times* and American Council on Consumer Interests newsletter. Discusses the literature on the causes of the rise and fall of this activism. Reports a decline in the consumer movement's news coverage and in overt support from business groups. Suggests that this change may reflect either an actual decline in the movement or a greater emphasis by the movement on "quieter activities." Proposes additional research on consumer group membership and finances. Introductory overview on changes in consumer activism ignores rising business opposition as an important reason for declining legislative success. Generalizations in the text are more far-reaching than those in the conclusion. The former include conclusions that "overt activism" and "the vitality of the consumer movement" have declined. Yet, coverage by the *New York Times* reflects mainly consumer movement visibility and, to a lesser extent, influence, rather than the extent or intensity of activism. For example, there was a great deal of "noisy activism" in 1981 in opposition to the Reagan administration, but it was not reported as thoroughly as advocacy a decade earlier. Nevertheless, the analysis of data is sound and its interpretation not far off the mark.

614 SNOW, ARTHUR, and WEISBROD, BURTON A. "Consumerism, Consumers, and Public Interest Law." In *Public Interest Law: An Economic and Institutional Analysis*, edited by Burton A. Weisbrod, 395-445. Berkeley: University of California Press, 1978.

An economic and institutional assessment of public interest law activities on consumer protection in the 1970s. Provides an overview of consumer protection activities including litigation, mainly by consumer groups. Discusses reasons why business and government fail to provide adequate consumer protection. These reasons relate to "allocative efficiency" and to "income distributional equity" in private markets, and to failures of government intervention in these markets. Analyzes six public interest law actions in terms of their success in addressing market failures. These actions concern airline passenger protections, Federal Trade Commission regulation, drug price disclosures, and information held by the Federal Reserve Board. Evaluates the effect of public interest law activities on the consumer interest. Concludes that these activities "have the potential to make contributions toward correcting failures in the provision of consumer protection."

615 STEIN, KAREN. "A Political History of the Proposal to Create a Federal Consumer Protection Agency." In *Proceedings of the 25th*

General

Annual Meeting, American Council on Consumer Interests, 126-31. Columbia, Mo.: American Council on Consumer Interests, 1979.

A paper discussing the ten-year history of congressional proposals to establish a federal consumer protection agency. Sections review debate and action by successive congresses, the ninetieth through the ninety-fifth. Provides a useful overview of this political history, but draws no significant conclusions about the issue, the players, or the process.

616 TOLCHIN, SUSAN J., and TOLCHIN, MARTIN. *Dismantling America: The Rush to Deregulate*. New York: Oxford University Press, 1983. 323 pp.

A useful analysis and critique of the reduction in federal consumer and environmental regulation begun by Congress during the Carter administration and accelerated by the Reagan administration. Suggests an explanation for this deregulation. Explains how the Reagan administration weakened regulatory agencies. Critically evaluates the use of cost-benefit analysis. Examines the congressional and business attack on the Federal Trade Commission during Michael Pertschuk's term as chair. Discusses federal regulation of nuclear power plants. Argues that the "rush to deregulate" is harming society. Contains limited information on the Consumer Product Safety Commission, Food and Drug Administration, and National Highway Traffic Safety Administration and on the efforts of consumer advocates to defend these agencies.

617 VOGEL, DAVID. *Fluctuating Fortunes: The Political Power of Business in America*. New York: Basic Books, 1989. 337 pp.

An analysis of the influence of business on public policy decisions. Develops the argument that this power rises and falls largely in response to changes in economic conditions and the structure of politics. Separate chapters treat the privileged position of business between 1960 and 1966, the rise of consumerism between 1966 and 1969, business on the defensive between 1969 and 1972, the public interest movement, the politics of economic stagnation between 1973 and 1976, how business turned the tide between 1977 and 1980, the political resurgence of business, and business and the Reagan administration between 1981 and 1988. Concludes that business influence varies with public perception of the long-term strength of the economy, the degree of cooperation within the business community, and the dynamics of the political system. Also concludes that public interest groups have replaced labor as the "central countervailing force" to business, that government has expanded controls on corporate behavior,

General

and that business has become more active politically. This work considers consumer groups to be an important part of the public interest movement threatening business, especially in the late 1960s. But its analysis of changes in consumerist influence in national policy-making is, for the most part, not original. The discussion of the rise of this influence is based largely on Pertschuk (entry 611) and its decline on articles in major newspapers and the *National Journal*. What is original in its interpretation is an emphasis on economic conditions, and public perceptions of these conditions, as a factor in the fluctuating power of consumer advocates.

618 VOGEL, DAVID. *Lobbying the Corporation: Citizen Challenges to Business Authority*. New York: Basic Books, 1978. 270 pp.

Analyzes selected citizen challenges to business in the 1960s and 1970s. Focuses on civil rights, antiwar, shareholder, corporate disclosure, and corporate Third World protests. The only consumer protests receiving attention are the unsuccessful efforts of community groups to elect a representative to the board of directors of Northern States Power Company (pp. 89-94) and the campaign against the marketing of infant formulas in the Third World (pp. 189-92).

619 VOGEL, DAVID, and NADEL, MARK [VICTOR]. "The Consumer Coalition: Dimensions of Political Conflict." In *Protecting the Consumer Interest: Private Initiative and Public Response*, edited by Robert N. Katz, 7-28. Cambridge, Mass.: Ballinger Publishing Co., 1976.

An analysis of the politics of consumer protection in the mid-1970s using treatment of four issues–consumer protection agency, tariffs, sugar price supports, no-fault auto insurance–as case studies. Finds that a united business community does not always stand in opposition to a united consumer community. On sugar and no-fault business was divided, while on tariffs and no-fault consumer groups could not agree. Concludes that consumer politics are becoming more complex.

1960-1968 (KENNEDY, JOHNSON ADMINISTRATIONS)

620 "Colorado Food Chain Cuts Prices As Buyers Prepare for Boycott." *Wall Street Journal,* 17 October 1966, 8.

Briefly reports on a threatened supermarket boycott in Colorado, led by an ad hoc housewives' group, and on the promise of one of the targeted chains to lower food prices.

621 "Consumers' New Day." *Economist* 219 (2 April 1966): 37-38.
Discusses consumer legislation being considered by Congress such as truth in lending, truth in packaging, and drug safety. Examines the new activism at the Food and Drug Administration.

622 CORDTZ, DAN. "The Home Front: Consumer Legislation to Be Pushed This Year." *Wall Street Journal*, 25 February 1966, 1+.
Feature article discusses plans by consumer advocates to promote consumer legislation in Congress, especially truth in lending and truth in packaging bills. Notes the importance of labor lobbyists to this effort. Questions how strongly President Johnson will support the legislation. Explains several bills and identifies their congressional proponents.

623 DETMAN, ART. "New Generation." *Magazine of Marketing*, 15 May 1966, 36-38, 41.
A review of seven recently published books by "muckrakers." Two, including Nader's *Unsafe at Any Speed*, focus on automobile safety; one on how car owners are swindled; one on false advertising; one on the use of dangerous food additives; one on the marketing of unsafe or ineffective drugs; one on corruption pervading American society; and one (which does not belong in this group) by a lobbyist for nationally advertised brands who attacks discount houses and private labels. The review suggests that these abuses could well lead to tougher consumer protection laws.

624 DRAPER, ANNE. "Battleline: Consumer Rights." *American Federationist* 73 (February 1966): 8-15.
A review of major consumer bills before Congress that are supported by the AFL-CIO. Treats truth in packaging, truth in lending, therapeutic devices, meat inspection, auto tire standards, and trading stamps legislation. For each, discusses the legislation itself, problems it is intended to resolve, and the bill's legislative status.

625 GAEDEKE, RALPH MORTIMER. "Consumerism in the 1960s: A Study of the Development of, Underlying Reasons for, and Business Reactions to Today's Consumer Protection Movement." Ph.D. dissertation, University of Washington, 1969. 355 pp.
Uses federal government documents and responses to a questionnaire to examine consumerism in the 1960s – its character, causes, and impact on business attitudes. The questionnaire was completed by three groups of individuals – the business-oriented, the consumer-oriented, and federal employees involved with consumer protection. Finds that the consumer movement is a "fluid and hard-to-

define phenomenon" with a scope broad enough to include not only consumer issues but also environmental ones. Discovers that this movement has received widespread governmental support as evidenced by numerous federal, state, and local consumer laws. Suggests that the roots of consumerism are complex and include sociological, psychological, economic, and political factors. Learns that business reaction has been mainly critical and defensive. Proposes "normative guidelines" on how business should react to consumerism. For a more detailed summary, see the *DAI* 30 (1969): 2198.

626 GILMARTIN, Sister JEANINE. "A Historical Analysis of the Growth of the National Consumer Movement in the United States from 1947 to 1967." Ph.D. dissertation, Georgetown University, 1970. 188 pp.
See entry 101 for annotation.

627 HERMAN, THOMAS. "Betty Furness on Consumer Firing Line." *Wall Street Journal*, 20 September 1967, 18.
See entry 249 for annotation.

628 HOPKINSON, TOM M. "New Battleground–Consumer Interest." *Harvard Business Review* 42 (September-October 1964): 97-104.
An early article, for a business audience, on the rise of consumerism and the need for corporations to address underlying consumer concerns. Briefly reports on the growing public support for reforms and the increasing number of reforms proposed in Congress and state legislatures. Discusses the negative response of business to this consumerism and how business is unable to prevent government regulation. Recommends "consumer-oriented management" and examines the skills, orientation, thinking, and structures needed to implement such management.

629 JANSSEN, RICHARD F. "President Urges Congress to Enact Pending Consumer Protection Bills." *Wall Street Journal*, 6 February 1964, 24.
A report on President Johnson's "consumer interests" message to Congress. The president urged passage of specific consumer legislation and better communication between the federal government and consumers.

630 LAMPMAN, ROBERT J. "JFK's Four Consumer Rights: A Retrospective View." In *The Frontier of Research in the Consumer Interest*, edited by E. Scott Maynes, 19-33. Columbia, Mo.: American Council on Consumer Interests, 1988.

A paper that examines the origins and impact of the four consumer rights proposed by President Kennedy in 1962. Written by a member of the Council of Economic Advisers and Consumer Advisory Council (CAC) who participated in the drafting of Kennedy's message that enunciated the rights. Briefly discusses the CAC and subsequent consumer legislation passed by Congress.

631 MARGOLIUS, SIDNEY. "Consumer Rights: The Battle Continues." *AFL-CIO American Federationist* 74 (April 1967): 1-4.

Summarizes recent advances in consumer organization and protection including the establishment of many consumer groups, new consumer initiatives by the Federal Trade Commission and Food and Drug Administration, and the creation of state and local protection agencies. Suggests that the greatest need at this point is for federal and state consumer protection legislation. Especially important are a federal truth in lending law and state laws prohibiting unfair debt collection practices. Includes a sidebar with labor's consumer protection agenda.

632 MARGOLIUS, SIDNEY. "The Year of the Outraged Consumers." *AFL-CIO American Federationist* 67 (September 1960): 16-20.

Reviews the status of consumerism. Suggests that public support is still strong but that consumer groups have limited resources, limited knowledge of many issues, and growing financial dependence on government and business. Summarizes the post-World War II growth of consumer protections. Points to credit protections as the most important recent advance. Identifies housing costs, food costs, high finance charges, inadequate health insurance, shoddy merchandise, and auto insurance costs as issues that need to be addressed.

633 "One and One-Half Cheers for Congress." *Consumer Reports* 33 (February 1968): 80-82.

Discusses the Wholesome Meat Act and Flammable Fabrics Act Congress just passed. Outlines the causes, provisions, and limitations of each.

634 "One Man Anti-Oil Lobby." *Time* 103 (25 March 1974): 29+.

An article on consumerist Lee White, head of the Consumer Federation of America's Energy Policy Task Force. Describes his protests against rising oil prices and advocacy for legislation to create a national oil company.

1960-1968

635 RICHARDSON, [STEWART] LEE, [Jr.]. "Mass Communications and the Consumer Movement." In *Dimensions of Communication*, edited by Lee Richardson, 459-61. New York: Appleton-Century-Crofts, 1969.

An analysis of newspaper coverage of 1966 supermarket boycotts that suggests the mass media, particularly newspapers, played a critical role. The coverage of local and national boycott events in one metropolitan daily suggests that local boycott leaders were influenced by reporting on national events. Hypothesizes that mass communications media can influence the length and nature of public conflicts.

636 "A Scepter for King Consumer." *Business Week*, 30 March 1963, 106+.

A report on rising consumer complaints and government efforts to respond to these grievances. Focuses on initiatives taken by California state officials, including the appointment of consumer activist Helen Nelson as consumer counsel.

637 "Sellers Beware!" *Economist*, 30 December 1967, 1291.

A report on the progress of consumer legislation before Congress. Discusses the passage of bills creating a National Commission on Product Safety, tightening standards for flammable fabrics, and requiring states to toughen their meat inspection. Notes that truth in lending legislation failed [though it passed the next year].

638 SNYDER, JAMES D. "A Look behind the Consumer Crusades." *Sales Management*, 15 June 1966, 38-41.

Discusses the growth of the consumer movement in the mid-1960s, as evidenced by the introduction of congressional legislation, more active federal regulatory agencies, the establishment of state and local protection agencies, the organization of consumer groups, and their networking at events such as Consumer Assembly. Notes that the movement is unusual in that it started in Washington and spread to the grass roots.

639 "The Thirtieth ... A Year to Remember." *Consumer Reports* 31 (November 1966): 571-73.

Summarizes recent consumer protection activity such as congressional consideration of several bills and passage of one, more vigorous antitrust enforcement by the Federal Trade Commission, and the passage of state consumer protection laws. Discusses the growing need for even more protections, especially the creation of an independent federal consumer protection agency.

640 WHITESIDE, THOMAS. *The Investigation of Ralph Nader.* New York: Arbor House, 1977.

     See entry 480 for annotation.

641 "Who Speaks for the Consumer Now?" *Changing Times* 21 (July 1967): 41-44.

     An article on the organization of grass-roots consumer groups. Traces the history of consumerism throughout the century. Reports on a survey of current organizations that found they average about 250 members, mainly middle-class and well-educated, and their highest priority is truth in lending legislation.

642 ZIMMERMAN, FRED L. "Public Defenders: President and Congress Expected to Push Bills to Protect Consumers." *Wall Street Journal,* 17 January 1968, 1+.

     A feature article that discusses political prospects for consumer legislation in Congress. Identifies measures President Johnson is likely to support. Credits Ralph Nader with stimulating much of the congressional interest in several bills. Predicts that warranties and auto insurance will receive much attention, in part because constituents are complaining about these issues to Congress.

1968-1976 (NIXON, FORD ADMINISTRATIONS)

643 BERRY, JEFFREY M. *Lobbying for the People.* Princeton: Princeton University Press, 1977. 331 pp.

     See entry 24 for annotation.

644 "Big Fight over How to Protect the Consumer." *U.S. News and World Report* 80 (26 January 1976): 40-41.

     Reports on the Ford administration's efforts to preempt the congressional campaign for sweeping new consumer protections. Mentions critical consumer response. Sidebar lists consumer protections proposed or established by Congress and federal regulatory agencies.

645 BRALOVE, MARY. "The Meat Revolt: Stores, Packers, Farms Begin to Feel Impact of Housewives' Outrage." *Wall Street Journal,* 29 March 1973, 1+.

     A feature article reporting on a consumer revolt against high meat prices. Discusses an upcoming meat boycott scheduled for April 1, but notes that sales of beef and pork have already declined.

1968-1976

646 BURNHAM, DAVID. "Nader Today: His Main Interest Is in Getting Others Organized." *New York Times*, 13 June 1976, sec. IV, p. 20.
    See entry 416 for annotation.

647 "Congress & A Consumer Protection Agency." *Congressional Digest*, February 1971, 33-64.
    A lengthy section on the proposed Consumer Protection Agency. Comprises the following articles: A brief introduction to the issue. A history of the growing consumer protection role assumed by the federal government, which includes a summary of all consumer protection laws. An outline of the consumer functions of federal agencies. The provisions of the Consumer Protection Organization Act of 1970 which had just passed the Senate. A summary of legislation considered by the ninety-first Congress. A debate between proponents of the agency such as Ralph Nader and Congressman Benjamin Rosenthal and opponents such as Joseph Califano and a U.S. Chamber of Commerce representative.

648 "Consumerism: The Mood Turns Mean." *Marketing Magazine*, 15 July 1969, 27-41.
    Discusses the rise of consumerism and implications for marketers. Contains an introduction emphasizing the reasons for its growth, and sections on consumerism at the grass roots and consumerism in Washington. The latter focuses mainly on Virginia Knauer, consumer adviser to the president, and on consumerist criticism of federal agencies. Includes sidebars on Governor Reagan's opposition to consumerism, on New York City consumer commissioner Bess Myerson, on Virginia Knauer, on twelve consumer leaders in Congress, and on major consumer legislation.

649 "Consumers Seek Basic Rate Help." *Washington Post*, 19 October 1974, sec. E, p. 10.
    A short article on a new campaign to persuade states to approve "lifeline" electricity rates for consumers. Indicates that public interest research groups (PIRGs) and citizen action groups are pushing the plan.

650 CREWDSON, PRUDENCE. "Consumer Groups Look to Carter for Relief: Ford's Record Deplored." *Congressional Quarterly Weekly Report* 34 (23 October 1976): 3044-45.
    An article comparing the positions of the two presidential candidates, Ford and Carter, on consumer issues. Discusses consumer leader views of the two candidates.

651 "Drive to Protect the Buyer: Consumer Gets the Spotlight." *U.S. News & World Report*, 18 January 1971, 20-21.

Provides an overview of the current surge in consumerism. Summarizes consumer legislation Congress will consider in the coming year. Describes how the Federal Trade Commission and the Justice Department will increase consumer protection activities. Indicates that many businesses are trying harder to please consumers. Notes that consumer advocates criticize the administration for failing to support strong legislation.

652 DUBROW, EVELYN. "Consumers: New Try in the Congress." *American Federationist* 80 (March 1973): 1-5.

Discusses the prospects for consumer legislation in Congress. Explains that such legislation is difficult to pass because consumers are a "disparate group," special interests are powerful, and the Nixon administration is not sympathetic. Looks at consumer bills dealing with a consumer protection agency, no-fault insurance, warranties, consumer credit, fish inspection, and drug regulation. Describes the character of each and the problems each addresses.

653 ELLIOT, KAREN J. "A Closer Look: Consumer Advocates Push Print Media to Screen Advertising." *Wall Street Journal*, 6 June 1974, 1.

A feature article reporting on the growing consumerist demand that newspapers and magazines take more responsibility for their ads. Notes the refusal of the Federal Trade Commission to require such an assumption of responsibility.

654 FRASER, EDIE. "Consumer Legislative Update: 1974 in Perspective, Outlook for 1975." *Business and Society Review*, Winter 1974-75, 58-63.

Discusses consumer legislation in the past and upcoming congressional sessions. Notes that in 1974 many bills were introduced but very few passed. Predicts that in 1975 several pieces of legislation will be approved, including a consumer protection agency bill. Describes other consumer legislative initiatives. Most of the legislation the author predicted would be approved in 1975 still had not become law in 1990.

655 GAPAY, LES. "Energy Office Aide Quits, Criticizes Unit for Ignoring Public, Favoring Oil Firms." *Wall Street Journal*, 13 August 1974, 5.

See entry 504 for annotation.

656 GARDNER, JUDY. "Consumer Report: Factions in Prolonged Controversy Gird for Showdown on Strong Consumer Agency." *National Journal* 5 (3 March 1973): 312-20.

1968-1976

Lengthy article on the Washington debate over the proposed creation of a new consumer protection agency. Discusses the positions of leading House and Senate supporters and opponents, the president, Federal Trade Commission, business groups, and consumer advocates on the legislation. Notes that, even among supporters of such an agency, there are major disagreements. Includes sidebars on the two major bills and on the history of the debate.

657 GARDNER, JUDY. "Debate Intensifies over Banning Cancer-Causing Food Additives." *National Journal* 4 (30 September 1972): 1534-43.

A lengthy article on a proposal to revise and weaken the Delaney clause banning cancer-causing food additives. Reports disagreement among scientists on the issue. Discusses the views of federal regulators, members of Congress, industry, and consumer groups. Predicts continuing debate but no congressional action this year. Includes sidebars on Congressman Delaney, the controversy over DES, and presidential candidate McGovern's changing position on the amendment.

658 GARDNER, JUDY. "Energy Crisis Stimulates Public Interest Group Response." *National Journal* 6 (2 February 1974): 159-62.

Examines the response of consumer groups and other public interest organizations to energy shortages. Indicates these groups are calling for more reliable data and for consumer participation in government deliberations. Outlines the concerns of the Consumer Federation of America, Ralph Nader, Common Cause, and the National Consumers Congress. Notes the hope of consumer leaders that this issue can advance legislation to establish a consumer protection agency. Includes a sidebar on a Federal Energy Administration common panel.

659 GARDNER, JUDY. "Proposals to Help Buyers Fight Back When Wronged Get Increased Consideration." *National Journal* 5 (7 July 1973): 981-87.

A lengthy article examining proposals advanced to help consumers resolve individual complaints against sellers. Focuses mainly on strengthening class-action suits, small-claims courts, and informal business-consumer dispute-resolution mechanisms. Suggests there is insufficient congressional backing for class-action legislation but growing support for reform of small-claims courts. Includes sidebars on the National Institute for Consumer Justice, an appeals-court decision on class action, and Congressman Eckhardt's commitment to class action.

660 GARDNER, JUDY. "Spread of Departmental Consumer Office Fails to Abate Pressure for Separate Agency." *National Journal Reports* 5 (3 November 1973): 1627-35.

A lengthy article on the failure of special consumer offices and advisers in several federal agencies adequately to represent the consumer interest in policy-making. Discusses the special assistant to the president for consumer affairs and consumer offices in the Cost of Living Council, Department of Agriculture, Department of Transportation, Food and Drug Administration, postal service, Civil Aeronautics Board, and National Highway Traffic Safety Administration. Analyzes problems and weaknesses of these offices including lack of staff and funds, limited or nonexistent policy role, inadequate knowledge of consumer problems, and cynicism by activists who are still pushing for the establishment of a consumer protection agency.

661 "Goal for 1970: A Federal Consumer Advocate." *Consumer Reports* 35 (January 1970): 15-17.

Discusses different proposals to increase consumer representation within the executive branch. Criticizes President Nixon's proposal and urges "serious consideration" of Congressman Rosenthal's legislation, which is backed by Ralph Nader.

662 GOLD, GERALD. "Things to Fight about besides Food Prices." *New York Times*, 25 August 1973, 30.

See entry 153 for annotation.

663 "Help for Consumers on the Way." *U.S. News and World Report* 71 (15 November 1971): 34.

Briefly describes new congressional and federal regulatory initiatives to protect consumers. Includes information on proposals in eleven areas.

664 "The Irate Consumer." *Newsweek* 75 (26 January 1970): 63.

A report on Consumer Assembly, the nation's largest annual consumer meeting, in which speakers such as Ralph Nader stressed the consumer movement's powerlessness and lack of progress. Notes, however, that the movement has produced "a good many demonstrable results."

665 JENSEN, MALCOLM W., and FOLKES, THOMAS M. "A New Era in Consumer Safety." *FDA Consumer*, 10 February 1974, 10-14.

Discusses the passage of the Consumer Product Safety Act and the Consumer Product Safety Commission that it created. Summarizes the structure, functions, and authority of the commission. Treats the implications for industry.

666 KNIGHT, MICHAEL. "Aid to Consumers Growing in Nation." *New York Times*, 9 August 1970, 1+.

A page-one article on the growing interest of state and local governments in establishing consumer protections. Discusses new consumer laws and agencies in several states.

667 KOTZ, NICK. "The Consumer Crusade." *Progressive* 33 (April 1969): 33-37.

An essay on the daunting challenges facing consumer advocates. Reports that many federal laws are neither adequately funded nor enforced. Describes threats to consumers' health and safety and to their pocketbooks. Argues that advocates must institutionalize themselves to ensure that consumers have an adequate voice in federal policy-making. Discusses ways this institutionalization could be accomplished.

668 MARGOLIUS, SIDNEY. "Consumer Affairs: Progress Is Slight." *American Federationist* 76 (September 1969): 1-6.

Suggests that consumerism is gaining momentum and achieving results. Examples of progress include new state laws, a federal truth in lending law, President Nixon's appointment of Virginia Knauer as his consumer assistant, and increasingly consumer-conscious courts. Identifies rising prices and interest rates, auto insurance rate hikes and cancellations, and an inadequate federal packaging law as problems to address. Notes that, as an alternative to regulation, business is advocating consumer education, yet defines this so as to exclude informative labeling.

669 MORRIS, JOHN D. "Nader Says Consumer Power Must Be Developed and Used." *New York Times*, 16 January 1970, 19.

An article on the Consumer Federation of America's Consumer Assembly at which Ralph Nader stressed the consumer movement's powerlessness and called for the establishment of public interest law firms. Bess Myerson and Virginia Knauer also spoke at the assembly.

670 "New Help for Shoppers, Tighter Rules for Business." *U.S. News and World Report* 70 (8 March 1971): 68-69.

A report on President Nixon's proposals for new federal consumer protections. These emphasize helping consumers resolve individual problems, but include support for the creation of a federal consumer office to ensure that consumers are represented in regulatory decision making.

671 OFFICE OF CONSUMER AFFAIRS, DEPARTMENT OF HEALTH, EDUCATION, AND WELFARE. *State Consumer Action, Summary 1974.* Washington, D.C.: U.S. Government Printing Office, 1975. 271 pp.

A lengthy survey of state consumer laws and regulations enacted, revised, or repealed in 1974. Organized by issue and, within each issue, by state. An annual report begun in 1971 by the U.S. Office of Consumer Affairs.

672 "The Pressure Is On for Safer Products." *Business Week*, 4 July 1970, 36-37.

Discusses the final report of the National Commission on Product Safety, which recommended an "omnibus" product safety act and a new federal agency to set and enforce standards. Reports that businesses are becoming more concerned about safety, largely because of increasing product liability awards. Includes a list of unsafe and possibly unsafe products identified by the commission. Also lists safety legislation considered by Congress.

673 "The Rising Tide of Consumerism: An Interview with Edie Fraser." *Association Management* 27 (October 1975): 39-43.

An interview with a business consultant on consumerism. She reports evidence of growing consumer influence in Washington and offers suggestions to professional and trade associations about ways to respond.

674 RUGABER, WALTER. "Politics Thwarts Consumer Forces." *New York Times*, 4 January 1976, sec. III, p. 30.

An article on the lack of progress of national consumer groups working in Washington. Explains this failure in terms of a business-oriented president, greater consumer awareness of costs of regulation, and a greater tolerance of abuses in a post-Watergate world.

675 "Rush to Protect Consumers." *U.S. News and World Report* 68 (2 February 1970): 44-47.

Discusses the surge of consumerism reflected by the passage of federal, state, and local consumer protections and by the increase in consumer complaints. Treats efforts of business groups to respond to consumer dissatisfaction, and examines encouragement of these efforts by the White House consumer office and by the Commerce Department. Identifies consumer legislation that Congress is likely to consider in the upcoming session. Bills proposed by President Nixon are criticized by Ralph Nader.

676 SCHOENFELD, ANDREA F. "Bill to Create Advocacy Unit Will Be Revived in New Congress." *National Journal* 2 (19 December 1970): 2771-79.

A lengthy article on the status of legislation to create a federal consumer protection agency. Discusses the issues being debated, congressional views, administration views, business opposition, and consumer group support. Includes sidebars on the different consumer agency bills and on the new consumer affairs section in the Justice Department.

677 SCHORR, BURT. "Consumerism: Down but Not Out." *Wall Street Journal*, 8 March 1978, 16.

An editorial-page article on the health of consumerism. Reports that despite recent disappointments in Washington, advocates have widespread public support, are multiplying at the grass roots, are supported by consumerists in the Carter administration, and are developing new legislative initiatives.

678 SCHORR, BURT. "*Vox Populi*: Public Interest Units Gain More Influence with Federal Agencies." *Wall Street Journal*, 7 July 1975, 1+.

A feature article that describes the increasing influence of public interest organizations on the decisions of federal agencies. Discusses several groups, each of which focuses attention on one agency. Notes, however, that the some fifty groups with about 100 lawyers are far outnumbered by corporate lobbyists and experts and that some groups are short of funds.

679 SHAFER, RONALD G. "Consumer Bill Killed by Words." *Wall Street Journal*, 27 October 1972, 8.

An editorial-page article discussing the defeat of the consumer protection agency bill in the Senate. Attributes the loss not only to a filibuster by conservatives but also to Nixon administration opposition and to the unwillingness of some Senate supporters to show up for votes.

680 SINGER, JAMES W. "Consumer Representation Plans Fail to Silence Agency Advocates." *National Journal* 8 (27 March 1976): 402-406.

Describes the debate over the administration's plan to ensure consumer representation in department and agency decision making. Reports criticism from consumer advocates who view the plan as a strategy to block consumer protection agency legislation. Describes the plans of several departments. Includes a sidebar identifying those persons responsible for the plans in the several departments and agencies.

681 SNYDER, JAMES D. "Those Expletive Deleted Consumerists – What Are They Planning Next?" *Sales Management*, 27 May 1974, 18-22.

Develops the theme that "consumerists are on the move again." Suggests that the movement has changed over the past five years. Now it has a broader power base, places greater emphasis on enforcement than on passing laws, gives greater attention to broad policy issues, places top priority on more consumer input in regulatory decision making, and is more mature. Extensively quotes Virginia Knauer, special assistant to the president, and Ellen Zawel, a founder of the National Consumers Congress. Discusses the debate over a consumer protection agency bill. Includes a table identifying the director, number of staff, budget, sources of income, and principal concerns of twenty-one consumer groups.

682 "U.S. Consumer Groups: Livelier Than Ever." *U.S. News and World Report* 81 (6 December 1976): 90-91.

See entry 272 for annotation.

683 "The U.S.'s Toughest Customer." *Time* 94 (12 December 1969): 89+.

See entry 478 for annotation.

684 WARK, LOIS G. "Independent Consumer Agency Bill Moves toward Election-Year Fight in Senate." *National Journal* 3 (18 December 1971): 2499-2504; (25 December 1971): 2525-34.

A lengthy two-part article on legislation to establish a consumer protection agency. Reports on differing views within Congress and Ralph Nader's aggressive support for the bill. Analyzes individual features of the legislation. Describes the legislative process that led to the bill's passage by the House last year. Discusses the role of consumer groups, business, the administration, and the Senate on the issue. Predicts passage of legislation by the Senate.

685 WIGHTMAN, RICHARD. "Consumerism." *Supermarket News*, 13 April 1970, 1+.

Discusses President Nixon's impact on consumer issues. Based largely on interviews with Virginia Knauer, the president's consumer adviser; congressional representatives; consumer leaders; and supermarket industry leaders. Critics charge that the administration calls for tough consumer legislation but proposes weak legislation, and claim that it has failed to act in a timely manner. Knauer defends the president, noting she sees him frequently. Concludes that the administration has performed "reasonably well, but could do a great deal better."

1976-1980 (CARTER ADMINISTRATION)

686 ARIEFF, IRWIN B. "Consumer Groups Seek New Image." *Congressional Quarterly Weekly Report* 37 (20 January 1979): 88-90.
    An article on rising opposition to consumer movement initiatives in Congress. Links this opposition to growing public identification of consumer reforms with inflation and government spending. Discusses recent legislative and electoral defeats suffered by consumer groups. Reports that in the future these organizations will increasingly focus on antiinflation measures.

687 BLUMENTHAL, RALPH. "Consumer Leaders, in Reappraisal, Seek New Initiatives." *New York Times*, 15 February 1978, sec. I, p. 21.
    Discusses the "period of transition and appraisal" being experienced by the consumer movement. Suggests that the movement needs new "scandals" and initiatives "to keep the momentum from flagging." Indicates consumer groups plan to emphasize grass-roots organizing and support of proconsumer candidates. Discusses factors that have led to the reappraisal including defeat of consumer protection agency legislation, recruitment of movement leaders by the Carter administration, the creation of state protection agencies, and the passage of consumer laws. Quotes consumer leaders as predicting a backlash against the defeat of the agency bill.

688 "The COIN Campaign." *Social Policy*, January-February 1979, 58-59.
    Reports the establishment of a citizen campaign, Consumers Opposed to Inflation in the Necessities (COIN), to fight inflation. The effort will focus on the price of food, energy, licensing, and health care. It will release a consumer price index ("CPI") for these necessities each month and will seek to mobilize citizen activity throughout the country. Gar Alperowitz and Mark Green will serve as special advisers.

689 "Consumer Activists Launching Shadow Energy Department." *Wall Street Journal*, 12 February 1979, 16.

A short article on the creation of a "shadow department of energy" by consumer activists critical of the U.S. Department of Energy. Indicates the new group will urge DOE employees to inform it of departmental problems.

690 "Consumerists Try to Regain Clout." *Business Week*, 29 May 1978, 107.
A report on the reaction of Washington-based consumer groups to the defeat of the consumer protection agency bill. Indicates that Ralph Nader and the Consumer Federation of America will work on grass-roots issues, including campaigning against anticonsumer members of Congress. Notes that White House consumer adviser Esther Peterson has been given some of the powers that would have been vested in the proposed agency. Suggests that the groups have lost influence.

691 "Consumers: Too Much Power?" *Economist*, 4 June 1977, 52.
Discusses the proposed federal consumer protection agency that would be empowered to press other federal regulatory agencies to act in the consumer interest. Suggests that although this seven-year-old proposal recently was approved by a House committee, its future is in doubt.

692 DEMKOVICH, LINDA E. "Consumer Groups See End in Sight after Long Fight over Agency." *National Journal* 9 (29 January 1977): 174-77.
Reports on the continuing campaign to create a federal consumer protection agency. Discusses the key issues Congress is debating. Speculates on President Carter's role in the controversy. Evaluates prospects for the legislation.

693 DEMKOVICH, LINDA E. "Consumer Leaders Hope That Carter Will Go to Bat for Them." *National Journal* 8 (4 December 1976): 1738-44.
A lengthy article on the condition and prospects of national consumer groups on the eve of the Carter presidency. Quotes Consumer Federation of America executive director Carol Foreman and Congress Watch director Joan Claybrook extensively. Discusses prospects for the consumer protection agency bill and other consumer legislation. Reports consumer leaders as expressing cautious optimism. Includes a sidebar briefly describing major national groups.

694 DEMKOVICH, LINDA E. "Consumer Movement Finds the Going Tough on Capitol Hill." *National Journal* 9 (6 August 1977): 1233-35.
Discusses the lack of progress of consumer legislation in the ninety-fifth Congress. Identifies reasons for this lack of movement.

1976-1980

Focuses on legislation to establish a consumer protection agency and to make class-action suits easier.

695 DEMKOVICH, LINDA E. "Even a White House Pep Rally May Not Save the Agency." *National Journal* 9 (25 June 1977): 996-99.
   Reports on the poor prospects for congressional passage of a consumer protection agency bill even though the president supports it. Examines reasons for the lack of sufficient congressional backing. Quotes consumer leaders as blaming business lobbying and quotes business as citing insufficient public support. Discusses Esther Peterson's role in the congressional battle.

696 DEMKOVICH, LINDA E. "Where Is the Consuming Public on the Proposed Consumer Agency?" *National Journal* 9 (10 December 1977): 1912-14.
   Suggests that the failure of the consumer protection agency bill reflected mainly public apathy. Cites congressional sources as saying they heard from no or few constituents who supported the legislation, even in districts targeted by consumer groups. Describes the slippage of House support during the course of the session. Includes a sidebar on Congressman Foley's opposition to the legislation.

697 FOREMAN, LAURA. "Carter's Raiders: The Outsiders Are In." *New York Times*, 20 April 1977, sec. III, p. 1+.
   A lengthy article on public interest advocates who have joined the Carter administration, including Robert Greenstein, Carol Tucker Foreman, Joan Claybrook, Michael Pertschuk, Peter Schuck, Harrison Wellford, and Peter Petkas. Quotes Ralph Nader as approving of these appointments.

698 FRASER, EDIE. "Consumerism in 1978." *Business and Society Review* 24 (Winter 1977-78): 81.
   A brief summary of consumer legislation considered by Congress in 1977. Suggests that the consumer movement is "alive and well," partly because of increased government funding. Includes a sidebar on major consumer legislative initiatives in 1978.

699 GORDON, MARY S., ed. *People Power: What Are Communities Doing to Counter Inflation*. Washington, D.C.: U.S. Office of Consumer Affairs [late 1970s]. 411 pp.
   A lengthy report on what local groups are doing to reduce consumer costs in the areas of food, housing, energy, and health. Emphasizes cooperative and self-help approaches yet does discuss

efforts to organize tenants, residential ratepayers, and users of the health-care system. Lists organizations working on each issue.

700 HINDS, MICHAEL deCOURCY. "Nader Expanding Consumer Efforts." *New York Times,* 27 September 1979, sec. I, p. 31.
　　See entry 436 for annotation.

701 KARR, ALBERT R. "Inside View: Former Consumerists Now in Agencies Find New Jobs Frustrating." *Wall Street Journal,* 15 December 1977, 1+.
　　See entry 323 for annotation.

702 KRAMER, LARRY. "Consumer Battles to Go On." *Washington Post,* 10 September 1978, sec. F, p. 2.
　　An article on the consumer movement after the defeat of consumer protection agency legislation. Suggests that the movement has made great progress in increasing consumer representation in the executive branch. Discusses the plans of new Consumer Product Safety Commission head Susan King.

703 KRAMER, LARRY. "Consumer Groups Gird against Inflation." *Washington Post,* 14 January 1979, sec. H, p. 20.
　　An article on the top priorities of consumer groups in the coming year. For the Consumer Federation of America and National Consumers League, the first priority is inflation, but for Ralph Nader, it is giant monopolies. Briefly discusses consumer regulatory agencies. Suggests grass-roots activism is "on the upswing."

704 KRAMER, LARRY. "Consumer Movement Hits Mid-Stride." *Washington Post,* 13 January 1978, sec. C, p. 9+.
　　An article on the maturing of the consumer movement. Reports successes that include the appointment of advocates to key administration positions, increased public participation in regulatory proceedings, proconsumer regulatory initiatives, and rising "consumer consciousness." Discusses the lack of progress of consumer protection agency legislation.

705 KRAMER, LARRY. "Consumers Promised More Aid." *Washington Post,* 20 January 1978, sec. B, p. 8.
　　A short article on the Consumer Federation of America's Consumer Assembly, which featured speeches by FTC head Michael Pertschuk and FDA head Donald Kennedy.

1976-1980

706 LEEPSON, MARC. "Consumer Protection: Gains and Setbacks." In *Consumer Protection: Gains and Setbacks*, 1-20. Washington, D.C.: Congressional Quarterly, 1978.

   The first report in a book by *Congressional Quarterly* staffers on various consumer problems and proposed reforms. A well-researched account of the current status and future of the consumer movement. Discusses the defeat of a consumer agency bill, criticism of the Consumer Product Safety Commission, Ralph Nader's organizations and influence, President Carter's appointment of consumer leaders to top government positions, and the movement's lack of unity.

707 McPHERSON, MYRA. "Former Consumer Activist Doing Job from Inside." *Washington Post*, 17 November 1977, sec. A, p. 2.
   See entry 325 for annotation.

708 MAYER, CAROLINE E. "A Rude Awakening for Activists in Government." *U.S. News & World Report* 84 (6 March 1978): 52+.
   See entry 326 for annotation.

709 MINTZ, MORTON. "Rights of Consumer Groups Attacked." *Washington Post*, 4 April 1979, sec. D, p. 7.
   An article on a ruling by a district court that Ralph Nader's consumer organizations cannot sue on behalf of the general public. Also discusses the Justice Department's contention that Consumers Union should not be allowed to sue on behalf of consumers. Reports the reaction of CU.

710 "Nader-Led Coalition Seeks Federal Charters for Large Companies." *Wall Street Journal*, 13 December 1979, 11.
   A short article on a new coalition of consumer and labor groups, led by Ralph Nader, to secure passage of legislation requiring large corporations to obtain federal charters. Describes other features of the legislation including a required notification of plant closings.

711 "Nader: Success or Excess?" *Time* 110 (14 November 1977): 76+.
   See entry 457 for annotation.

712 "A New Agency for Consumers: Sizing Up the Chances." *U.S. News and World Report* 82 (30 May 1977): 46.
   A report on growing support for a federal consumer protection agency. Outlines arguments for and against the unit. Notes that this issue has been debated within Congress for years.

713 PAPPAS, VASIL. "Westinghouse Bid to Settle Uranium Suits out of Court Faces Consumer Opposition." *Wall Street Journal*, 8 April 1977, 10.

A report on a campaign, led by the Environmental Action Foundation, to press public service commissions in eleven states to investigate out-of-court settlements between utilities and Westinghouse on uranium contracts the latter canceled. Both consumer and environmental groups participated in the effort.

714 *Public Interest Perspectives: The Next Four Years*. Proceedings from the first major gathering of public interest advocates. Washington, D.C.: Public Citizen, 1977. 218 pp.

A transcript of a conference organized by Public Citizen on the future of public interest advocacy. After keynote addresses by Ralph Nader and Jerry Wurf, sessions focused on structural change, the budget process, funding challenges, tactics, working with the Carter administration, citizen involvement, litigation, regulatory agencies, citizen organizing, lobbying, and communications. Lists participating organizations and their representatives.

715 ROSENBAUM, DAVID E. "Public Affairs Groups, Now on the Outside, Expect Access to Power under Carter." *New York Times*, 1 December 1976, sec. II, p. 6.

See entry 331 for annotation.

716 SARASOHN, JUDY. "Consumers Count Few Victories in 1979." *Congressional Quarterly Weekly Report* 38 (12 January 1979): 108-11.

An article discussing the increasing number of congressional defeats suffered by consumer groups. Describes issues on which these organizations won and lost. Reports consumer reaction blaming growing business influence and President Carter's lack of leadership, as well as the business response that consumer advocates are out of touch with their constituents. Includes a sidebar on President Carter's executive order requiring consumer programs in executive branch offices.

717 SCHARFENBERG, KIRK. "The Community as Bank Examiner." *Working Papers for a New Society* (September-October 1980): 30-35.

Examines the new efforts by community groups to use the Community Reinvestment Act (CRA) to force banks to meet the credit needs of low-income and lower-middle-income communities. Reports on about sixty such challenges and dozens of bank agreements to make available mortgage money. Assesses future prospects of this type of organizing. Concludes that it offers a promising new strategy that empowers citizens as it helps them meet their credit needs.

718 SINGER, JAMES W. "Consumer Offices in the Agencies – the Best the Activists Can Expect?" *National Journal* 12 (6 September 1980): 1478-79.

Discusses the executive order requiring most executive branch departments and agencies to develop plans for ensuring consumer representation. Quotes consumer leaders as being relatively satisfied with the order, considering the unwillingness of Congress to fund a separate agency or public participation. Briefly describes consumer programs of the Food and Drug Administration, Department of Transportation, Department of Commerce, and Health and Human Services.

719 SINGER, STEVE. "States Tax Big Oil." *Working Papers for a New Society*, July-August 1980, 5-6.

Discusses the national campaign initiated by the Citizens Labor Energy Coalition to persuade states to create a new tax on oil companies. Describes efforts in New York and Connecticut.

720 VALENTINE, JOHN. "Brewing Boycott: Rising Coffee Prices Are Beginning to Stir Consumer Protests." *Wall Street Journal*, 3 January 1977, 1+.

A feature article reporting that the rise in coffee prices has stimulated an emerging consumer boycott in the United States and other countries including Canada, Britain, West Germany, and Australia. Indicates that the New York City consumer affairs commissioner issued a boycott call to 400 activists around the country. Notes that many consumers interviewed had not heard of the boycott while others would not honor it.

721 WALSH, EDWARD. "Foes of Oil Decontrol Fail to Budge Carter." *Washington Post*, 2 June 1979, sec. A, p. 1.

A page-one article on sharp criticism by consumer advocates of President Carter's decision to decontrol oil prices, which followed a meeting with him.

1980-1989 (REAGAN, BUSH ADMINISTRATIONS)

722 BODNAR, JANET. "Whatever Happened to the Consumer Movement?" *Changing Times* 43 (August 1989): 45+.

A lengthy article on the growth and increased influence of the consumer movement in Washington. Outlines the movement's agenda. Discusses the performance of the Federal Trade Commission, Consumer Product Safety Commission, and local protection agencies. Describes the emergence of conservative consumer groups, such as Consumer Alert, that favor free-market solutions. Profiles Consumer Alert, Consumer Federation of America, Consumers Union, and Public Citizen.

723 BROWN, MERRILL. "Consumerists Look to Cover Grassroots." *Washington Post*, 11 January 1981, sec. L, p. 4.
    A report on the priorities of national consumer groups during the Reagan administration. Suggests that these will be protecting past gains by using the courts and organizing at the grass roots. Quotes consumer leaders as expressing apprehension about the new administration.

724 "Catering to King Consumer." *Fortune* 108 (14 November 1983): 43-44.
    A short article on increasing support for consumer interests in Congress. Suggests that when the issues are highly visible, these interests usually win.

725 COOPER, ANN. "Low-Income Customers Discover Down Sides of Phone, Banking Deregulation." *National Journal* 17 (26 January 1985): 204-205.
    Discusses the negative impacts of banking and telephone deregulation on the poor. Reports on the efforts of national consumer advocates to win lifeline protections for these consumers.

726 DAHL, JONATHAN. "Consumers Gain Unlikely Victory in Antitrust Action in New Mexico." *Wall Street Journal*, 5 June 1984, 37.
    Reports on a successful price-fixing lawsuit, initiated by six teachers and later supported by the state attorney general, against natural gas suppliers. Gas customers, including the teachers' school district, won $121 million in price reductions.

727 DUKE, PAUL, Jr. "Consumer Groups View Bill Inserts as a Potent Force against Utilities." *Wall Street Journal*, 23 October 1985, 57.
    See entry 281 for annotation.

728 EGAN, JAMES. "The Woman Who Blew the Whistle on the Electric Company." *Family Circle*, 19 April 1983, 114+.
    A report on Dorothy Spielman's successful crusade against the South Norwalk Electric Works. Spielman's dissatisfaction stemmed

from rising rates and seemingly unfair billing practices. After complaining in vain to various government agencies, she attracted the interest of two local newspapers. Their coverage of the issue led to a city investigation that resulted in the arrest of seven utility officials.

729 EMSHWILLER, JOHN R., and CAMP, CHARLES B. "On and On Grinds Fight over Old Fords That Slip into Reverse." *Wall Street Journal*, 14 April 1988, 1+.

A lead article that discusses the seventeen-year controversy over pre-1980 Ford cars that sometimes back up when in park. Reports differing views of the company, on the one hand, and of new regulator Joan Claybrook and the Center for Auto Safety, on the other. Describes the debate within the Department of Transportation and continuing litigation.

730 HINDS, MICHAEL deCOURCY. "Consumer Groups' Dishonor Roll of '87." *New York Times*, 5 December 1987, 56.

A lengthy article that treats consumer abuses in 1987 as identified by a dozen national advocacy groups. Problems relate to automobiles, recreational vehicles, home-equity loans, children's television, food, and drugs. Reports that advocates blame the Reagan administration and its regulatory agencies for many of these problems.

731 HINDS, MICHAEL deCOURCY. "The Consumer Movement: Whatever Happened." *New York Times*, 21 January 1983, sec. I, p. 21.

An article on the decline of the consumer movement because of Reagan administration policies. Suggests that the demands of consumer advocates "have been balanced and often outweighed by the need to stimulate the economy, to promote new drug development, . . . and to protect auto makers against product liability claims by not requiring new safety technology." Quotes administration officials on the need to reduce consumer regulations. Reports the advocate response that this "deregulation" is shortsighted and will cost society more money in the long run.

732 HINDS, MICHAEL deCOURCY. "A Subdued Nader Works to Organize Consumers." *New York Times*, 27 April 1982, 20.

See entry 437 for annotation.

733 KRAMER, LARRY. "The Tide of Consumer Influence Is in the Grip of a Strong Undertow." *Washington Post*, 13 January 1980, sec. G, p. 12.

An article on the goals of national consumer groups in the 1980s. Identifies them as ensuring consumers adequate information and increasing the economic and political power of consumers through cooperatives, new telecommunications technologies, and checkoff mechanisms.

734 McGUIRE, E. PATRICK. "Consumerism Lives! ... and Grows." *Across the Board* 17 (January 1980): 57-62.
An article based on interviews with corporate consumer affairs executives and consumer leaders on the current status and future of consumerism. Suggests that, despite the failure of congressional consumer legislation, consumers are growing more demanding. Notes the disillusionment of some activists with government regulation and their increasing emphasis on state reforms and on litigation. Reports that corporate representatives acknowledge the influence of advocates on their companies. Predicts that the consumer issues of the 1970s, such as the establishment of a consumer protection agency and greater public participation, will continue in the 1980s. In retrospect, most have not.

735 MAYER, ROBERT N. "The Consumer Politics of Trade Restrictions: The Case of Domestic Content Requirements." *Journal of Consumer Affairs* 18 (Winter 1984): 343-54.
A timely analysis of the consumer politics of trade restrictions with special focus on proposed domestic content requirements for imported cars. Outlines arguments for and against content legislation. Notes that no major consumer groups actively opposed this legislation and two even passively endorsed it. In analyzing congressional votes, finds that members of Congress supporting content requirements were likely to cast proconsumer votes on other issues. Discusses reasons for the position of consumer groups on the issue and the risks it entails. This study assumes that free trade is always in the consumer interest, without considering the complexity of trade relations with Japan, which was the sole target of the legislation. It also ignores the role of most major consumer groups in opposing other kinds of trade restrictions. Domestic content legislation may have been a special case because it was pushed by the United Auto Workers, a longtime supporter of consumer protection, and had no chance of passing the Senate or being signed into law by the president. Nevertheless, the study raises important issues that advocates should consider.

736 "Nader's Anti-Business Bust." *Time* 115 (28 April 1980): 51.
A report on "Big Business Day," which consisted of demonstrations organized by Ralph Nader against large corporations. Indicates that the crowds were "sparse" and that the Corporate

Democracy Act the rallies promoted is unlikely to pass soon. Quotes the reactions of several business leaders.

737 NICHOLSON, TOM. "Onward, Consumer Soldiers." *Newsweek* 101 (25 April 1983): 56.
A report on the growth of grass-roots consumer activism. Mentions the Citizen/Labor Energy Coalition, Telecommunications Research and Action Center, Massachusetts Fair Share, Consumer Action, and California Public Interest Research Group. Notes that Congress is becoming more supportive of consumerist concerns, especially related to antitrust legislation.

738 O'NEILL, BARBARA, and WHITNER, CATHARINE. "Shaping Public Policy to Enhance Family Well-Being: Lobbying for a County Consumer Affairs Office." *Journal of Home Economics*, Fall 1986, 17-21.
An article by two home economists on how they and colleagues helped establish a consumer protection office in Suffolk County, New Jersey. Notes their use of a state official, local officials, and the media. Includes fifteen "hints" about lobbying successfully for a local consumer office.

739 PASZTOR, ANDY. "State Regulators Take Up Battle against Rising Natural Gas Prices." *Wall Street Journal*, 21 January 1983, 25.
A report on growing opposition by state utility regulators to rising gas prices. Credits "public clamor" orchestrated partly by grass-roots activists as a stimulus to this opposition. Briefly discusses the federal debate about fully deregulating gas prices.

740 PERTSCHUK, MICHAEL. *Giant Killers*. New York: W. W. Norton, 1986. 252 pp.
The lively, perceptive story of five public interest victories in Congress and the advocates who made them possible, written by a leading public interest advocate who chaired the Federal Trade Commission in the Carter administration. Focuses on the Cigarette Labeling Act of 1984, preservation of the Tuolumne Wild River in California, Voting Rights Act of 1982, defeat of the MX missile in 1984, and defeat of the medical profession's campaign to secure an antitrust exemption. The chapter on the latter discusses at length the role of Congress Watch lobbyist Jay Angoff in opposing the proposed exemption. In the preface, the author identifies five conditions that must usually be present for public interest lobbyists to prevail. In the conclusion, he observes that all the highlighted lobbyists come from

working-class, largely apolitical families, and few attended elite colleges. He also echoes David Cohen who has suggested that the role of the public interest lobbyist is "priestly and prophetic."

741 ROSEWICZ, BARBARA. "Consumer Lobbies Gain Ground on Capitol Hill by Parlaying Tactics, Timing on Banking Bills." *Wall Street Journal*, 5 October 1987, 54.

Examines the campaign initiated by national consumer groups to pass new consumer banking protections. Emphasizes the importance of research that reveals consumer abuses and is widely reported on by the press. Shows how consumer lobbyists work with reform-minded members of Congress and their staffers.

742 SADDLER, JEANNE. "Holding Action: Consumer Groups Try to Keep Earlier Gains As Their Power Wanes." *Wall Street Journal*, 31 December 1986, 1+.

A lead article that assesses the efforts of national consumer groups to defend protections under attack by the Reagan administration. Suggests that public support for consumerism has declined and discusses reasons for this decline. Describes the increasing willingness of consumer groups to join with business on legislative and information campaigns. Underestimates the institutional strength of consumer groups and thus fails to anticipate the surge of consumerism later in the decade.

743 SCOTT, SARAH. "Consumer Advocates Wait Anxiously for the Pendulum to Swing Their Way." *National Journal* 13 (10 January 1981): 57-58.

Reports on congressional opposition to funding of consumer participation in federal regulatory proceedings even before President Reagan took office. Critics charge that this "public participation" financing represents a backdoor way of creating the consumer protection agency rejected by Congress. Public interest groups cite several examples of the success of this consumer representation.

744 SHENON, PHILIP. "Nader, after Eight Years, Is Back on the Inside." *New York Times*, 10 May 1989, sec. II, p. 6.

See entry 474 for annotation.

745 SINCLAIR, MOLLY. "Consumer Groups Seek New Focus of Action." *Washington Post*, 7 February 1985, sec. C, p. 3.

An article on a Consumer Federation of America Consumer Assembly that featured Ralph Nader as a speaker. Nader criticized several groups for their lack of vigor in protecting consumers. Reports differences in strategy and style among national groups.

746 SMITH, DARLENE BRANNIGAN, and BLOOM, PAUL N. "Is Consumerism Dead or Alive? Some Empirical Evidence." In *The Future of Consumerism*, edited by Paul N. Bloom and Ruth Belk Smith, 61-74. Lexington, Mass.: Lexington Books, 1986.
   See entry 69 for annotation.

747 THORNTON, JEANNYE, and TAYLOR, RONALD A. "Reagan's War on Red Tape Draws Blood." *U.S. News and World Report* 92 (18 January 1982): 62-63.
   A report on efforts of the Reagan administration to reduce consumer regulations and on the opposition of consumer groups. Briefly describes "deregulation" at the Federal Trade Commission, Consumer Product Safety Commission, National Highway Traffic Safety Administration, Food and Drug Administration, and Department of Agriculture. Notes two proconsumer initiatives by these agencies. Discusses the attempt of consumer groups to defend existing regulations.

748 WHITE, EILEEN. "Phone Activists: Jump in Local Rates Since AT&T Breakup Is Spurring Protests." *Wall Street Journal*, 27 September 1985, 1+.
   A lead article reporting grass-roots opposition to rising local phone rates. Indicates that these rates have replaced electric rates as the top-priority consumer utility issue. Describes how national advocacy groups, state-funded utility advocates, and grass-roots organizations are working together against rate increases and local measured service. Focuses most attention on the debate in Pennsylvania.

749 "Who Will Protect Consumers Now?" *Changing Times* 35 (June 1981): 17-20.
   An article on new challenges facing the consumer movement, particularly the Reagan administration's attack on consumer protections. Reports consumerist criticisms of the Consumer Product Safety Commission, Federal Trade Commission, and Food and Drug Administration. Notes the increasing importance of grass-roots organizing. Discusses the funding problems of consumer groups and their priority issues.

11. Political Impacts

750 APPLETON, LYNN M. "Explaining Laws' Making and Their Enforcement in the American States." *Social Science Quarterly* 66 (December 1985): 839-53.

An instructive analysis of the enactment and enforcement of state consumer protection laws. Theorizes that consumer lawmaking can be largely explained in terms of the demand for law, while law enforcement can mainly be explained by the supply of state resources. Develops indices for the independent variables of mass need, elite need, interest groups, and fiscal capacity, and for the dependent variables of lawmaking and enforcement. Finds that the quality of the laws is most closely associated with the demand factor of high income levels ("elite need") and unrelated to the scope of state consumer agency operations ("interest groups"). Discovers that law enforcement is most closely correlated with population mobility ("mass need") and the state's fiscal capacity. Thus, while the theory that lawmaking is related to demand factors and enforcement to supply factors is largely verified, it does not explain all the variation in consumer protection.

751 FLICKINGER, RICHARD. "The Comparative Politics of Agenda Setting: The Emergence of Consumer Protection as a Public Policy Issue in Britain and the U.S." *Policy Studies Review* 2 (February 1982): 429-44.

Using a review of the literature and interviews with British government, retailer, and consumer representatives, examines how and why consumer protection became an important policy issue in Britain and the United States during the 1960s and early 1970s. Reviews the development of consumer protection policies in the two countries. Discusses indicators of the agenda status of proposed policies.

Concludes that consumer protection is a discretionary agenda item under the direct control of government policymakers. Suggests that these policymakers initially were attracted to consumer protection as a strategy for restraining inflation but later turned to other approaches. Minimizes the role played by consumer groups in placing consumer protection on the public agenda, by noting the passage of much legislation before the organization of most U.S. groups and also noting the defeat of their top legislative priority, a federal consumer protection agency. Fails to list important consumer legislation passed in the early 1970s that was pushed by consumer lobbyists. Yet, provides a different and useful perspective on the influence of national consumer organizations than that held by most consumerists and their critics.

752 FORD, GARY T. "Adoption of Consumer Policies by States: Some Empirical Perspectives." *Journal of Marketing Research* 15 (February 1978): 49-57.

An analysis of the factors associated with state consumer laws to try to explain why some states are more consumer protection-oriented than others. Correlates urbanization, education, retail sales, and percentage of whites with state statutes. Finds that these independent variables explain more than half of the variance in protection laws. Also discovers four clusters of states with similar legislation – "laggard states" (mainly from the South), "legal remedies states," "leader states" (most from the West Coast, upper Midwest, and mid-Atlantic regions), and "heartland states" (most from the Mideast and Midwest). Learns that different states lead in the adoption of specific consumer laws.

753 HANDLER, JOEL F. *Social Movements and the Legal System*. New York: Academic Press, 1978. 252 pp.

An assessment of the success of litigation by public interest organizations. Examines thirty-eight cases in the areas of environmental protection, consumer protection, civil rights, and social welfare. Attempts to explain the outcome of each case using five clusters of variables – the characteristics of the groups, costs and benefits, bureaucratic contingencies, judicial remedies, and characteristics of the public interest litigators. Concludes that public interest groups find it difficult to gain tangible results from litigation, except where a problem can be solved on the basis of a rule change. Acknowledges, however, that this litigation may confer a number of indirect benefits – publicity, funding, consciousness-raising, and legitimacy – that are difficult to measure. The chapter on consumer protection reviews fourteen examples of litigation in areas such as consumer credit, food and drugs, utility rates, and air travel. These conform to patterns in the other cases examined in the study. The chapter also includes a perceptive summary of Nader-related groups, the Consumer Federation of America, the Center for Auto Safety, and other consumer organizations based on earlier academic research and articles in *National Journal*.

754 KEISER, K. ROBERT. "The New Regulation of Health and Safety." *Political Science Quarterly* 95 (Fall 1980): 479-91.
　　An analysis of how regulatory policies have been formulated and implemented by federal health and safety agencies–Food and Drug Administration, National Highway Traffic Safety Administration, Consumer Product Safety Commission, and Occupational Safety and Health Administration. Focuses on those factors that either encourage or hinder regulatory activism. Concludes that the government has significantly increased its commitment to reduced injuries and fatalities. Identifies the major barrier to regulatory activism not as capture but as "immobilization," because of agency domination by "conservers" most interested in convenience and security. Argues that this immobilization has been overcome by the mobilization of constituency support by political entrepreneurs and interest groups such as the Health Research Group. Notes that two areas of disagreement are the degree to which safety protections are an individual or social responsibility and the level of economic costs caused by health and safety regulations that is acceptable.

755 KNIGHT, MICHAEL. "Aid to Consumers Growing in Nation." *New York Times*, 9 August 1970, p. 1+.
　　See entry 666 for annotation.

756 MAYER, ROBERT [N.]. *The Consumer Movement: Guardians of the Marketplace*. Boston: Twayne Publishers, 1989. Ch. 5.
　　See entry 57 for annotation.

757 MAYER, ROBERT N., and SCAMMON, DEBRA L. "Intervenor Funding at the FTC: Biopsy or Autopsy." *Policy Studies Review* 2 (February 1983): 506-15.
　　See entry 327 for annotation.

758 MEIER, KENNETH J. "The Political Economy of Consumer Protection: An Examination of State Legislation." *Western Political Quarterly* 40 (June 1987): 343-60.
　　An analysis of factors related to state consumer protection laws. Hypothesizes that these statutes reflect industry pressures, consumer groups, bureaucratic forces, and elected officials. Develops indices of

these four independent variables and correlates them with the extent of state consumer protection. Finds that all four variables explain over half of the variation in consumer protection laws. Discovers that industry pressures are the weakest influence on these statutes. Explains this finding in terms of the countering of small-business opposition to consumer legislation by big-business support. Learns that "urbanism" is the indicator most highly correlated with strong protection laws. Suggests that this association reflects the fact that in urban states consumer activists are more likely to come in contact with other advocates. A more likely explanation is that, because their markets are larger and more impersonal, urban states have greater consumer protection needs.

759 NADEL, MARK V[ICTOR]. *The Politics of Consumer Protection.* Indianapolis: Bobbs-Merrill, 1971. 257 pp.
　　See entry 609 for annotation.

760 NADEL, MARK VICTOR. "The Unorganized Interests: Consumers in the Policy Process." Ph.D. dissertation, Johns Hopkins University, 1971. 372 pp.
　　See entry 610 for annotation.

761 NADEL, MARK V[ICTOR], ed. "Symposium on Consumer Protection Policy." *Policy Studies Review* 2 (February 1983): 417-549.
　　Twelve articles by social scientists from different fields on consumer protection policies. Issues addressed are the rationale for and emergence in the United States and Britain of these policies, the uses of consumer information and education as a substitute for direct regulation, Federal Trade Commission policies, and two alternatives to regulation – a strict liability system and mediation/arbitration.

762 PERTSCHUK, MICHAEL. *Giant Killers.* New York: W. W. Norton, 1986. 252 pp.
　　See entry 740 for annotation.

763 VOGEL, DAVID. *When Consumers Oppose Consumer Protection.* St. Louis: Center for the Study of American Business, Washington University, 1989. 40 pp.
　　An analysis of four cases in which consumers opposed federal regulations restricting their choices. These cases involved opposition to the seat belt interlock system, motorcycle helmet requirements, the ban on saccharin, and FDA approval of new drugs to be used in the treatment of AIDS. Suggests that, in the last twenty-five years, there have been few instances of consumer opposition to consumer

regulations. Finds that the four cases share three characteristics: first, eliminating the regulation did not force consumers to be exposed to related health and safety threats; second, consumers opposing the regulation believed that it made them worse off; third, each case was highly visible. Concludes that these instances of consumer backlash and the apparent indifference of consumers to regulation-related costs on business have encouraged Congress to reduce consumer health and safety threats by restricting the choices of corporations rather than those of consumers.

12. Economic Impacts

GENERAL

764 AMERICAN ENTERPRISE INSTITUTE. *Regulation*. Washington, D.C.

A journal published between 1977 and 1985 by a conservative "think tank" for the purpose of evaluating government regulations. The articles by academics and other experts include assessments of food, drug, cigarette, and motor vehicle safety regulations. Intended to be written "in a readable style," according to the journal, they do not contain documentation of references.

765 KOTLER, PHILIP. "What Consumerism Means for Marketers." *Harvard Business Review* 50 (May-June 1972): 48-57.

A discussion of the implications of consumerism for corporations, particularly marketers. Argues that consumerism was inevitable, will be enduring, will be beneficial, is promarketing, and can be profitable through the introduction of needed new products and through the adoption of a companywide consumerist orientation. Although inadequately documented and occasionally simplistic in its analysis, represents a useful discussion of the significance and implications of consumerism for a general business audience.

766 MAYER, ROBERT [N.]. *The Consumer Movement: Guardians of the Marketplace*. Boston: Twayne Publishers, 1989. Ch. 6.

See entry 57 for annotation.

General

767 MAYER, ROBERT N., and BURTON, JOHN R. "Distributional Impacts of Consumer Protection Policies: Differences among Consumers." *Policy Studies Journal* 12 (September 1983): 91-105.

An important article on the distributional effects of consumer protection policies. Reviews research related to safety, performance, information, and price that assesses the impact of factors such as income, age, geographic region, and household size. For instance, research on safety suggests that regulations may increase prices paid by low-income households by a higher percentage than those paid by the more affluent, yet may reduce risk more for the poorly educated than for the well-educated. Concludes that it is difficult to reach conclusions about the overall distributional impacts of consumer protection policies. Recommends that these impacts receive more attention from researchers and from policymakers. Some of the research examined incorporates the biases of many economists. For example, restrictions on high-priced credit to low-income consumers are considered to be undesirable. Yet, if such restrictions cause these consumers to defer certain purchases, they may enhance their welfare.

768 MICHMAN, RONALD D. "Impact of Consumerism: A Response Needed in Product Planning." *Business and Economic Dimensions* 9 (May-June 1973): 7-11.

Discusses the implications of consumerism for product planning. Specifically, examines the relationship of consumerism to the marketing concept and its impacts on the prepurchase buying phase, the purchase itself, and the postpurchase experience. Suggests that consumerism will endure and that business should develop the new opportunities it presents.

BOYCOTTS

769 PRUITT, STEPHEN W., and FRIEDMAN, MONROE. "Determining the Effectiveness of Consumer Boycotts: A Stock Price Analysis of Their Impact on Corporate Targets." *Journal of Consumer Policy* 9 (December 1986): 375-88.

Examines the effect of twenty-one consumer boycotts on their corporate targets through analysis of changes in the stock prices of the companies. Finds that announcements of these boycotts seem to depress stock prices considerably. Yet was unable to determine reasons for the apparent success of the boycotts. Suggests that corporate managers should take threatened boycotts seriously.

CONSUMER INFORMATION

770 DAY, GEORGE S. "Assessing the Effects on Information Disclosure Requirements." *Journal of Marketing* 40 (April 1976): 45-52.

A review of the available evidence on the behavioral effects of consumer information disclosure at the point of sale. Suggests reasons why, to date, there is so little of this evidence. Discusses research related to a hypothesized hierarchy of effects, information effectiveness, segment differences, long-run effects, and indirect effects on producer and retailer behavior. Concludes that the evidence suggests that disclosures have little effect on buyer behavior but increase buyer confidence. Outlines the implications of this evidence for future research and for industry.

771 DAY, GEORGE S., and BRANDT, WILLIAM K. "Consumer Research and the Evaluation of Information Disclosure Requirements: The Case of Truth in Lending." *Journal of Consumer Research* 1 (June 1974): 21-32.

An evaluation of the consumer impact of truth-in-lending disclosures based on analysis of survey data from initial interviews with 793 Californians and second interviews with 196 of them. Finds that these disclosures had relatively little effect on credit search and usage behavior. Suggests the possibility that their use by a small minority was sufficient to police the market. Urges more effective consumer education to help consumers understand and use truth-in-lending disclosures.

772 DYER, ROBERT F., and MARONICK, THOMAS J. "An Evaluation of Consumer Awareness and Use of Energy Labels in the Purchase of Major Appliances: A Longitudinal Analysis." *Journal of Public Policy & Marketing* 7 (1988): 83-97.

An analysis of the level of awareness of appliance energy labels by recent purchasers of refrigerators and washers, and of changes in energy awareness of purchasers before and after mandatory energy labels. Using a consumer mail panel, researchers sampled groups of recent purchasers before and after labels were required. They found that younger, two-income, first-time buyers were most aware of labels; that after required labeling, reported knowledge of appliance energy efficiency increased significantly; and that significant percentages of buyers were aware of the labels and used the information in their purchases, especially of refrigerators. Discusses implications for marketing of these appliances.

Consumer Information

773 GREENE, BRANDON F.; ROUSE, MARK; GREEN, RICHARD B.;
and CLAY, CONNIE. "Behavior Analysis in Consumer Affairs: Retail
and Consumer Response to Publicizing Food Price Information."
Journal of Applied Behavior Analysis 17 (Spring 1984): 3-21.

An analysis of the consumer benefits of food price surveys
conducted by a public interest research group (PIRG). Compares the
behavior of food prices in large chains and smaller independent stores
in two cities – one where price information was made available to
consumers and one where it was not. Finds that this information
restrained prices in the independent stores but not in the chain. Also
learns that many consumers used the information as a basis for store
selection. Provides no evidence that price surveys increase collusion
among retailers.

774 HADDEN, SUSAN G. *Read the Label: Reducing Risk by Providing
Information.* Boulder, Colo.: Westview Press, 1986. 275 pp.

The first major evaluation of the public policy implications of
product labeling. Chapter 1 reviews the history of labeling. Chapter 2
defines a theoretical basis for labeling as a method of risk control.
Chapters 3-8 assess the implementation of labeling requirements in five
areas – drugs, consumer products, workplace conditions, food, and
pesticides. Chapters 9-11 criticize the theoretical assumptions
underlying these requirements and propose changes in labels and their
formats and content to control risk more effectively.

775 HUTTON, R. BRUCE, and WILKIE, WILLIAM L. "Life Cycle Cost:
A New Form of Consumer Information." *Journal of Consumer Research*
6 (March 1980): 349-60.

An authoritative analysis of the potential effectiveness of providing
information to help consumers minimize life-cycle costs (and energy
consumption) on household appliances. Reports the results of an
experiment involving an experimental group, who received life-cycle
cost information, and a control group, who did not. Found that
consumers receiving the information were much more accurate in
estimating the costs of appliance features, in understanding cost
relationships involving energy, and in dealing with the complexity of the
information presented. Concludes that life-cycle cost information is "a
superior information form." But notes potential problems in supplying
this information to consumers in the marketplace so that it would assist
purchasing decisions.

776 KELLEY, WILLIAM T., and GORSE, ETIENNE. "The Fair
Packaging and Labeling Act of 1966." In *New Consumerism: Selected*

Readings, edited by William T. Kelley, 425-49. Columbus, Ohio: Grid, 1973.

An assessment of the impact of the Fair Packaging and Labeling Act of 1966 based on review of government reports and articles in the trade press. Discusses the deceptive practices that led to its passage, the law itself, and its effects. Concludes that it has done little to protect consumers because of split jurisdictions, widespread exemptions, noncompliance, and nonenforcement.

777 McELROY, BRUCE, and AAKER, DAVID A. "Unit Pricing Six Years after Introduction." *Journal of Retailing* 55 (Fall 1979): 44-56.

Analyzes the responses of over 1,000 California shoppers to unit pricing at a supermarket chain. Finds that many consumers use a mature unit-pricing program and that they value it highly. Also learns that many shoppers use other in-store information including item prices and "special" or "on sale" signs.

778 RUSSO, J. EDWARD. "The Value of Unit Price Information." *Journal of Marketing Research* 14 (May 1977): 193-201.

An important evaluation of unit price information by measuring its value to consumers and to retailers. Reviews research on retailer costs of maintaining unit pricing and consumer benefits of this pricing. Describes a research design in which consumer purchases in two supermarkets with shelf prices, unit price lists, or no unit price information were examined. Reports that shelf tags resulted in a 1 percent consumer savings, while both tags and unit price lists led to a 3 percent savings. Indicates also that the list format caused a 5 percent increase in the market shares of store brands. Concludes that unit pricing can benefit both consumers and retailers.

779 SCHMITT, JACQUELINE; KANTER, LAWRENCE; and MILLER, RACHEL. *Impact of the Magnuson-Moss Warranty Act: A Comparison of 40 Major Consumer Product Warranties before and after the Act.* Staff report to the Federal Trade Commission, Washington, D.C., June, 1979.

A Federal Trade Commission staff report on the effects of the Magnuson-Moss Warranty Act that compares the warranties of forty products before and after the statute was enacted. Reports that the law appeared to improve the reliability, length, scope, and remedies of warranties and to limit their exclusions and limitations of consumers' rights.

780 STERN, LOUIS L. "Consumer Protection Via Increased Information." *Journal of Marketing* 31 (April 1967): 48-52.

Consumer Information

A discussion by a marketing professor of the trends in consumer protection legislation, especially required information disclosures, and the need for such disclosures. Treats terms of sale, standards and grade labeling, consumer advisory services, and full disclosure. Concludes that improved disclosures represent not only the most economical and least restrictive type of consumer protection but also a persuasive argument against additional restrictions on advertising.

781 URSIC, MICHAEL. "An Empirical Analysis of the Effectiveness of the Magnuson-Moss Act." In *Proceedings, 31st Annual Conference of the American Council on Consumer Interests*, edited by Karen P. Schnittgrund, 198-201. Columbia, Mo.: American Council on Consumer Interests, 1985.

A paper that reanalyzes data collected by the Federal Trade Commission on the effectiveness of the Magnuson-Moss Act. Concludes that the law increased the availability of warranties and the proportion of shoppers reading them but also decreased the ability of warranties to be understood. Recommends that the FTC take steps to address the latter problem.

782 ZANGER, ALBERT. "What Was the Impact of the Choate Study on the Cereal Market?" In *New Consumerism: Selected Readings*, edited by William T. Kelley, 285-300. Columbus, Ohio: Grid, 1973.

Evaluates the effects of a critical study by Robert B. Choate of the healthfulness of breakfast cereals. Concludes that the study resulted in temporary brand switching, improvements in cereal formulations, and greater emphasis on nutrition in cereal ads. Based largely on information from newspaper articles and the trade press.

CONSUMER PROTECTION

783 NICKS, STEPHEN J. "Lemon Laws in the United States: More Hype Than Help." *Journal of Consumer Policy* 9 (March 1986): 79-80.

Evaluates lemon laws passed in over thirty states since 1982 to assist consumers in resolving complaints about defective new cars. Suggests that the existence of many different state laws and the lack of centralized reporting requirements make it difficult to assess impact with any precision. Concludes that the threat of consumer resort to lemon-law remedies probably has improved the speed and seriousness with which manufacturers and dealers resolve complaints, yet actual use of these remedies has not been as great as advocates predicted. Cites no data to support the latter conclusion. Acknowledges that lemon laws are so new in many states that consumers may still be getting used to them.

ECONOMIC REGULATION / DEREGULATION

784 CRANDALL, ROBERT W.; GRUENSPECHT, HOWARD K.; KEELER, THEODORE E.; and LAVE, LESTER B. *Regulating the Automobile*. Washington, D.C.: Brookings Institution, 1986. 202 pp.
   See entry 789 for annotation.

785 DARDIS, RACHEL; GARKEY, JANET; and ZHANG, ZHIMING. "Deregulation of Trucking in the United States – Implications for Consumers." *Journal of Consumer Policy* 12 (1989): 19-38.
   Evaluates the costs and benefits of trucking deregulation in 1980. Defines benefits in terms of the effects of relaxed entry restrictions and changes in operating restrictions, and defines costs in terms of the impacts on highway safety. Calculates that in a five-year period, average annual logistics cost savings totaled $38 billion. Finds that, when speed and miles driven were controlled, deregulation reduced fatality rates; yet it also increased miles driven, thus raising costs. Recommends improved highway systems to accommodate increased truck traffic.

786 MAYER, ROBERT N.; ZICK, CATHLEEN; and BURTON, JOHN R. "Consumer Representation and Local Telephone Rates." *The Journal of Consumer Affairs* 23 (Winter 1989): 267-84.
   An evaluation of the effects of methods of public utility commissioner selection, commissioner terms of office, and type of proxy advocacy on local phone rates. Finds that the method of selection has no relation to these rates, but finds that the term of office and the types of advocacy do. Specifically, longer commissioners' terms and independent consumer counsels are associated with lower rates. Also shows that higher-income states tend to have lower rates, possibly because they are more likely than lower-income states to have flat-rate service options rather than local measured service.

787 SNOW, ARTHUR, and WEISBROD, BURTON A. "Consumer Interest Litigation: A Case Study of *Nader v. Allegheny Airlines.*" *Journal of Consumer Affairs* 16 (Summer 1982): 1-22.
   An analysis of the efficiency and equity aspects of Ralph Nader's attempt to eliminate airline overbooking by suing Allegheny Airlines. Concludes that the achievement of Nader's stated goal would not have served consumer interests in efficiency, but that these interests were underrepresented in airline and regulatory decision making and that the

principal result of the lawsuit, a Civil Aeronautics Board rule requiring disclosure, did promote efficiency. Observes that publicity and other nonlitigation activity, as well as court or regulatory decisions, are needed to correct market and government failures.

PRODUCT SAFETY

788 ASCH, PETER. *Consumer Safety Regulation: Putting a Price on Life and Limb.* New York: Oxford University Press, 1988. 172 pp.

A perceptive analysis of the current status of consumer safety regulation and the debate between economists and consumer advocates over its desirability. Written for laypersons as well as for economists, attempts to bridge the gap between these "market traditionalists" and advocates. Chapter 1 introduces the debate over safety. Chapter 2 outlines the nature of safety regulation in the United States and Britain. Chapters 3 and 4 review economic and noneconomic arguments for this regulation. Chapter 5 discusses issues related to consumer misperception of risk. Chapter 6 analyzes how federal safety agencies develop policy. Chapter 7 reviews evidence on the economic impacts of important policies. Chapter 8 presents concluding observations. It argues that efficiency must remain as a criterion of safety policy. It also suggests that the differences between economists and advocates on safety regulation reflect their views of the ways markets function and of the extent to which individuals are competent judges of their own welfare. It concludes that there is a role for both groups.

789 CRANDALL, ROBERT W.; GRUENSPECHT, HOWARD K.; KEELER, THEODORE E.; and LAVE, LESTER B. *Regulating the Automobile.* Washington, D.C.: Brookings Institution, 1986. 202 pp.

A cost-benefit analysis of safety, fuel emissions, and fuel efficiency for motor vehicles. Concludes that the overall costs of these regulations exceed their benefits; however, finds that the benefits of the safety standards alone are greater than their costs. An unbiased effort to assess automotive safety regulation that deserves careful attention. Its limitations are inherent in such assessments: For example, the benefits of improved air quality cannot be determined with any precision. Also, the assumption that, in the absence of fuel efficiency standards, fuel efficiency would have improved substantially is open to question, particularly in light of new research showing that consumers tend to ignore lifetime product costs in purchase decisions.

790 DARDIS, RACHEL; AARONSON, SUSAN; and LIN, YING-NAN. "Cost Benefit Analysis of Flammability Standards." *American Journal of Agricultural Economics* 60 (November 1978): 695-700.

Examines the role of cost-benefit analysis in assessing product safety regulations, and applies such analysis to an evaluation of flammability standards for children's sleepwear. Discusses potential costs and benefits of safety regulations. Concludes that, despite a lessening of consumer choice, the flammability standards were cost-effective. Notes that any indirect costs and the benefits of reduced pain and suffering were difficult to calculate and thus were not included in the analysis.

791 DARDIS, RACHEL, and LEFKOWITZ, CAMILLE. "Motorcycle Helmet Laws: A Case Study of Consumer Protection." *Journal of Consumer Affairs* 21 (Winter 1987): 202-20.

Examines the losses to society in 1981 from the earlier repeal or weakening of state motorcycle helmet laws. Finding that these losses far exceeded the cost of helmets to riders, concludes that helmet laws are cost-effective in preventing serious injuries. Reviews the arguments for and against these statutes. Notes that the total costs of motorcycle accidents are relatively small.

792 HANSEN, KEITH A. "The Cancer Scare: Did It Hurt the Cigarette Industry?" In *New Consumerism: Selected Readings*, edited by William T. Kelley, 301-34. Columbus, Ohio: Grid, 1973.

A detailed analysis of antismoking campaigns and their impact on smoking. Discusses popular reaction to these campaigns, why people smoke, the role of government and other groups in these campaigns, and industry responses. Concludes that the campaigns have been and will continue to be ineffective. If the author were to revise the study today, he would undoubtedly qualify this conclusion.

793 LOWRANCE, WILLIAM W. *Of Acceptable Risk*. Los Altos, Calif.: William Kaufmann, 1976. 180 pp.

A study written for the National Academy of Sciences on safety. Addresses problems such as the way we assess hazards, differences between scientific and political debates, how we can determine what risks the public is prepared to accept, and why controversies about alleged hazards continue. Individual chapters discuss measuring risk, judging safety, public concerns, remedies, and DDT as a case study. Chapter 4 includes a discussion of the role of advocacy groups in public policy debates on safety.

Product Safety

794 McAULIFFE, ROBERT. "The FTC and the Effectiveness of Cigarette Advertising Regulations." *Journal of Public Policy & Marketing* 7 (1988): 49-64.

Critically assesses the effectiveness of federal regulation of cigarette advertising over the past thirty years. Reviews FTC policies toward this advertising and research on its effects. Suggests that these regulations have reduced competition in the industry, use of filter-tip cigarettes, and industry incentives for developing safer cigarettes; also suggests they have not discouraged smoking. Concludes that regulators should be cautious in implementing new policies.

795 McGUIRE, THOMAS. "An Evaluation of Consumer Protection Legislation: The 1962 Amendments: A Comment." *Journal of Political Economy* 83 (September-October 1975): 655-61.

A critique of Peltzman's study (entry 797) that concluded new-drug regulations impose considerable costs on consumers. After noting that his use of consumer-demand theory is questionable, finds specific flaws in his procedures for carrying out the analysis. Suggests that he underestimated gains from an increase in consumer information and exaggerated the costs related to stricter screening of new drugs. Concludes that Peltzman's analysis "provides no real evidence" to justify repeal of the regulations.

796 PELTZMAN, SAM. "The Effects of Automobile Safety Regulation." *Journal of Political Economy* 83 (August 1975): 677-725.

Argues that auto safety regulations have not affected the highway death rate. Contends that the decline in occupant fatalities has been offset by a rise in pedestrian deaths because of an increase in "risky driving." Convincingly rebutted by Robertson (entry 800).

797 PELTZMAN, SAM. "An Evaluation of Consumer Protection Legislation: The 1962 Drug Amendments." *Journal of Political Economy* 81 (September-October 1973): 1049-91.

Evaluates the 1962 drug amendments, which require premarketing approval of all new drug claims, in terms of costs and benefits. Argues that while they did reduce consumer waste on ineffective drugs, they also resulted in a significant decline in drug innovation, which, by limiting competition, costs consumers $250-500 million annually. Uses consumer-surplus analysis and "expert" drug evaluations as the basis for this estimate. The application of these methods is criticized by McGuire (entry 795).

798 PELTZMAN, SAM. *Regulation of Automobile Safety*. Washington, D.C.: American Enterprise Institute for Public Policy Research, 1975. 53 pp.

A more detailed version of the author's *Journal of Political Economy* article (entry 796). See that annotation for a summary of the argument.

799 PELTZMAN, SAM. *Regulation of Pharmaceutical Innovation: The 1962 Amendments*. Washington, D.C.: American Enterprise Institute for Public Policy Research, 1974. 118 pp.

A more detailed version of the author's *Journal of Political Economy* article on drug regulation (entry 797). See that annotation for a summary of the argument.

800 ROBERTSON, LEON S. "A Critical Analysis of Peltzman's 'The Effects of Automobile Safety Regulation.'" *Journal of Economic Issues* 11 (September 1977): 587-600.

A critique of a study by Sam Peltzman (entry 796) that concluded that auto safety regulation has led to an increase in pedestrian deaths because it has encouraged "risky driving." Argues that Peltzman used data that included fatality rates related to unregulated as well as regulated vehicles; also charges that he utilized inappropriate proxy measures in his analysis. After adjusting his model for these factors, shows that pedestrian deaths did not increase, thus implying no increase in risky driving.

801 SMITH, BETTY F., and DARDIS, RACHEL. "Cost-Benefit Analysis of Consumer Product Safety Standards." *Journal of Consumer Affairs* 11 (Summer 1977): 34-46.

Examines the role of cost-benefit analysis in assessing consumer product safety standards. Applies this analysis to an evaluation of flammability standards for children's sleepwear. Identifies the types of direct and indirect costs and benefits of safety standards. Shows that the benefits of the sleepwear standards exceed costs under several assumptions. Notes the limitations of cost-benefit analyses. Concludes, nevertheless, that such analysis is useful for policymakers, particularly in comparing alternative safety programs.

802 VISCUSI, W. KIP. "Consumer Behavior and the Safety Effects of Product Safety Regulation." *Journal of Law & Economics* 28 (October 1985): 527-53.

Empirically assesses the impact of Consumer Product Safety Commission regulations on product safety. In examining home accident

Product Safety

data, finds no significant effects from CPSC regulation. In studying poisoning rates, discovers no decline after the safety cap requirement. Suggests that safety regulations may induce a lulling effect on consumer behavior that partially or wholly offsets any safety benefits. For a critique of this research, see Zick (entry 806).

803 VISCUSI, W. KIP. "The Lulling Effect: The Impact of Child-Resistant Packaging on Aspirin and Analgesic Ingestions." *American Economic Review* 74 (May 1984): 324-27.
     Examines the possibility that protective bottle cap requirements on aspirin and certain other drugs decreased consumer safety by reducing parental caution. Analyzes the problem conceptually, proposing an empirical test. Reports that overall the child-resistant bottle cap regulation had no effect on aspirin poisonings and an adverse effect on analgesic poisonings. Concludes that this regulation lulled consumers into being less safety-conscious. According to Mayer (entry 57), in Viscusi's statistical model his "inclusion of the lagged value of the dependent variable" may "overwhelm the possible influence of other independent variables."

804 VISCUSI, W. KIP. *Regulating Product Safety*. Washington, D.C.: American Enterprise Institute for Public Policy Research, 1984. 116 pp.
     The most comprehensive and thorough conservative critique of the Consumer Product Safety Commission. Examines the rationale for product safety regulation, modes of intervention, the CPSC's regulatory strategy, the general character of CPSC policies, and costs and benefits of eleven products regulated by the agency. Proposes abolition of the CPSC and transfer of its functions to the executive branch, the elimination of the agency's section 15 authority, substitution of consumer information and penalties for current standards and bans, and improvement of the agency's data base and cost-benefit analysis. Acknowledges the imprecision of this analysis but gives the benefit of doubt to business. Includes analysis of product-related accident and death trends that has been criticized by Zick (entry 806).

805 WIGGINS, STEVEN N. "Product Quality Regulation and New Drug Introductions: Some New Evidence from the 1970s." *Review of Economics and Statistics* 63 (November 1981): 615-19.
     Building on Peltzman (entry 797), uses new data from the 1970s to examine the effects of the 1962 drug amendments on the introduction of new drugs. Estimates the effects of regulation on research spending. Investigates the effects of regulation on the types of drugs being produced. Finds that in this period, regulation reduced the rate of new

drug innovations. Because of the difficulty of scientifically establishing a product's effectiveness, indicates that scientists are "several steps away from final policy conclusions." Research supported in part by the Pharmaceutical Manufacturers Association.

806 ZICK, CATHLEEN D.; MAYER, ROBERT N.; and SNOW, LAVERNE ALVES. "Does the U.S. Consumer Product Safety Commission Make a Difference? An Assessment of Its First Decade." *Journal of Consumer Policy* 9 (March 1986): 25-40.

An evaluation of the effectiveness of the Consumer Product Safety Commission based on analysis of changes in accidental home death rates. Suggests that studies by the Consumer Federation of America (CFA), claiming a significant effect on these rates, and by Viscusi, finding no effect, are methodologically deficient. Concludes that the CPSC did save thousands of lives but far fewer than CFA estimated. Notes, however, that lack of data prevented controlling for the effects of any rise in product liability litigation.

13. Business Responses

ATTITUDES OF THE BUSINESS COMMUNITY

807 BARKSDALE, HIRAM C., and FRENCH, WARREN A. "Response to Consumerism: How Change Is Perceived by Both Sides." *MSU Business Topics* 23 (Spring 1975): 55-67.
See entry 346 for annotation.

808 GAEDEKE, RALPH M. "What Business, Government, and Consumer Spokesmen Think about Consumerism." *Journal of Consumer Affairs* 4 (Summer 1970): 7-18.
See entry 348 for annotation.

809 GAZDA, GREGORY MACE. "A Study of the Attitudes of Businessmen, Consumers, and Consumerists toward Consumerism." Ph.D. dissertation, Arizona State University, 1974. 195 pp.
See entry 111 for annotation.

810 GAZDA, GREGORY M[ACE], and GOURLEY, DAVID R. "Attitudes of Businessmen, Consumers, and Consumerists toward Consumerism." *Journal of Consumer Affairs* 9 (Winter 1975): 176-86.
See entry 112 for annotation.

811 HOPKINSON, TOM M. "New Battleground–Consumer Interest." *Harvard Business Review* 42 (September-October 1964): 97-104.
See entry 628 for annotation.

Attitudes of the Business Community

812 "Nader Is a Good Guy, Says U.S. Chamber of Commerce Chief." *Wall Street Journal*, 19 September 1978, 19.

A short article reporting a speech by the U.S. Chamber of Commerce's new president, Edward Rust of State Farm Insurance, in which he said Ralph Nader is trying to make the free-enterprise system work as it is supposed to. A subsequent article noted that the chamber said the speech reflects the views of Rust, not of the chamber.

BUSINESS PRACTICES

813 "Associations Answer Consumerism Challenge." *Association Management* 23 (January 1971): 24-27.

A laudatory report on the response of 250 trade and professional associations to Virginia Knauer's challenge to help members resolve consumer complaints. These associations offered to notify individual companies of grievances received by Knauer's White House office. Briefly describes several cases.

814 BELKIN, LISA. "Consumerism and Business Learn Together." *New York Times*, 13 April 1985, 48.

See entry 311 for annotation.

815 "Business Responds to Consumerism." *Business Week*, 6 September 1969, 94-96.

A lengthy special report on the "consumerism boom" and the ways businesses are responding to it. Reports that members of Congress, having discovered that consumerism is popular with voters, have passed three major bills recently and are introducing dozens more. Attributes consumerism's popularity to growing product complexity, business expansion, rising consumer expectations, and anomie. Discusses business attempts to respond to consumerism that include consumer research, voluntary product standards, improved product quality and repairability, and improved customer service. Treats the problems of federal agencies' enforcement of new laws. Includes sidebars on product liability, Whirlpool's customer programs, and a tire recall.

816 THE CONFERENCE BOARD. *The Challenges of Consumerism: A Symposium*. New York: The Conference Board, 1971. 90 pp.

Ten papers by academics, business leaders, government officials, and a consumerist on consumerism and its implications for business. Focuses on consumer problems and concerns and ways these can be addressed. Little mention of the work of consumer organizations.

817 DAY, GEORGE S., and AAKER, DAVID A. "Industrywide Responses to Consumerism Pressure." *Harvard Business Review* 50 (November-December 1972): 120-24.

Analyzes business responses to consumerism and how they can be improved. Responses include research, education, the introduction of proconsumer policies, and the establishment of consumer affairs departments. Examines barriers to such consumer initiatives. Discusses the emergence of trade association leadership for coordinating and disseminating research, consumer and dealer education, development of standards, and complaint handling. Concludes that business must address underlying problems in ways that may not boost short-run sales or profits and that may include establishing an independent group to represent the consumer interest within the organization.

818 DRUCKER, PETER. "Consumerism: The Opportunity of Marketing." In *Consumerism: Viewpoints from Business, Government, and the Public Interest*, edited by Ralph M. Gaedeke and Warren W. Etcheson, 252-58. San Francisco: Canfield Press, 1969.

An address to marketers that argues that the "total marketing concept" has failed to anticipate consumer desires and thus has allowed consumerism to develop. Urges marketers to stop viewing consumers as a threat and to become consumerist leaders.

819 EVANS, JOEL R., ed. *Consumerism in the United States: An Inter-Industry Analysis*. New York: Praeger Publishers, 1980. 452 pp.

An examination of consumerism in ten industries: appliance, banking, clothing, household products, mail-order, petroleum, pharmaceutical, the professions, retailing, and lead/asbestos/fluorocarbons. The chapter on each contains a historical description of related consumerism and a discussion of the roles of consumer groups, government, the industry, and individual companies. The research was conducted by ten M.B.A. students at Hofstra University over a two-year period. Much of the data used were gathered by questionnaires completed by trade associations and individual companies, though response rates were low. Like many master's theses, the chapters are well researched but are limited by rigid organization, stilted style, and lack of insight. The book is valuable mainly as an introduction to consumerism in the selected industries and as a source of business reaction to this advocacy.

820 FERNSTROM, MEREDITH. *Consumerism: Implications and Opportunities for Financial Services*. Report published by the American Express Company in 1984.

Business Practices

See entry 573 for annotation.

821 GROSE, JACK NORMAN. "A Study of the Marketing Strategies Used by the Cigarette Industry with Emphasis on Those Designed to Counter Consumerism during the Period 1964 to 1973." D.B.A. dissertation, Mississippi State University, 1974. 180 pp.

Documents and analyzes the marketing strategies of the cigarette industry to counter antismoking consumerism following publication of the Surgeon General's 1964 report. Shows how the study, which linked smoking to lung cancer, led to efforts by consumerists to discourage smoking and impose restrictions on the industry. Evaluates the impact of consumerism on sales, profits, and earnings of cigarette companies. Concludes there was not "a sustained negative effect" because of the effectiveness of the industry's marketing strategies. For a more detailed summary, see *DAI* 35 (1975): 7469A.

822 KOTLER, PHILIP. "How to Anticipate Consumerism's Coming Threat to Banking." *Banking* 65 (January 1973): 20-22.

An article by a marketing professor addressed to bankers on ways they can respond to growing consumerism. Suggests reasons that banks are increasingly the focus of attention by activists. Identifies potentially questionable banking practices. Recommends a new marketing orientation that stresses better monitoring of customer concerns and reform of those practices that are being criticized.

823 PRESTBO, JOHN A. "Seller Beware: Consumer Proposals Bring About Changes in American Business." *Wall Street Journal*, 21 June 1971, 1+; 1 July 1971, 1+.

A feature article reporting on new efforts by corporations to respond to a growing number of consumer complaints and antibusiness attitudes. These responses include the establishment of complaint departments and toll-free hotlines, the creation of consumer affairs positions, and restructuring to enhance the importance of customer service departments. Suggests that unlike the early 1900s and 1930s, consumers today are most concerned with "safe, reliable products and services that perform as advertised and that are repaired or remedied promptly when they fail."

LOBBYING

824 "Business Lobbying: Threat to the Consumer Interest." *Consumer Reports* 43 (September 1978): 526-31.

Lobbying

Explains how business has increased the effectiveness of its federal lobbying to counter consumer advocates. Notes that it has copied techniques used by public interest groups–generating many letters from constituents to members of Congress, filing lawsuits, and seeking to influence the media. Contrasts the number and resources of business lobbyists with those of consumer activists in Washington. Describes specific lobbying strategies of business–finding a longtime supporter or a contributor to communicate with a legislator, sending chief executives to lobby Congress, funding congressional campaigns through political action committees (PACs), and seeking to influence columnists and editorial writers. Emphasizes public financing of congressional campaigns as a way to check growing business influence on public policy. Includes a sidebar on "public interest law firms" financed by business.

825 PERTSCHUK, MICHAEL. *Revolt against Regulation*. Berkeley: University of California, 1982. 165 pp.
    See entry 611 for annotation.

826 SCHWARTZ, GEORGE. "The Successful Fight against a Federal Consumer Protection Agency." *MSU Business Topics* 27 (Summer 1979): 45-57.
    An examination of the nine-year legislative battle over the establishment of a federal consumer protection agency that reveals how companies and their associations can and do influence the political process. Reviews the legislative history of the proposal, the contending sides, their debate, and their strategies. Cites as important reasons for the defeat of the proposal the business strategy of delay and Ralph Nader's unwillingness to compromise.

827 "The Unmaking of a Consumer Advocate." *Consumer Reports* 37 (February 1972): 80-83.
    An analysis of the emasculation of the 1971 Consumer Protection Act by business lobbyists. Attributes their political influence not only to an extensive Washington grass-roots lobbying operation but also to huge campaign contributions. Includes a sidebar identifying those congressional leaders with influence over the bill.

828 VOGEL, DAVID. *Fluctuating Fortunes: The Political Power of Business in America*. New York: Basic Books, 1989. 337 pp.
    See entry 617 for annotation.

14. Criticisms of the Movement

ACADEMIC

829 ADAMS, JAMES RING. "Measuring the Worth of Consumerism." *Wall Street Journal*, 24 November 1972, 6.

An editorial page article on a conference of economists criticizing consumerism. Discusses microeconomic research suggesting that the costs of consumer regulations frequently outweigh their benefits. Also reports a consumerist response that such research inflates costs and understates social benefits.

830 BROFFMAN, MORTON H. "Is Consumerism Merely Another Marketing Concept?" *MSU Business Topics* 19 (Winter 1971): 15-21.

A revised version of a speech that argues that current consumerism goes beyond previous marketplace criticisms to question the structure of business institutions and their marketing efforts. Criticizes some consumer advocates and business leaders for being doctrinaire. Concludes that, despite its excesses, consumerism has had a constructive effect on business.

831 CREIGHTON, LUCY BLACK. *Pretenders to the Throne: The Consumer Movement in the U.S.* Lexington, Mass.: D. C. Heath, 1976. 142 pp.

See entry 36 for annotation.

832 GARRETT, DENNIS E. "Consumer Boycotts: Are Targets Always the Bad Guys?" *Business and Society Review*, Summer 1986, 17-21.

Academic

> Discusses the "rebirth" of consumer boycotts and the moral issues they raise. Describes ethical arguments for and against these boycotts. Outlines a "framework for guiding future analysis" of the issue.

833 GUSTAFSON, ALBERT W. "Consumerism and the Free Enterprise System: An Overview of Recent Trends." *Alabama Business* 46 (August 1976): 2-4, 10.

> An evaluation of consumerism that focuses on the benefits and costs of government regulation. Provides a useful overview of alleged costs but does not report the results of related research.

834 HOLSWORTH, ROBERT D. *Public Interest Liberalism and the Crisis of Affluence.* Boston: G. K. Hall, 1980. 158 pp.

> A lengthy essay evaluating the "public interest liberalism" of Ralph Nader from a humanistic, environmentalist perspective. Chapter 1 examines the development of this liberalism in the 1960s. Chapter 2 locates Nader between conventional politicians and radical critics. Chapter 3 explains Nader's "defensive liberalism" and identifies its contributions and limitations. Chapter 4 argues that Nader's liberal reformism cannot deal adequately with ecological problems. Chapter 5 discusses two earlier economists, Simon Patten and Thorstein Veblen, who wrote critically about an earlier crisis of affluence. Chapter 6 critically evaluates the perspective that only authoritarian regimes can adequately restrain ecologically damaging growth. This essay perceptively analyzes the limits of consumerist reformism, yet offers somewhat idealistic solutions that assume the possibility of rapid cultural change.

835 KLEIN, ROGER. "Consumerism Gets the Brush-Off." *New York Times*, 26 November 1972, sec. III, p. 12.

> An article by an economist who criticizes consumerists for neglecting the costs of proposed reforms. Uses research by Peltzman on drugs (entry 797) to illustrate his point.

836 KROLL, ROBERT J., and STAMPFL, RONALD W. "The New Consumerism." In *American Council on Consumer Interests: 27th Annual Conference Proceedings*, edited by Carol B. Meeks, 97-100. Columbia, Mo.: American Council on Consumer Interests, 1981.

> A paper arguing that traditional consumerism is declining while a "new consumerism" is taking its place. Defines traditional consumerism as being antibusiness, focusing on noneconomic issues, supporting "benefit rights" solutions to problems, and assuming widespread agreement among consumers about problems and remedies. Suggests

that consumers are increasingly becoming antiunion and antigovernment, giving economic issues higher priority, favoring "opportunity rights" solutions, and diversifying their views of consumerism. By 1990, however, traditional consumer groups had regained some of the public support they lost in the late 1970s, and no new set of consumer organizations had been established.

837 LAZARUS, SIMON. *The Genteel Populists*. New York: Holt, Rinehart and Winston, 1974. 303 pp.
    See entry 54 for annotation.

838 SCHRAG, PHILIP G. "Consumerism Today: A Movement Still in Its Infancy." In *Consumerism*, edited by Mary Gardiner Jones and David M. Gardner, 89-99. Lexington, Mass.: Lexington Books, 1976.
    An assessment by a law professor of consumer protection needs and opportunities related to disclosure, product safety, harsh contracts, the courts, consumer remedies, and inflation. Suggests that poverty be made a top consumer priority.

839 SHAPIRO, STANLEY J. "Marketing and Consumerism: Views on the Present and the Future." *Journal of Consumer Affairs* 7 (Winter 1973): 173-78.
    An essay by a marketing professor that evaluates the consumerist critique of marketing. Suggests that, despite its imperfections, the present system may serve society better than a highly regulated one. Recognizes, however, that consumerist criticism of marketing has served useful social purposes. Predicts continuing confrontation between consumerism and marketing but less public support for consumerism in the future.

840 VOGEL, DAVID. "The Public-Interest Movement and the American Reform Tradition." *Political Science Quarterly* 95 (Winter 1980): 607-27.
    A provocative analysis of the political philosophy of public interest organizations and its political implications. Suggests that the principal goal of these organizations is to increase their influence in government decision making and to reduce that of business. Describes three types of reforms that they believe will accomplish this purpose – procedural reforms such as public disclosure, liberalized standing requirements, and due process for whistle-blowers; public subsidy of their advocacy through RUCAGs (later called citizen utility boards), public participation funding, and liberalized tax laws restricting lobbying; and agency representation through, for example, a new consumer protection agency. Argues that these reforms are similar to those in the

Academic

Progressive period, which sought to increase public participation in the political process, but differ from New Deal liberalism, which sought to increase government authority. Criticizes the public interest program for "insufficiently recognizing that public subsidy is not, and cannot be, free"; it will increase public interest dependence on government vulnerability to business pressure. Notes that business has increasingly taken advantage of procedural reforms won by public interest groups. Observes that the major effect of public interest advocacy has been not to make government more accountable to citizens and increase its legitimacy for regulating business, but only to increase its size. The political philosophy treated is largely that of Ralph Nader and his organizations in the 1970s. In the 1960s and 1980s, public interest groups focused most of their attention on specific problems affecting consumers.

841 VOGEL, DAVID. *When Consumers Oppose Consumer Protection*. St. Louis: Center for the Study of American Business, Washington University, 1989. 40 pp.
See entry 763 for annotation.

BUSINESS

842 GUZZARDI, WALTER, Jr. "The Mindless Pursuit of Safety." *Fortune* 9 (April 1979): 54-64.
A critique of the increasing use of product recalls by federal regulatory agencies. Focuses mainly on recalls by the National Highway Traffic Safety Administration, yet also discusses those by the Consumer Product Safety Commission and product bans and seizures by the Food and Drug Administration. Also laments an "explosion in the number of lawsuits." Concludes that this "mindless pursuit of safety" will harm more people than it will help. Recommends greater use of cost-benefit studies.

843 MILLONES, PETER. "Harassment Laid to Consumerism." *New York Times*, 18 February 1970, 1+.
A page-one report of a Better Business Bureau conference in which the president of the New York bureau accused consumerists of "harassment, . . . prejudice, and emotion" that threaten business with "a depressing decline." Most of the audience are reported to have responded enthusiastically to his speech.

Business

844 NICKEL, HERMAN. "The Corporation Haters." *Fortune* 10 (16 June 1980): 126-36.

Argues that there is an anticorporation network of activists that carries on the spirit of the New Left. Includes Ralph Nader and his organizations in this coalition. Identifies the Interfaith Center on Corporate Responsibility as a principal coordinator of the network. Examines in detail the campaign against the marketing of infant formula in Third World countries.

845 ROCHE, JAMES P. "The Attack on Free Enterprise." *Michigan Business Review* 23 (July 1971): 18-23, 31.

A speech by the chairman of General Motors that defends the free-enterprise system against consumerist criticisms. Faults consumer protection for adding to business costs and hindering its ability to compete in international markets.

846 WEBSTER, GEORGE D. "Standards Are Required for the Regulation of Consumer Groups." *Association Management* 31 (September 1979): 20+.

An article by the general counsel of the American Society of Association Executives advocating standards of conduct and disclosure for consumer organizations. Criticizes Consumers Union and other groups as "self-appointed." Objects to public participation funding for consumer organizations.

CONSERVATIVE

847 BENNET, JAMES T., and DiLORENZO, THOMAS J. *Destroying Democracy: How Government Funds Partisan Politics*. Washington, D.C.: Cato Institute, 1985. 561 pp.

An attempt funded by conservative foundations to show that tax funds appropriated for social purposes have been diverted to support left-liberal political advocacy. Chapter 5 focuses on the consumer movement. Finding little evidence of government funding of major groups except a Department of Agriculture contract to the Consumer Federation of America, VISTA grants to PIRGs, and "witness fees" to several groups testifying in Federal Trade Commission hearings, all in the late 1970s, it tries to show that these organizations have "destabilized the free enterprise system through regulation, the attempted nationalization of industry, and plain harassment." This chapter reports only a small portion of the government funding of consumer advocacy groups during the Carter administration. Yet by

Conservative

1985 virtually all of this funding had ceased. Although the book criticizes Ralph Nader as one of the "destroyers of democracy," it identifies no government funding of his Washington-based network of organizations.

848 BENNETT, JAMES T., and DiLORENZO, THOMAS J. "Tax-Funded Unionism III: Front Organizations." *Journal of Labor Research* 8 (Spring 1987): 179-89.
See entry 334 for annotation.

849 BRUNK, MAX E. "The Anatomy of Consumerism." *Journal of Advertising* 2, no. 1 (1973): 9-11+.
A short article that is more a critique than the analysis of consumerism it claims to be. Emphasizes that consumer protection has imposed economic costs and limited individual freedom. Useful only as an outline of conservative arguments against consumerism.

850 FRIEDMAN, MILTON, and FRIEDMAN, ROSE. *Free to Choose.* New York: Harcourt Brace Jovanovich, 1979. 338 pp.
A popular critique of government intervention in private markets. Chapter 7 evaluates government regulation in consumer markets by the Interstate Commerce Commission, Food and Drug Administration, Consumer Product Safety Commission, Environmental Protection Agency, and Department of Energy. It argues that market competition more effectively protects consumers than does regulation and has the additional virtue of not restricting consumer choice.

851 GRAYSON, MELVIN J., and SHEPHARD, THOMAS R. *The Disaster Lobby: Prophets of Ecological Doom and Other Absurdities.* Chicago: Follett Publishing Co., 1973. 256 pp.
A one-sided conservative critique of "prophets of doom," including Ralph Nader and other consumerists, who have denied citizens the right to purchase and benefit from "the miracles of modern science and technology." In a chapter entitled "The Pot Stirrers," attacks Nader for costing consumers billions of dollars and denying them the right to choose in the automotive market. In this chapter and the next, also criticizes Esther Peterson, Betty Furness, Bob Choate, the Federal Trade Commission, and other consumerists. Ignores research on the benefits of consumer regulations and citizen support for them.

852 ISAAC, RAEL JEAN, and ISAAC, ERICH. *The Coercive Utopians: Social Deception by America's Power Players.* Chicago: Regnery Gateway, 1983. 325 pp.

An alarmist conservative critique of a "new class" of left/liberal intellectuals who work through universities, foundations, government, media, the churches, and public interest groups to gain power and undermine American democracy. In one chapter, treats Ralph Nader's advocacy and that of groups he has inspired such as the public interest research groups (PIRGs).

853 PETERSON, MARY BENNETT. *The Regulated Consumer*. Los Angeles: Nash Publishing, 1971. 271 pp.

A book in the Principles of Freedom series with an introduction by Milton Friedman. A critique of "interventionist" regulation, with chapters on federal regulation by the Food and Drug Administration, Department of Justice's Antitrust Division, Federal Trade Commission, National Labor Relations Board, Interstate Commerce Commission, Civil Aeronautics Board, and Federal Communications Commission. In the chapter on the FDA, discusses the development and current character of consumerism. Identifies Virginia Knauer, Bess Myerson, and Ralph Nader as consumerist leaders who are pressing for government intervention. Ignores the support of consumer advocates for procompetition measures such as more vigorous antitrust enforcement and airline deregulation.

854 REYNOLDS, ALAN. "What Does Ralph Nader Really Want?" *National Review* 17 (28 February 1975): 219-23.

A conservative critique of Ralph Nader's political ideology and program. Summarizes Nader's worldview, which emphasizes using government power to reduce and regulate corporate power. Finds fault with his assumptions that large corporations are too powerful, that laws benefit these corporations, and that greater health and safety regulation is desirable. Emphasizes that there are "complex trade-offs" in such regulation to which Nader "rarely gives adequate consideration." Criticizes much Nader-inspired research as sloppy and biased.

855 STANG, ALAN. "Ralph Nader: The Autocrat and the Establishment." *American Opinion*, January 1975, 35-48+.

A right-wing critique of Ralph Nader. After attacking *Unsafe at Any Speed*, develops the theme that Nader is a "consumer fraud" with a hidden agenda to collectivize the country. Outlines links to alleged left-wing groups and individuals, such as the Ford Foundation, which supposedly "has given millions to innumerable outright Communist operations."

Conservative

856 WINTER, RALPH K. *The Consumer Advocate versus the Consumer.*
Washington, D.C.: American Enterprise Institute for Public Policy
Research, 1972. 16 pp.

A conservative critique of consumer advocacy, in particular its
proposal for a consumer protection agency, by a law professor. Outlines
the ideology and solutions of advocates. Criticizes this ideology for
neglecting the costs of regulation, for using inadequate economic
theory, for ignoring consumer preferences, and for denying consumers
choice. Discusses five types of legitimate regulation. Faults the proposed
consumer protection agency. Although somewhat theoretical and
simplistic, the analysis of consumerism and the discussion of the role of
regulation are essentially correct. But the critique of consumer advocacy
ignores such economic and political realities as well-documented
consumer problems, lack of adequate consumer redress, limited
resources of advocates, influence of business in politics, and the
adversarial nature of the public policy-making process.

PRESS

857 BOYD, MARJORIE. "The Protection Consumers Don't Want."
Washington Monthly, September 1977, 29-34.

Argues that legislation creating a Consumer Protection Agency
was defeated largely because of lack of public support. Traces this to
unintended negative effects of consumer laws and regulations already
on the books. Discusses the Truth in Lending Act, Employee
Retirement Income Security Act (ERISA), Poison Prevention
Packaging Act, and Consumer Product Safety Commission. Suggests
that laws sometimes inconvenience consumers, raise prices, and
increase legal costs. Recommends simpler, more limited laws whose
effects are well-thought-out beforehand. This article exaggerates public
disillusionment with consumer protections and neglects other important
factors such as the strength of business lobbying and public apathy to
federal policy-making. Yet, unlike advocate analyses of the defeat of the
agency, it correctly points out that there was very little grass-roots
support for this measure.

858 BRODER, DAVID. "Citizen's Beef." *Washington Post*, 12 December
1975, sec. B, p. 7.

An op-ed essay by a prominent columnist on Ralph Nader's
criticism of President Carter one month after Carter assumed office.
Defends Carter against Nader, suggesting that the president's earlier
meeting with Nader was a political mistake, that Carter is fairly

conservative, and that he could well appoint tough regulators in the future.

859 HARRIS, MARLYS. "What Have Consumer Groups Done for You Lately?" *Money* 11 (October 1982): 18-28.

A one-sided critique of the consumer movement. Faults consumer groups for refusing to merge with each other, for abandoning issues, for being too adversarial, for refusing to disclose their finances, for taking "less than voluntary" contributions from students, and for retaining funds from a price-fixing settlement. Notes the rise of business-supported conservative consumer groups that seek to neutralize the impact of more liberal advocacy organizations. *Money* refused to print any of numerous letters correcting inaccuracies and responding to criticisms in the article.

860 SHEPARD, THOMAS R., Jr. "We're Going Too Far on Consumerism." *Reader's Digest* 98 (February 1971): 147-50.

A condensed version of a speech by a publisher which argues that consumerism is limiting individual freedom and threatening business productivity. Specifically criticizes reforms to limit the number or sizes of food products and to require the installation of seat belts in cars. More an impassioned general defense of the free-enterprise system than a carefully reasoned, well-documented critique of consumerism.

861 YOUNG, LEAH. "A Chink in Nader's Armor?" *New Republic*, 2 September 1972, 11.

A discussion of Ralph Nader's lack of support for national no-fault automobile insurance legislation. Notes that the trial lawyers, who oppose no-fault, have contributed funds to Nader activities. Quotes one advocate as suggesting that Nader tolerates an inefficient tort system in which lawyers are overcompensated so they "[will] be around for other things." Suggests why most state insurance officials, many insurance companies, and trial lawyers oppose no-fault. See Nader's response (entry 577).

RADICAL

862 BURLINGHAM, BO. "Popular Politics: The Arrival of Ralph Nader." *Working Papers for a New Society*, Summer 1974, 5-14.

See entry 415 for annotation.

Radical

863 EDWARDS, RICHARD C. "An Appeal to Tired Activists: A Radical
Looks at the Consumer Movement." In *Consumerism*, edited by Mary
Gardiner Jones and David M. Gardner, 129-40. Lexington, Mass.:
Lexington Books, 1976.

A critique addressed to "tired activists" by an armchair socialist.
Characterizes the consumer movement as "largely ignored" and "largely
out of money." Describes three unsatisfactory models the movement
uses to counteract the antisocial impacts of business: a "community of
interests" model, an "institutional" model, and an "aroused citizenry"
model. Argues that consumer activists should join with others who are
trying to achieve democratic socialism. By 1990, the movement for this
socialism had disappeared, but the consumer movement had
institutionalized itself in Washington, D.C., and many states. Edwards
might respond that consumer reforms have failed to address serious
social problems such as poverty and alienation.

864 GARTNER, ALAN, and RIESSMAN, FRANK. *The Service Society
and the Consumer Vanguard*. New York: Harper and Row Publishers,
1974. 266 pp.

A radical analysis of how the growth of a "service society" and its
contradictions create the potential for a consumer-oriented economy.
Includes a critique of the consumer movement as too reformist, too
disorganized, and too weak to realize this potential. Suggests that
women, minorities, and youth, who hold most service jobs, offer greater
hope for effecting radical changes. An original and provocative
discussion of social and economic changes in the United States.
Expresses far too much optimism that service workers will serve as
advocates for consumers as well as for themselves. Fails to anticipate
growing consumer dissatisfaction with monopoly services (e.g.,
government, some utilities) and the harsh effects on workers of
competition in private service markets (e.g., banking, food services).

865 HORNSBY-SMITH, MICHAEL P. "The Structural Weaknesses of the
Consumer Movement." *Journal of Consumer Studies and Home
Economics* 9 (December 1985): 291-306.

A Marxist analysis of the consumer movement that concludes it is
politically impotent. Relying heavily on an article by Jeremy Mitchell
(entry 60), reviews the movement's growth and character. Suggests that
it serves mainly the educated middle class and does not seriously
challenge the dominance of business. Outlines pluralist and conflict
approaches to the analysis of the relation of consumer organizations to
the political process. Argues, but does not document, that there is
substantial corporate dominance of the marketplace. Identifies five
structural weaknesses of the movement: lack of communication with

Radical

consumers, inability to mobilize, refusal to act aggressively, acceptance of existing marketing arrangements, and ideological support for these arrangements. Hypothesizes that consumerism rises and falls with discretionary income. An excellent framing of two theories for evaluating the consumer movement. Yet fails to demonstrate that a conflict approach is more valid than a pluralist one.

15. International Consumer Movement

WORLDWIDE

866 ABRAHAM, MARTIN, and ASHER, ALLAN. "Dangerous Products: Consumer Interpol." In *Consumers, Transnational Corporations, and Development*, edited by Ted Wheelwright, 263-75. Sydney, Australia: Transnational Corporations Research Project, University of Sydney, 1986.

A discussion of an international clearinghouse of information on hazardous consumer products. Examines industry dumping practices and the failure of governments to check these that led the International Organization of Consumers Unions (IOCU) to establish Consumer Interpol. Describes the structure, operation, and early impacts of this information source.

867 ALLAIN, JEAN-PIERRE. "Consumer Organization and Representation in Developing Countries." In *The Frontier of Research in the Consumer Interest*, edited by E. Scott Maynes and ACCI Research Committee, 506-9. Columbia, Mo.: American Council on Consumer Interests, 1988.

A short paper on the consumer movement in the Third World. Distinguishes four types of groups. Summarizes the character of the movement in Asia, Latin America, and Africa. Briefly discusses the International Organization of Consumers Unions (IOCU) and the UN consumer guidelines.

868 "Asians Form Group on Hazardous Products." *New York Times*, 5 October 1982, sec. I, p. 11.

Worldwide

An article on the creation of a new investigative network, Consumer Interpol, that will report on hazardous products being sold in Asia and will seek to restrict or ban them. The project is associated with the International Organization of Consumers Unions (IOCU). Quotes several Asian advocates on the need for such an effort.

869 AUERBACH, ALEXANDER. "The Consumer Movement Abroad: Still in the First Stages. . . ." *Washington Post*, 7 January 1973, sec. K, p. 10+.

An article suggesting that the consumer movement is far less advanced in other parts of the world than in the United States. Indicates that in industrialized countries rules favor sellers, not buyers, and that developing nations often adopt U.S. product safety and selling practices. Contains little information on the movement in specific countries.

870 BAROVICK, RICHARD L. "The Public Interest Goes International." *Business and Society Review* 34 (Summer 1980): 53-54.

Discusses the growing interest of activist organizations in the international conduct of multinational corporations. Reviews the efforts of the *Multinational Monitor, Mother Jones*, Center for Development Policy, the Institute for Policy Studies, and institutional investor groups.

871 BERTON, LEE. "Crusading Consumers." *Wall Street Journal*, 12 July 1968, 32.

A lengthy review of consumer advocacy outside the United States. Reports that twenty nations have passed basic consumer protection legislation and that eighty consumer protection groups have been organized. Focuses on organizations in Britain, Malaysia, Sweden, Jamaica, Israel, France, the Netherlands, and Japan.

872 CIOCCA, HENRY G. "The Infant Formula Controversy." *Journal of Contemporary Business* 7, no. 4 (1978): 37-56.

A response by a Nestlé representative to critics of their marketing infant formula in the Third World. Accuses the critics of distortion of the company's position and simplistic solutions. Discusses infant mortality and breast-feeding in the Third World.

873 "European Housewives' Choice." *Economist* 199 (15 April 1961): 245-46.

A discussion of a report on consumer protection prepared for the European Productivity Agency. This publication evaluates three methods for improving shopper efficiency – product testing and reports based on this research, product labels that list ingredients, and quality seals awarded to goods that pass tests. It points out the limitations of each. It also recommends eliminating laws restricting consumer organizations and passing others protecting consumers.

874 "Exporting Hazardous Products." *Consumer Reports* 49 (February 1984): 104-5.

Examines the issue of exporting products banned in the United States to other countries. Reports on the Reagan administration's lack of concern for these exports and the efforts of Consumers Union and the International Organization of Consumers Unions to block them. Summarizes the arguments for and against these exports. Urges the U.S. government to prohibit them.

875 FAZAL, ANWAR. "The Consumer Movement Is Alive and Well." In *Proceedings, 29th Annual Conference of the American Council on Consumer Interests*, edited by Karen P. Goebel, 1-4. Columbia, Mo.: American Council on Consumer Interests, 1983.

A speech to the American Council on Consumer Interests that takes the form of a letter to Colston Warne. Suggests the emergence of a "fourth wave" of consumerism in the 1980s in which the movement becomes global. Describes new worldwide consumer protection networks. Issues the challenge of eliminating "violence," "waste," and "manipulation" from the world marketplace. Takes the United States to task for being the only developed country to oppose international consumer protections. Challenges ACCI members to participate in the worldwide consumer movement.

876 GAEDEKE, RALPH M[ORTIMER], and UDO-AKA, UDO. "Toward the Internationalization of Consumerism." *California Management Review* 17 (Fall 1974): 86-92.

Examines consumer protection in a world of multinational corporations and increased trade. Notes that the United States has relatively tough safety standards but that it exempts a number of imported products. Reports the results of a survey of the governments of fifty-eight countries that finds a lack of agreement about who should set quality and safety standards for traded products. Discusses differences in the responses of industrialized and nonindustrialized countries. Describes international organizations involved in consumer protection, including the International Organization of Consumers Unions (IOCU). Proposes the establishment of a UN Consumer Protection Institute to act as a clearinghouse of information about potentially harmful products that are traded.

Worldwide

877 GREER, WILLIAM. "The Third World Looks at Consumerism." *New York Times*, 31 May 1986, 52.
See entry 172 for annotation.

878 HARLAND, DAVID. "The United Nations Guidelines for Consumer Protection." *Journal of Consumer Policy* 10 (September 1987): 245-66.
Describes and evaluates the general guidelines for consumer protection adopted by the UN General Assembly in 1985. Summarizes and assesses the general principles and specific guidelines covering seven areas. Concludes that the guidelines represent a compromise between advocates and others including the Reagan administration, yet represent a "valuable starting point" for developing comprehensive consumer policy and a "useful framework" for assessing existing policies.

879 INTERNATIONAL ORGANIZATION OF CONSUMERS UNIONS. *Consumer Currents*. The Hague, Netherlands.
A newsletter, published ten times annually, containing news relevant to consumer advocates, particularly those in the Third World. Short articles summarize newspaper and magazine articles and publications from consumer groups. Recent issues have emphasized news on food, infant formula, the environment, pesticides, and tobacco.

880 INTERNATIONAL ORGANIZATION OF CONSUMERS UNIONS. *Proceedings of the 12th IOCU World Congress*. The Hague: IOCU, 1987.
Proceedings of the most recent World Congress of the International Organization of Consumers Unions. Includes transcripts of speeches given in general assemblies and in seminars on such issues as transnational corporations, foreign debt, consumer safety, and the consumer movement in Spain. Also includes summaries of several dozen workshops, congress resolutions, and a list of participants.

881 KAUFMAN, IRA, and CHANNON, DEREK. "International Consumerism: A Threat or Opportunity?" *Industrial Marketing Management* 3 (October 1973): 1-12.
An article by two British business professors on the international consumer movement. Identifies four unique characteristics of modern consumerism. Suggests that consumer movements in different countries experience four stages–crusading, popular movement, managerial, and bureaucratic. Locates movements in several nations in this life cycle. Outlines an input-output model for helping understand corporate responses to consumerism. Argues that business should take the offensive in responding to consumerist challenges by better satisfying consumer wants and needs.

Worldwide

882 MAYER, ROBERT. *The Consumer Movement: Guardians of the Marketplace*. Boston: Twayne Publishers, 1989. Ch. 7.
See entry 57 for annotation.

883 MORELLO, TED. "No Dumping–by Order." *Far Eastern Economic Review*, 3 November 1983, 74-75.
Describes the International Organization of Consumers Unions (IOCU), a federation of consumer advocacy groups from different countries. Focuses greatest attention on IOCU's Penang, Malaysia, office and its director, Anwar Fazal, who also serves as IOCU president. Discusses IOCU efforts to ban hazardous or ineffective products by helping the UN identify unsafe products, by maintaining a monitoring system for these products (Consumer Interpol), and by lobbying governments. Provides information on IOCU's staffing and funding and on the Consumer Association of Penang, a Malaysian affiliate of IOCU.

884 O'GRADY, M. JAMES. "Protecting Consumers around the World." *Canadian Business Review* 5 (Spring 1978): 16-19.
Discusses international consumerism with a special focus on the International Organization of Consumers Unions (IOCU). Outlines the development of product-testing organizations in several industrialized countries. Describes the growing number of grass-roots organizations in all regions of the world. Includes a sidebar on IOCU that identifies its structure and many member organizations.

885 PETERSON, ESTHER. "The Case against 'The Case against the UN Guidelines for Consumer Protection.'" *Journal of Consumer Policy* 10 (December 1987): 433-39.
See entry 590 for annotation.

886 POST, JAMES E. "International Consumerism in the Aftermath of the Infant Formula Controversy." In *The Future of Consumerism*, edited by Paul N. Bloom and Ruth Belk Smith, 165-78. Lexington, Mass.: Lexington Books, 1986.
An examination of the growth of consumerism in the Third World. Suggests that this expansion has been strongly influenced by the Nestlé boycott related to the company's marketing of infant formula. Identifies the principal concerns of Third World consumerism as the appropriateness of products and the appropriateness of marketing practices. Suggests that the boycott helped give rise to new concepts in consumer protection–demarketing, public purpose, legitimate market, and marketing codes of conduct.

Worldwide

887 POST, JAMES E., and BAER, EDWARD. "Demarketing Infant Formula: Consumer Products in the Developing World." *Journal of Contemporary Business* 7, no. 4 (1978): 17-35.

Evaluates the marketing of infant formula in the Third World. Discusses the products, criticism of their marketing, and the industry response. Argues that there are serious problems of consumer misuse and related injury. Recommends that manufacturers "demarket" this product in the Third World.

888 SAPIRO, ANDRIEN, and LENDREVIE, JACQUES. "On the Consumer Front in France, Japan, Sweden, U.K., and the U.S.A." *European Business*, Summer 1973, 43-52.

A survey of the consumer movements in Japan, the United States, England, France, and Sweden. Finds that in Japan, the movement is aggressive but unsophisticated; in the United States, it is "a vast social force" both militant and political; in England, its development is limited so long as it remains independent of political parties; in Sweden, its support by unions, cooperatives, and the social democrats has allowed it to establish effective government protection mechanisms; and in France, it has been weakened by government intervention. Concludes that consumerism is not a radical but rather a neoliberal movement.

889 THORELLI, HANS B. "Consumer Policy in Developing Countries." In *Proceedings of the 29th Annual Meeting, American Council on Consumer Interests*, edited by Karen P. Goebel, 147-53. Columbia, Mo.: American Council on Consumer Interests, 1983.

A paper that examines consumer risks in Third World countries and proposes policies to minimize them. Describes research on Third World consumption that reveals structural problems such as lack of quality control, lack of ability to preserve fresh food, predatory practices of sellers, and poverty. Suggests that the short-term prospects for reform are very poor because of the cartelized nature of markets ("cryptocapitalism") and the absence of consumer advocates. Proposes a program of consumer emancipation based on consumer protection, education, and information, which will help establish open markets.

890 VALENTINE, JOHN. "Brewing Boycott: Rising Coffee Prices Are Beginning to Stir Consumer Protests." *Wall Street Journal*, 3 January 1977, 1+.

See entry 720 for annotation.

891 WARNE, COLSTON E. "The Worldwide Consumer Movement." In *Consumerism: Viewpoints from Business, Government, and the Public*

Worldwide

Interest, edited by Ralph M. Gaedeke and Warren W. Etcheson, 17-19. San Francisco: Canfield Press, 1972.

A short article on the growth of a worldwide consumer movement. Suggests that consumer protection in Europe is quite similar to that in the United States. Notes emerging Asian consumer groups. Suggests that the movement's unresolved problem is developing methods of assisting the poor in nations "that have never known an honest civil service and that have low levels of business ethics and consumer competence."

892 WEIDENBAUM, MURRAY. "The Case against the UN Guidelines for Consumer Protection." *Journal of Consumer Policy* 10 (December 1987): 425-32.

A critique of the UN consumer protection guidelines by an academic who served in the Reagan administration. Argues that the guidelines represent an infringement on the sovereign rights of nations and that they promote greater government intervention in private markets. Suggests that the UN should focus instead on its role as international peacekeeper. For a critique of this critique, see Peterson (entry 885).

893 WEINTRAUB, BERNARD. "Consumer Activism Up in Poor Nations." *New York Times*, 1 July 1970, 4.

An article on growing consumer activism in Asia and Africa. Describes efforts in Malaysia, Ghana, India, and Pakistan.

894 WEINTRAUB, BERNARD. "Specialists of 30 Nations Discuss Help for Poor." *New York Times*, 30 June 1970, 43.

A report on the International Organization of Consumers Unions' World Congress in West Germany in which the failure of the organization to deal with problems of the poor and the Third World was addressed. IOCU has been funded and dominated by product-testing organizations in the United States and Europe.

895 WHEELWRIGHT, TED, ed. *Consumers, Transnational Corporations, and Development*. Sydney, Australia: Transnational Corporations Research Project, University of Sydney, 1986. 390 pp.

A collection of eighteen papers on the relationships between transnational corporations, economic development, and consumer interests. Examines corporate abuses in the areas of food, pesticides, drugs, tobacco, and alcohol. Treats consumer mobilization against infant formula, dangerous products, and corporate crime. Explores the future of international consumerism. Many of the papers represent

Worldwide

revised versions of addresses given at a conference of the International Organization of Consumers Unions.

AMERICAS

896 BOURGEOIS, JACQUES C., and BARNES, JAMES. "Viability and Profile of the Consumerist Segment." *Journal of Consumer Research* 5 (March 1979): 217-28.

Compares responses from 267 consumerists and 968 other Canadians to try to explain differences between the two groups. Finds that consumerists are better educated, more likely to be managers or professionals, more likely to be middle-class or upper-middle-class, less likely to enjoy shopping, more independent and self-confident in their relation to sellers, more critical of advertising, more likely to read "establishment" newspapers, and less exposed to the broadcast media than are nonconsumerists. Concludes that consumerists may constitute 15 percent of the population and are influential with other consumers. Suggests that consumerism may be only one expression of a more general "social activist" orientation.

897 GOLDSTEIN, JONAH. "Public Interest Groups and Public Policy: The Case of the Consumers' Association of Canada." *Canadian Journal of Sociology* 12 (March 1979): 137-55.

Examines the history of the Consumers' Association of Canada (CAC) to reveal the limitations of a "general organization" as opposed to a "constituency group." Discusses the role and limitations of public interest groups in capitalist democracies. Suggests that the history of the CAC can be divided into two periods. In the first, 1947-67, the organization was led mainly by middle-class and upper-class women who practiced "accommodation politics" with business and political leaders who "politely tolerated" them. In the second, 1968-77, the group expanded its membership and activities to include legal advocacy before the courts and regulatory agencies. But it had problems reconciling professionals and volunteers, defining priorities, and aggressively advocating reforms without jeopardizing government funding. Concludes by discussing reasons why constituency groups can be more effective advocates.

898 McCOOK, EDITH. "Consumers' Association of Canada." *Canadian Labour* 8 (October 1963): 5-7.

A brief report on the structure and activities of the Consumers' Association of Canada, written by a participant.

899 MOFFETT, MATT. "Mexican Consumers Have a Stout Friend in Arturo Lomeli." *Wall Street Journal*, 18 January 1988, 1+.

Lead article profiles Arturo Lomeli, longtime consumer advocate in Mexico. Describes problems such as short-weighting that face Mexican consumers. Describes the almost insurmountable obstacles he confronts.

900 MORNINGSTAR, HELEN J. "The Consumers' Association of Canada: The History of an Effective Organization." *Canadian Business Review* 4 (Autumn 1977): 30-33.

An article by a leader of the Consumers' Association of Canada on the organization. Discusses its founding, consumer bulletin, current structure, policies, activities, and funding.

901 OLLEY, ROBERT E. "The Canadian Consumer Movement: Basis and Objectives." *Canadian Business Review* 4 (Autumn 1977): 26-29.

An article by a professor/consumerist on the concerns and objectives of Canadian consumer groups such as the Consumers' Association of Canada. Discusses four areas of concern – quality of life, environment, social responsiveness and participation, and conserving. Predicts growing consumerist participation in diverse forums, some groping and internal disagreement as consumerists define "new syntheses and paradigms," and both a scarcity of resources and a "self-confident desire to expand."

902 SEVERO, RICHARD. "Consumer Units Gain in Caribbean." *New York Times*, 6 May 1973, 11.

An article on the growth of the consumer movement in the English-speaking Caribbean that is focusing on defective or unsafe products. Discusses the National Consumers League in Jamaica, the Bahan Consumers League, and the Caribbean Consumer Council, which coordinates the activities of the groups.

903 ZIEGEL, JACOB S. "Consumerism in Canada." *Canadian Banker* 78 (November-December 1971): 4-6.

An article by a professor/consumerist that examines the rise of consumerism in Canada. Notes that it has grown recently because of urbanization, affluence, and "an overwhelming disparity in sophistication and bargaining power" between sellers and buyers. Discusses recent Canadian consumer protection initiatives in the areas of safety, deception and fraud, disclosure, and representation.

Asia

ASIA

904 CHIRA, SUSAN. "Defuse Goals Set by Naders of Japan." *New York Times*, 14 July 1986, sec. IV, p. 10.

An article on the Japanese consumer movement which suggests that, since about 1975, it has not been confrontational. Discusses the support of some groups for restrictions on food imports, but fails to note that these organizations are backed by agricultural cooperatives. Indicates that membership in consumer groups is declining and that they are not influential in policy-making.

905 CLIFFORD, MARK. "Citizens Begin to Battle for Their Rights." *Far Eastern Economic Review*, 8 September 1988, 96-97.

A brief description of emerging Korean consumer organizations, especially the Citizens Alliance for Consumer Protection in Korea (CACPK). Notes that the leadership of these organizations is largely well-educated, middle-class women. Indicates that there is a nationalistic strain in consumer advocacy criticizing tobacco and food imports.

906 "Fighting for Consumer Rights." *Beijing Review* 45 (11 November 1985): 28.

Describes the new China Consumers' Commission (identified by a 1989 article as the China Consumers' Association). Identifies the major goals of the organization as complaint resolution, the elimination of substandard products from the market, and consumer information dissemination.

907 GARNER, ROY. "Lobbies/Consumer Organizations: More a Barrier Than a Force for Reform." *Far Eastern Economic Review*, 11 June 1987, 92-93.

Argues that Japan's consumer organizations are on the decline because of falling membership and conflicting goals. Faults these groups for their ties to and financial dependence on agricultural cooperatives, which explains their opposition to food imports.

908 HARTLEY, WILLIAM D. "Nipponese Naderism: Japanese Consumers Doff Docile Image, Stiffen Their Demands." *Wall Street Journal*, 29 January 1971, 1+.

A feature article discussing the growing consumer revolt in Japan led by homemakers. Describes a boycott of color television sets called by the National Federation of Women's Organizations. Identifies the most critical consumer problem as high prices on basic commodities such as food and housing.

909 HINDS, MICHAEL deCOURCY. "Consumer Protection 101 for Chinese." *New York Times*, 12 September 1988, sec. IV, p. 1.

An article on the China Consumers' Association, whose leaders were visiting New York City. Notes that they have 865 regional offices but only a $60,000 budget, which they use mainly to handle individual consumer complaints.

910 HONG, LIU. "Association Champions Consumer Rights." *China Reconstructs* 38 (November 1989): 41-43.

Describes the four-year-old China Consumers' Association. Outlines emerging consumer problems that gave rise to its organization. Discusses its founding, structure, funding, and activities, which have emphasized complaint resolution and the development and promotion of model consumer laws by provinces and cities. Identifies the organization's principal constraint as lack of funding.

911 JAPAN CONSUMER INFORMATION CENTER. *Consumer Policy in Japan*. Tokyo: Japan Consumer Information Center, 1989. 51 pp.

A booklet by a government-funded agency that describes consumer policy in Japan, including federal and local consumer protection, the Information Center, and "redress of consumer damages." One chapter provides an overview of private consumer organizations. Contains a chronology of major consumerist events from 1945 to 1989.

912 KIM, YONG HEE. "Consumerism in Southeast Asia: The Case of South Korea." In *Proceedings, 31st Annual Conference of the American Council on Consumer Interests*, edited by Karen P. Schnittgrund, 220-22. Columbia, Mo.: American Council on Consumer Interests, 1985.

A paper discussing consumerism in South Korea. Suggests that it was "triggered" by the failure of the government to give adequate attention to consumer goods industries and to Korean protectionism, which forced consumers to purchase inferior domestic products. Identifies the first consumer activists as women upset by "predatory" practices of sellers. Describes the major consumer organizations but notes their lack of support. Recommends additional research to reveal consumer needs that can serve as the basis for government regulations and for improved consumer education.

913 KIRKPATRICK, MAURINE A. "Consumerism and Japan's New Citizen Politics." *Asian Survey* 15 (March 1975): 234-46.

Asia

An informative analysis of the growth of consumerism in Japan in the early 1970s. Argues that the consumer movement has become a vehicle for expressing public dissatisfaction with an "increasingly mass consumption society." Reports on a survey of consumer groups that found over 1,000 with some ten million members. Indicates that women were instrumental in organizing and leading these groups. Suggests that government support not only helped the organizations expand but also gave them legitimacy. Describes the boycotts against canned goods containing cyclamates and against televisions with inflated list prices as instrumental in the growth of public support for consumerism. Presents survey data suggesting that most supporters will never join consumer groups.

914 LUTFY, CAROL. "The Docile Charm of the Japanese Consumer." *Eastern Economic Review*, 3 November 1988, 79-81.
    Examines the ineffectiveness of Japanese consumer organizations. Reports they have few members, little money, and ties to producer groups. Indicates, for example, that the most important group, the Japan Consumers Union, has 4,000 members and ties to agricultural interests that explain why it opposes food imports. Suggests an explanation as to why Japanese consumers are so "docile."

915 MORELLO, TED. "No Dumping–by Order." *Far Eastern Economic Review*, 3 November 1983, 74-75.
    See entry 883 for annotation.

916 NEWMAN, BARRY. "Watchdogs Abroad." *Wall Street Journal*, 8 April 1980, 1+.
    Discusses consumer problems in Malaysia and a consumer organization, the Consumer Association in Penang, that is trying to solve them. Suggests that many of these problems result from the marketing by multinationals of products banned in the developed world.

917 PETERSON, ESTHER. "International Perspective: Consumer Issues in Mainland China." In *Proceedings, 33rd Annual Conference of the American Council on Consumer Interests*, edited by Vickie L. Hampton, 321-24. Columbia, Mo.: American Council on Consumer Interests, 1987.
    See entry 593 for annotation.

918 RAJAKARUMA, LUCIEN. "Consumer Protection in Ceylon." *Washington Post*, 1 January 1972, sec. A, p. 19.
    An article on the creation by the government of 2,000 consumer committees throughout Ceylon to monitor the performance of public

and private institutions. Reports on the debate over these "people's committees."

919 SHOHEI, MAKI. "The Postwar Consumer Movement: Its Emergence from a Movement of Women." *Japan Quarterly* 23 (April-June 1976): 135-39.

Analyzes the emergence of a Japanese consumer movement. Finds that it began and remains primarily a grass-roots movement led by homemakers. Reports that it is not well organized or funded. Suggests that an essential precondition of further growth is an increase in "the consciousness of popular sovereignty" among the Japanese.

EUROPE

920 BIERVERT, BERND; MONSE, KURT; and ROCK, REINHARD. "Alternatives for Consumer Policy: A Study of Consumer Organizations in the FRG." *Journal of Consumer Policy* 7 (September 1984): 343-58.

Assesses the "efficiency" of four consumer organizations in West Germany that receive substantial government funding. Bases this evaluation on analysis of 1,600 documents and interviews with 124 officials of the organizations, government, and business. Discusses the emergence of consumer problems such as drinking water pollution and chemicals in food that cannot be solved by the traditional consumerist emphasis on market transparency. Finds that consumer organizations have failed to address adequately these types of problems because of their financial dependence and their lack of individual members who could apply pressure to government officials. Instead, the groups have focused on increasing market efficiency by assisting individual consumers. Proposes a model for the more effective representation of consumer interests.

921 BODDEWYN, J. J. "The Swedish Consumer Ombudsman System and Advertising Self-Regulation." *Journal of Consumer Affairs* 19 (Summer 1985): 140-62.

One of a series of studies by the author on advertising self-regulation and outside participation in different countries. Examines this self-regulation and the roles of government and consumer groups in Sweden. Concludes that Swedish consumer protections on advertising rely largely on government-issued guidelines based on business self-regulation and resulting from negotiations with business. Describes the role of the consumer watchdog in regulating advertising. Characterizes

Europe

the Swedish consumer movement as fragmented, highly specialized, individualized, and influenced by unions and large corporations.

922 "Consumer Forces Told to Eat Cake." *New York Times*, 15 January 1971, 47.

An article on consumerism in Europe, which it calls weak in comparison with that in the United States. Discusses the abolition of the Consumer Council in Britain, the small budget of the League of Consumer Organizations in West Germany, and the weakness of private consumer groups in Sweden. Also mentions consumer groups in France and Belgium.

923 COUNCIL OF EUROPE. *The Collective Interests of Consumers*. Strasbourg, France: Council of Europe, 1980. 104 pp.

A report on measures permitting government agencies or private organizations to protect consumers. Includes replies from fifteen countries to a questionnaire that requested information about private associations or agencies. Some responses only list organizations while others describe them briefly.

924 FLETCHER, WINSTON. "A Setback in the Long March of Consumerism." *New Statesman*, 2 June 1978, 733.

A short report on a debate about the merits of consumerism. Summarizes the critical arguments of business representatives. Suggests that these representatives underestimate public support for consumerism.

925 FLICKINGER, RICHARD. "The Comparative Politics of Agenda Setting: The Emergence of Consumer Protection as a Public Policy Issue in Britain and the U.S." *Policy Studies Review* 2 (February 1982): 429-44.

See entry 751 for annotation.

926 FORBES, J[AMES] D. *The Consumer Interest: Dimensions and Policy Implications*. London: Croom Helm, 1987. 341 pp.

See entry 39 for annotation.

927 HOLLMANN, HERMANN H. "Consumer Protection Movement in Western Europe and Its Impact on Business." *International Contract* 2 (June-July 1981): 259-76.

An overview of consumer protection in Western Europe that discusses institutional developments, political and legislative developments, and trends and impacts of the latter. Includes separate treatments of West Germany, the United Kingdom, France, Scandinavia, Austria, the Netherlands, and Italy. Concludes that "the concept of consumerism is expanding" with significant implications for business.

928 KRONHOLZ, JUNE. "Consumerism European-Style." *Wall Street Journal*, 20 November 1979, 24.

An editorial-page article on problems the European Economic Community creates for consumerists. On the one hand, individual nations are sometimes reluctant to enact consumer protections that will be opposed by other countries. On the other hand, the EEC is reluctant to propose standards for the whole European community that will be resisted by individual members.

929 LEE, JOHN M. "Doubts Voiced in Britain As Nader Airs His Views." *New York Times*, 21 October 1971, 17.

See entry 445 for annotation.

930 McROBERT, ROSEMARY. "Nader's British Raiders." *New Statesman*, 29 October 1971, 581.

See entry 449 for annotation.

931 MARTIN, JOHN, and SMITH, GEORGE W. *The Consumer Interest.* London: Pall Mall Press, 1968. 280 pp.

An examination of the rise of British consumerism and the reasons for its emergence and growth. Part 1 reviews the history of consumer cooperatives and consumer groups. Part 2 investigates changes in the marketplace that stimulated consumerist activity. Part 3 discusses the laws relevant to consumers and their enforcement. Part 4 examines and evaluates the "consumer response" in the areas of education, product testing, labeling, consumer advice, and local consumer groups. The work also describes consumer groups in the United States, Scandinavia, other European countries, and Commonwealth countries. Concludes that British consumerists have little influence on government policy-making. Suggests that they consider organizing a consumer party and a union of consumers.

932 MOSBY, ALINE. "Let Them Eat Cake." *Washington Post*, 20 January 1974, sec. L, p. 7.

An article on the growth of consumerism in France. Discusses the National Consumers' Institute and adverse consumer reaction to a strike of shopkeepers.

Europe

933 NADEL, MARK V[ICTOR], ed. "Symposium on Consumer Protection Policy." *Policy Studies Review* 2 (February 1983): 417-549.
    See entry 761 for annotation.

934 NELLES, WILFRIED. "Consumer Self-Organization and New Social Movements." *Journal of Consumer Policy* 6, no. 3 (1983): 251-72.
    Analyzes the increased number of self-help organizations in West Germany. Based on examination of these groups in the Cologne/Bonn region, estimates there are more than 30,000 in the country with between 300,000 and 500,000 members. Categorizes these organizations as focused on personal and cultural identity (e.g., women's groups), housing and living area (e.g., tenants' associations), environment, and the alternative economy (co-ops). Hypothesizes that the growth of these groups reflects "increasing systematic control of socialization and reproduction" and that they strive for "cultural emancipation." A challenging article because of its theoretical orientation.

935 ORGANISATION FOR ECONOMIC COOPERATION AND DEVELOPMENT. *Consumer Policy in OECD Countries: 1985*. Paris: OECD, 1985.
    An annual report on principal developments in consumer policy in twenty-one OECD countries during the previous year. Includes a chapter summarizing these changes and chapters on changes in each nation. The latter discuss institutional developments and "regulatory or other action" relating to consumer protection and education.

936 PACE, ERIC. "Ombudsman for Consumers Urged in Scandinavia." *New York Times*, 14 April 1970, 5.
    An article on the growing interest in Scandinavia of establishing consumer watchdogs to protect consumers and a school curriculum to educate citizens. Suggests that Sweden, Norway, and Denmark have "an edge in consumer protection over other countries."

937 PESTOFF, VICTOR A. "Exit, Voice, and Collective Action in Swedish Consumer Policy." *Journal of Consumer Policy* 11 (March 1988): 1-27.
    An impressive analysis of the relationship between markets, politics, and nongovernmental organizations in Swedish consumer policy. Introduces four theoretical concepts for understanding this relationship – exit and voice, collective action, countervailing power, and integrated organizational participation in public policy-making. Describes five stages in the development of consumer influence – initiation, expansion, consolidation, retrenchment, and decentralization. Emphasizes the importance of government

intervention on behalf of consumers to ensure their representation in policy-making. Notes, however, that this advocacy is not assured, particularly in the current period of political malaise. Contains theory that could usefully be applied to consumer policy development in other countries.

938 ROBERTSON, JEAN, and ROBERTSON, ANDREW. "Consuming Fire." *New Statesman*, 10 November 1967, 654.

A short but wide-ranging article on consumerism in Britain. Discusses briefly a Michael Young speech at a Consumer Assembly, the priorities of British consumers, an attack on *Which?* by the Institute of Economic Affairs, and an evaluation of that criticism.

939 ROSE, LAWRENCE L. "The Role of Interest Groups in Collective Interest Policy-Making: Consumer Protection in Norway and the United States." *European Journal of Political Research* 9 (March 1981): 17-45.

See entry 67 for annotation.

940 SMITH, GEORGE [W.]. *The Consumer Interest*. London: John Martin Publishing, 1982. 331 pp.

An analysis of the consumer interest in major economic, industrial, commercial, and social issues, and of the successes and failures of British consumer groups in representing consumer views and meeting consumer needs between 1968 and 1980. Concludes that these organizations have failed to persuade policymakers and the public that they accurately represent the views of most consumers. Suggests that the British consumer movement needs its own Ralph Nader. Chapter 10 contains a useful description of public agencies and private groups working to protect consumers in Britain.

941 THORELLI, HANS B., and THORELLI, SARAH V. *Consumer Information Handbook: Europe and North America*. New York: Praeger, 1974. 525 pp.

A study of independent consumer information programs maintained by public and private organizations in Europe and North America. Part 1 examines prototype programs in comparative testing (Consumers Association, England), informative labeling (varndeklarationshamaden, Sweden), and quality certification (Qualité-France). Part 2 includes chapters on consumer organizations and information programs in sixteen nations. Chapter sections on individual product-testing agencies typically discuss objectives and governance, finances, personnel, publications, media outreach, activities, impacts, and ancillary activities. The chapter on the United States devotes more attention to Consumers Union than to all other organizations and programs. Part 3 examines a number of international organizations including the International Organization of Consumers Unions (IOCU). The executive summary to the book contains interesting generalizations about the number, funding, sponsorship, public awareness, clientele, and other characteristics of the information programs.

942 TIVEY, LEONARD. "The Politics of the Consumer." *Political Quarterly* 39 (April-June 1968): 181-94.

Addresses the issue of the lack of effective consumer representation in Britain. Explains why trade unions, cooperatives, the Consumers Association, the National Federation of Consumer Groups, specialized consumer organizations, the Consumer Council, and the government cannot provide this representation. Discusses reasons for the weakness of the consumer movement. Proposes the creation of a consumers alliance, including all consumer organizations, that would try to influence national public policy-making.

943 WESSWICK, LOUISE. "A Comparison of Consumer Affairs in Scandinavia and the U.S." In *Proceedings, 29th Annual Conference of the American Council on Consumer Interests*, edited by Karen P. Goebel, 294-99. Columbia, Mo.: American Council on Consumer Interests, 1983.

Compares consumer education and protection in Scandinavian countries with those in the United States. Consists mainly of separate descriptions of consumer affairs in Denmark, Sweden, and Norway. Concludes by identifying similarities and differences between Scandinavian consumer practices and those in the United States. The most striking differences are that the former are funded largely by the government, are more centralized, and feature consumer watchdogs who help enforce consumer laws.

Author Index

References are to entry numbers, not pages. Where a work is entered in more than one section, only the entry bearing a full annotation is indexed.

Subject Index

National Health Planning and
Resources Development Act of
1974, 328
National Highway Traffic Safety
Administration, 129-30, 229, 323,
339, 343-44, 441, 448, 463, 616, 660,
747, 754, 842
National Institute for Consumer
Justice, 659
National Insurance Consumer
Organization, 13
National Labor Relations Board, 853
National Public Interest Research
Group, 200
National Recovery Administration,
82, 94
Natural Gas Policy Act, 571
Nelson, Helen, 3, 142-43, 482, 576,
636
Nestlé, 872, 886
Netherlands, 77, 871, 927
New Deal, 54, 64, 74, 82, 104, 143, 840
New Jersey, 90, 297
New Jersey Consumers League, 273,
297
Newman, Edwin, 34
New Mexico, 726
New York, 90, 266, 719
New York City, 234
New York City Department of
Consumer Affairs, 404-6, 720
New York Consumer Assembly, 330
New York PIRG, 13, 300
New York State Consumer Advisory
Committee, 100
New York State consumer counsel,
100
New York Times, 477
Nixon, Richard, 258, 656, 661, 668,
670, 675, 685
Nolf, Nancy, 2
Norris, William, 427
Northeastern Minnesota Consumers
League, 270
Northern Rockies Action Group, 606
Northern States Power Company,
294-95, 618
Norway, 67

Occupational Safety and Health
Administration, 754
Office of Management and Budget,
581
Office of Price Administration, 82
Ohio Public Interest Campaign, 13
Olson, Mancur, 290
Oreffice, Paul, 427
Oregon, 282

Pachtner, Kathryn, 308
Packwood, Robert, 34
Pakistan, 893
Patten, Simon, 834
Pennsylvania, 266, 748
People's Republic of China, 593, 906,
909-10
Pertschuk, Michael, 34, 326, 483-86,
508, 616, 697, 705
Peterson, Esther, 34, 104, 145, 246-47,
249-50, 255-257, 312-13, 315, 317-
18, 437, 488, 492, 495-97, 690, 695,
851
Petkas, Peter, 697
Pharmaceutical Manufacturers
Association, 805
Pickens, T. Boone, 427
Pittle, R. David, 275-76, 499
Poison Prevention Packaging Act, 857
President's Committee on Consumer
Interests, 101, 246, 610
President's Consumer Advisory
Council, 101, 141-44, 246, 630
President's Council on Environmental
Quality, 323
Professional Insurance Agents, 312-13
Progressive period, 54, 64, 74, 85, 433,
840
Project on Corporate Responsibility,
207
Proposition 103, 209, 429, 434
Public Citizen, 11, 13, 29, 196, 200,
203, 206, 210, 221, 227-35, 324, 462,
714, 722
Public Citizen Litigation Group, 202,
236-38, 612
Public Citizen's Congress Watch, 13,
29, 147, 202, 206, 740